The Power of Life or Death

The Power of Life or Death

A critique of medical tyranny

Fabian Tassano

Foreword by Thomas Szasz

Duckworth

First published in 1995 by
Gerald Duckworth & Co. Ltd.
The Old Piano Factory
48 Hoxton Square, London N1 6PB
Tel: 0171 729 5986
Fax: 0171 729 0015

© 1995 by Fabian Tassano

All rights reserved. No part of this publication
may be reproduced, stored in a retrieval system, or
transmitted, in any form or by any means, electronic,
mechanical, photocopying, recording or otherwise,
without the prior permission of the publisher.

A catalogue record for this book is available
from the British Library

ISBN 0 7156 2642 6 Hbk
ISBN 0 7156 2697 3 Pbk

Typeset by Ray Davies
Printed and bound in Great Britain by
Biddles Ltd, Guildford and King's Lynn

Contents

Foreword by Thomas Szasz   vii
Preface   xi

Part I. Medical Power

1. The health care agenda   3
2. The development of medical paternalism   13
3. Medical professionals: facts and fictions   25
4. Patients: passive victims   39
5. The good of society   51
6. The restriction of medical resources   65

Part II. Power at the Edge of Life

7. Life-or-death decisions   85
8. Wanting to die   91
9. Wanting not to be treated   107
10. Wanting to live   123
11. Moral syllogisms   143
12. Conclusions   155

Bibliography   167
Sources of quotations   171
Index   175

Foreword

Never in history have physicians been able to help their patients as much as they can today, yet they are more dissatisfied with being doctors than ever before. Similarly, never in history have patients received so much benefit from medical care as they do today, yet they are more dissatisfied with being patients than ever before. How can this be? The answer stares us in the face. In the twentieth century, medicine has become increasingly allied with the state and now functions as an arm of it. Power debauches those who hold it, and debases those who are held under it. Medical power is no exception.

This new source of power has, of course, its apologists, called Clinical Ethicists, and its system of justification, called Medical Ethics. The advent of Medical Ethics as a distinct discipline – embraced by philosophers corrupted by the statist-medical establishment; taught in medical schools along with sciences such as biochemistry and physiology; parading its pretentious psychobabble in its own professional journals; and respected by the courts as a Solomonic Science – marks the birth of phoney patient rights, and the death of genuine Lockean (inalienable) rights.

There is a spooky similarity between the naive conceit with which the Communists boasted that it is the duty of the state to protect people from greedy farmers and rapacious landlords, and the naive conceit with which we boast that it is the duty of the state to protect people from dangerous drugs and depraved quacks. To fulfil their self-imposed duty, the Communists united the market and the state and declared that people now enjoyed 'consumer autonomy'. To maintain this fiction, the authorities tried to prevent people from securing for themselves goods or services outside the state-controlled system and reserved their most savage punishments for those guilty of the crime of 'self-location' (border abuse or illegal emigration).

Mutatis mutandis, to fulfil their self-imposed duty, the Medical Paternalists united medicine and the state and declared that people now enjoyed 'patient autonomy'. To maintain this fiction, the authorities try to prevent people from securing for themselves medical goods or services outside the state-controlled system and reserve their most savage punishments for those guilty of the crime of 'self-medication' (substance abuse or illegal drug use).

It need hardly be said – but, today, it must be said – that when the market in consumer goods is a state monopoly, consumer autonomy is an oxymoron; and that when the market in medical goods is a state monopoly, patient autonomy is an oxymoron. Few people today realise that illegal immigration and illegal drug use are quintessentially modern crimes.

Consider how we actually live. A person goes into the forest and eats a mushroom he finds growing there; or into the fields, and smokes a weed he finds sprouting among the corn stalks; or to a pond, and licks the skin of a toad he finds swimming there. Judicial agents of the state pronounce every one of these persons a criminal and punish him. Medical agents of the state pronounce every one of them to be a 'patient' and 'treat' him (against his will).

Moreover, these are but minor manifestations of a pervasive Medical Muslimism – that is, an ethic and politics of unquestioning submissiveness, not to Allah, but to a Medical Leviathan. (The word 'muslim' means *submission* [to the will of Allah]. I use the term Medical Muslimism to denote a social belief system founded on the proposition that it is the duty of the citizen to submit to the superior wisdom of the agents of the Therapeutic State.) Regardless of how well informed an ordinary citizen might be about medical matters, he cannot buy a test of his blood or stool, or an X-ray of his chest or knee, or penicillin or opium to treat his infection or relieve the pain of his fatal cancer. There are good reasons for such controls, counters Conventional Wisdom. No doubt there are. There were good reasons for executing the men who translated the Bible into English and for the Catholic Index of Prohibited Books.

Today, no Normal Man views his lack of access to the information, drugs and technology available to physicians as a restriction on his personal liberty, much less as an interference with his autonomy or individual rights. This is the basic issue that Fabian Tassano examines in this important book. His thesis – which he supports with clear evidence and convincing reasoning, and with which I agree – is that never before was the power of the medical establishment as secure or unlimited as it is today.

Persons with career aspirations – especially in politics, law, medicine, and the media – now either praise the alliance between medicine and the state or avoid the subject. Criticism of the powers of statist medicine is as unwelcome today as was criticism of the powers of statist religion in the past. This is why – although the concerns that animate Mr Tassano's critique are not new – the most perceptive critics of medical power, not surprisingly, have been artists. For example, W.H. Auden warned:

> In all technologically advanced countries today, whatever political label they give themselves, their policies have, essentially, the same goal: to guarantee to every member of society, as a psychophysical organism, the right to physical and mental health. The positive symbolic figure of this goal is a

naked anonymous baby, the negative symbol, a mass of anonymous concentration camp corpses. ... What is peculiar and novel to our age is that the principal goal of politics in every advanced country is not, strictly speaking, a political one, that is today, it is not concerned with human beings as persons and citizens, but with human bodies. (W.H. Auden, *The Dyer's Hand, and Other Essays*, New York: Vintage, 1968, p. 87.)

The Argentinian writer Adolfo Bioy-Casares put it even more starkly:

When man believed that happiness was dependent upon God, he killed for religious reasons. When man believed that happiness was dependent upon the form of government, he killed for political reasons. After dreams that were too long, true nightmares ... we arrived at the present period of history. Man woke up, discovered that which he always knew, that happiness is dependent upon health, and began to kill for therapeutic reasons ... It is medicine that has come to replace both religion and politics in our time. (Adolfo Bioy-Casares, 'Plans for an escape to Carmelo', *New York Review of Books*, April 10, 1986, p. 7.)

Science, Law and Common Sense dismiss such warnings as mindless rejections of medical progress. Alas, if only it were that simple.

Preface

This book has not been written for medical ethicists or for workers in the health care industry but for users of medical services who are interested in knowing about their position as clients, particularly with regard to life-saving treatments. I have therefore made no particular attempt to place my analysis within the context of the contemporary 'medical ethics' literature, much of which appears to be aimed at supporting, or at least accommodating, the current practice of medical authoritarianism which I regard as repugnant and unacceptable.

To the ideologically sensitive reader, I apologise for not being gender-neutral in my use of personal pronouns. Achieving this in a consistent way would have exacted too high a cost, in my view, in terms of readability.

I have avoided the use of the term 'patient' since it carries precisely those connotations about the nature of medicine which I believe need to be rejected: subordination, passivity and diminished status.

My thanks go to Dr Charles McCreery for his invaluable help in making numerous comments and suggestions, both on content and style. I am also grateful to Professor Antony Flew for constructive remarks. I have benefited from discussions with a number of members of the medical profession, in particular Dr H.R. Hewitt, and with many medical clients. I should like to thank John Brownlow of Twenty Twenty Television for providing me with useful material about the Dr Loucas case (chapter 3). The title of chapter 11 was suggested to me by a seminar given by Dr Grant Gillett.

The opinions expressed in the book, and any factual errors, are of course my responsibility alone.

Versions of Chapters 8 and 9 were previously published as Notes by the Libertarian Alliance.

This book is dedicated to the memory of William and Dorothy Green.

F.T.

Part I

Medical Power

1

The health care agenda

Medical monopoly

It is a truism that in an economic transaction involving the provision of a service for payment, the supplier and the consumer have different interests. To begin with, there is a difference of interests with regard to *value*. The supplier generally wants to provide the least possible and to do so at the highest possible price, while the consumer wants the greatest possible benefit and to pay the minimum price. But there are also more subtle differences of interest. Each party has views about the way the service should be provided, about the appropriate level of quality, and about the rules governing the transaction.

Such differences of interest are often resolved via the mechanism of a competitive market. Competitive markets give each party a certain amount of bargaining power which ensures that the terms of transaction will to some extent reflect each party's interests. A competitive market depends on there being more than one, and preferably many, parties of each type. Choice and the profit motive will then tend to ensure that the benefits of interaction are split relatively evenly between suppliers and consumers. If a supplier tries to arrange a deal with a customer which is biased too far in his own favour, the likelihood is that another supplier will offer a better deal in order to take the business away from his rival. Profit maximisation by *competitive* suppliers produces benefits for consumers, since suppliers (a) will have a tendency to undercut one another, resulting in lower prices, and (b) will be relatively motivated to do things as efficiently as possible.

The economic argument most often cited against a *monopoly* is that profit maximisation leads it to charge a price for its product which is excessive. However, a situation in which the supplier of a service is not subject to any competition also has other effects. In a more general sense, there is relatively little incentive for such suppliers to tailor their services to the precise wishes of their customers. What incentive there is depends on customer demand having some responsiveness to changes in the quality of service provided. If, however, the service provided is an *essential* one which consumers cannot do without, the responsiveness will be low, and the incentive of a monopoly supplier to adapt to customer wishes is likely to be minimal.

The insulation from customer wishes of a monopoly supplying an essential service will have two important consequences in addition to the question of price. First, the terms and quality of the service provided are likely to depend almost entirely on the preferences of suppliers. Secondly, the efficiency of the service provided is likely to be poor.

The medical services of industrialised countries have for some time now functioned as quasi-monopolies, in the sense that medical practitioners are subject to minimal competition. This has come about through the creation of a licensing system for the practice of medicine, and through the development of strong professional associations which include among their objectives the protection of members from market forces, for example by prohibiting advertising. There is therefore a likelihood that the two features of monopoly described above will characterise, at least to some extent, the quality of medical care provided. In other words, we would expect the terms of the service to reflect predominantly the preferences of suppliers, and we might also anticipate the existence of chronic inefficiencies.

With regard to the question of inefficiencies, there is certainly some evidence in favour of the hypothesis that medical services do indeed suffer from a level of carelessness and incompetence considerably worse than that which we might expect given the quantity of resources provided to them. However, it is not easy to assess this aspect of the situation objectively. Medical professions have been careful to protect themselves from scrutiny and criticism. One of the ways this has been achieved is by the creation of an image of the health care worker as one who is necessarily doing his best and whose motives may not be questioned. Another way is by asserting that the work of medical practitioners can only be objectively judged by other practitioners, a claim which has largely been accepted by other professional groups as well as by the lay public.

This book, however, is concerned with the other of the two expected characteristics of medical monopoly. It is to be anticipated that practitioners subject to little or no market pressure will be able to shape the service they offer to suit their own needs, demands and preferences, and that they will gain a distinct dominance over their customers. In the case of a service which supplies essential needs, this will give suppliers an extraordinary degree of power.

Professional power

The central argument of this book is that the powers of the medical profession have, largely as a result of monopolisation, grown to unacceptable and dangerous levels. The assumption that doctors and other health care workers act in their clients' best interests rather than their own has been accepted with a minimum of discussion and has been used to endow doctors with increasing control over their clients. Moreover, the identifi-

1. The health care agenda

cation of health professionals with *moral* attributes has led to a belief that doctors may appropriately be charged with the task of making non-clinical decisions on behalf of society, such as whether treatment requested by a person in a specific instance is socially or morally acceptable. Power is, of course, subject to abuse in any profession, and there is no reason to think that doctors are less likely than any other social group to exercise their powers in ways that are unacceptable to their clients. Indeed, it is a hypothesis which should be considered that the control over people's bodies offered by medicine appeals to (among others) people who derive a questionable satisfaction from exercising such control, and that this makes abuse more, not less, likely.

Through a combination of factors, including perhaps a psychological need to believe that those who have power over one are benevolent, the medical profession appears to have become more or less immune from serious criticism. One might think, for example, that the recent revelation that British surgeons are in effect killing their clients by refusing them life-saving operations if they do not give up smoking would have led to a public outcry against the medical profession. Yet, some mild complaints aside, the matter soon disappeared from public attention and seemed to be accepted as simply another feature of life under the National Health Service.

The increasing discretion given to doctors to make decisions and to act as agents of the community, combined with a prevailing world view according to which doctors are moral agents *par excellence*, is leading to a situation in which doctors are using their position in ways that are anything but ethical. Although the concept of patient autonomy is allegedly being given increasing weight, there is limited evidence for the contention that this is influencing the behaviour of doctors in any way that represents a genuine shift of control in favour of clients. On the other hand, there is plenty of evidence to suggest that doctors' disregard of their clients' wishes is increasing rather than decreasing.

In Part I of this book, we shall look at the institutional and ideological setting of modern medicine. We shall examine the attitudes of doctors and their clients to each other, and those of the public to medicine in general; and we shall consider how the current practice of what we may call 'medical authoritarianism' (the tendency of health care workers to override their clients' wishes) has come about, and how it is being maintained.

In Part II, we will consider how the characteristics of contemporary medical practice affect issues regarding edge-of-life medicine. There are three main issues to be considered: individuals being denied life-saving treatment because of decisions made by doctors; individuals being unable to refuse treatment; and individuals being unable actively to end their own lives. There is also the matter of individuals who are unable, or are considered unable, to express their preferences with regard to life or death.

In this chapter, we will begin by briefly considering the evidence for the proposition that doctors are agents who, like other economic agents, seek to maximise their own interests and that, in the absence of commercial pressures, these interests involve the pursuit of professional power.

Patients' interests, doctors' interests

Of the various scientific and technological developments that have taken place over the last fifty years, the advances which have been made in medicine are arguably the most significant. It is one thing to be able to travel faster, or to have more convenient forms of entertainment; it is quite another to reshape one's face, engender children without sexual intercourse, or go on living despite the breakdown of a major organ. Socially and morally, medical technology clearly strikes much deeper than the technology of, say, space exploration or computer graphics.

Yet despite the seriousness of the issues which medical technology raises – issues about the value of life, about parenthood and about personal identity – what the technology is *about* is essentially the same as for any other technology: satisfaction of individual human needs and wants. While the idea that medical technology exists purely and simply to gratify the desires of individuals may be distasteful to some, it is clear that the only alternative view must be one based on the notion of collective interests which, if it differs at all from the former, would appear to call for some actions which result in individual *dis*satisfaction. Thus if we take the view, for example, that a particular treatment should be provided if and only if an appropriate committee of doctors considers it advisable, then there will inevitably be some who would otherwise have had treatment who are frustrated. As we shall see, there may also be some who *will* have treatment when they would not otherwise have chosen it.

We find ourselves in a situation in which an increasingly wide range of medical technology exists for the alleviation of disease, abnormality and other conditions found undesirable by their sufferers. Given this situation, we can imagine a theoretical ideal in which each individual is (i) perfectly informed about his condition (if any), and about what is available in the way of treatment; and (ii) able to access all the medical services and technology he wants.

There are five main reasons why medical practice does not match up to this ideal. First, there is a shortage of unbiased medical information available to clients.

Secondly, there are limits to the quantity of resources which can be devoted to medicine. Even if every person were perfectly informed, it is possible that an economy could not sustain the total aggregate demand for medical services.

Thirdly, access to the available technology is limited not only by reference to resource considerations, but also because of legal restrictions on its supply. For example, it is not possible to obtain an influenza vaccination simply by paying for it; you can only obtain it if your GP considers it appropriate.

Fourthly, there is resistance to the application of medical technology in certain areas for reasons which are usually described as 'moral' but which are perhaps best defined as having little or nothing to do with the physiological health of the consumer.

Fifthly, it is possible – in spite of the *prima facie* illegality of this – for treatment to be applied to someone against his wishes.

Doctors frequently tell us that their role is not simply one based on commercial considerations, but one which involves automatic obligations to each of their clients and to clients in general. The British Medical Association, for example, regularly asserts that doctors are expected to put patients' interests before their own. If this model of doctors is correct, then we might expect that one of the medical profession's objectives would be to maximise client satisfaction. We might therefore expect the profession's attitude to each of the five obstacles outlined above to be consistent with this objective. Given its ostensible standard of selflessness, we would expect doctors' attitudes *not* to be determined by any tendency towards the maximisation of their own powers.

It is therefore instructive to examine the actual behaviour of doctors with regard to the five issues in question.

A lack of information

The first of the areas which may shed some light on the motivation of doctors concerns information. What do the profession's attitudes in this area tell us about its priorities?

An important aspect of modern medical technology concerns what might be called the preference issue. Although the number of ways in which it is possible to interfere constructively with the human body has grown to impressive proportions, there are very few of these ways which do not carry risks or negative side effects. For most modern remedies there is a physiological or psychological price to be paid by the client. More than ever, therefore, medicine is about making choices – between different options, including that of leaving alone, with different benefits and disadvantages. Since these benefits and disadvantages will depend on the likes and dislikes of the client, which will vary from one individual to another, it is very important that these choices are made by clients themselves, and on the basis of adequate information.

As we shall see, however, the standard of information provision on the part of doctors is, on the whole, extremely poor. Indeed, the evidence suggests that some doctors are positively motivated to keep their clients in the dark. Not only do many doctors feel little obligation to inform clients about treatment options; they may not even tell their clients what is wrong with them, and may go so far as to enter them as subjects in experiments without their knowledge.

One possible response to poor client information is for the practitioner to make the decisions about treatment, on the assumption that he knows best what is in the client's interest. This is medical paternalism, a phenomenon which will be discussed in the next chapter. In a sense, paternalism has always been the preferred approach of the medical profession. However, a combination of advancing medical technology and the dominance of a system of medicine in which the client does not pay the doctor has made paternalism the *rule* of modern medical practice. Although there is a notional requirement for consent to treatment from the client, we shall see in later chapters that this provides little obstacle in practice to doctors getting their way.

What is wrong with doctors making decisions about treatment is not only that there are serious flaws in the assumption that a doctor's judgement on what is best for the client will invariably be better than the client's, or better often enough for it not to matter that a minority of clients are overridden against their interests, but also that the modern medical professional no longer has the client's welfare as his only consideration. In chapter 5 we will look at ways in which the interests of people other than the client himself are increasingly playing a part in the treatment decisions made by the doctors.

Resource constraints

Requiring people to pay for medical services, whether as the need arises or via private health insurance, is one way to achieve allocation of finite medical resources. Since the possibility of private medicine appears at first sight to increase the degrees of freedom of doctors, enabling them to take on both private and state-funded clients, one might expect them to defend the principle of being able to buy medical care if one chooses to, over and above what the state provides. Curiously, however, their support for this principle is muted. The British medical profession, for example, was a staunch opponent of the Conservative Government's attempts to privatise certain services provided by the NHS. It has consistently called for greater funding of the NHS, implicitly supporting higher taxation, and therefore in effect a shift of resources from the private sector. The BMA's handbook on medical ethics complains that a system of private medicine can lead to over-treatment for those who can afford to pay, and that failure to treat those who cannot pay is 'perceived by many people' to be immoral.

What are the reasons for this attitude on the part of doctors to the resourcing of the health service? The profession itself would perhaps account for it in terms of its ethical beliefs, although even if this were true, we might question to what extent the preferences of a group of persons whom we employ or hire to serve us should carry weight in determining what sort of services they provide. There is, however, another reason why the profession may favour state medicine, which has to do with the greater decision-making powers which its members have under such a system.

A system of medicine which is not linked directly to the sacrifice of resources by individual clients is liable to suffer from excess demand. There are essentially three main ways in which this problem may be resolved. First, the range of available services may be restricted to those which *can* be offered, under the existing budget, to all who demand them. Secondly, in areas of excess demand services can be allocated by lottery or on a first come, first served basis. Thirdly, allocation decisions can be made by a process of subjective selection.

Now it is not clear which of these options maximises aggregate consumer satisfaction; nor, indeed, that this is the criterion on which a choice between them should be made. It might be argued that the third has the capacity of maximising satisfaction, provided the allocation decisions are made in an appropriate way. However, this seems to ignore the high degree of *dis*satisfaction created in clients who are deliberately excluded, as opposed to being refused on the basis of non-availability or of losing a probabilistic gamble. More seriously, what grounds are there for believing that allocation decisions will maximise, rather than minimise, satisfaction? What evidence do we have for the supposition that a person, or a group of people, is *able* to make decisions on behalf of others which will produce the maximum of happiness, or the minimum of unhappiness, or indeed that they will necessarily make those particular decisions even if they know what they are?

What *is* clear, on the other hand, is which of these options maximises the power of doctors. Complete elimination of certain services may require decisions involving the profession, but these decisions are likely to be closely scrutinised. Having to serve all clients equally, or in strict order of arrival, or on a random basis, gives doctors little scope for using their own discretion. Allocating scarce resources on the basis of 'rational' case-by-case decisions, on the other hand, offers almost unlimited scope for the exercise of power.

We will see that doctors have little objection to making case-by-case decisions about medical allocation. Some, indeed, favour a system in which they are given wide discretion in this respect. Here again, health workers are allotting duties to themselves which go beyond that of doing the best for their individual clients. The impact of their allocation preferences on issues such as euthanasia will be considered in Part II.

The restriction of technology

A third area in which it is illuminating to examine the implicit attitudes of the medical profession is that of medical technology, by which I mean principally drugs and medical equipment.

In the last hundred years, as the medical profession has become increasingly organised and powerful, it has been able to campaign successfully for most of the available medical technology to become accessible to clients only via its own members. As a result, most of the more potent medical treatments and aids are now not available to laymen. *Prima facie*, preventing access to medical technology decreases consumer freedom and hence consumer satisfaction. The argument against this has traditionally been that harm is prevented in certain cases by not allowing individuals complete access to what is available. However, it is doubtful that this is applicable in every case where medical technology is restricted. For example, why is it not possible to have an X-ray without the approval of a doctor? It is not merely that a qualified person has to *administer* such restricted tests or treatments, but that they cannot lawfully be given at all, simply on the basis of one's own decision or willingness to purchase; a doctor must give authorisation. For certain cases in which innocuous treatments are restricted, it seems highly likely that the restriction has only negative effects. For instance, in Britain it is not possible to obtain influenza vaccine except through a doctor. However, there are frequently shortages of the vaccine, particularly during 'flu epidemics, so that doctors start to apply rationing and many people who ask for it have to go without. It seems unlikely that chronic shortages would occur with such regularity if drug companies were competing for an over-the-counter market in the vaccine.

It is questionable therefore whether the restriction of medical technology really benefits the consumer. What is not in doubt, however, is that such restriction increases the power of doctors. Indeed, it may be argued that the enormous power of the medical profession depends precisely on this restriction.

We shall see in chapter 6 that doctors are keen to protect their monopoly of medical technology. In cases where there is an argument for making a treatment or aid more liberally available, so that consumer satisfaction would be increased by deregulation, there is relatively little support for this argument from the profession. On the contrary, the tendency on its part is to call for increased regulation, including over areas which have been unregulated in the past.

The refusal to release medical technology has an important bearing on the question of euthanasia. It is because of the automatic assumption that clients can never be allowed access to the most potent medicines that the question of an ill person ending his own life is almost invariably linked with the idea of his being killed by a doctor.

Ideological obstacles

The possibility of tampering with nature arouses a certain amount of disapproval. This is particularly true in cases where medicine provides a service which can enhance a person's life, rather than treating a sickness, as for example with reproductive technology, or plastic surgery.

There is clearly a potential conflict in this situation between the individual's wishes and the attitude of the society in which he lives. The question is, what should the position of the medical profession be on such matters?

We shall see that the profession is, on the whole, suspicious of client autonomy and tends to side with social prejudice rather than consumer sovereignty. Moreover, the profession appears to consider itself to be a source of authority on moral issues. It tends to reject the interference of government or law in its workings, preferring to leave ethical decisions to the discretion of its members.

Coercive medicine

A final area of interest with regard to doctors' motives concerns the question of treatment without consent.

It should surely be a fundamental principle of medical practice that treatment is *never* applied against the expressed wishes of an adult client. Yet we find that treatment is on occasion given by medical professionals against the wishes of a competent client. Moreover, the profession as a whole gives a qualified endorsement to this behaviour.

Indeed, we shall find that it is beginning to be argued that treatment without consent may in certain circumstances be applied even where it is the interests of someone other than the client which are being served.

The power of life or death

The evidence with respect to each of the five issues examined will suggest that the medical profession is not particularly concerned with the problem of maximising client satisfaction. On the other hand, its behaviour *is* consistent with a desire to maximise its own powers, not only in the clinical sphere, but on a wider social level.

Yet despite this, the image of itself which the profession presents to the outside world is that of a group of people operating only by the most selfless standards. Indeed, at the same time as it appropriates greater powers for itself, the profession asserts its claim to moral purity with increasing intensity. These two trends are clearly not unrelated: in order to adopt more coercive and authoritarian positions, doctors must be immune from suspicion concerning their motives.

The most potentially worrying aspect of the drive to increase the powers of the medical profession is that most users of medicine appear to find no fault with the profession's implicit claim to represent the forces of good. If this is true, it suggests that most people regard this claim as legitimate. Given a situation in which one group of people seek to maximise their power over others and believe they have the right to do so, and in which those others feel they have no right to object, what are the likely ultimate consequences?

In the following chapters, we will consider what consequences have already been engendered by this situation, and what future developments are being urged on us. To what extent is medicine determined by the preferences of doctors rather than by those of clients? In particular, when clients' wishes become particularly significant, namely when decisions of life or death are made, how much authority do those wishes have? The area in which this issue is most frequently debated is that of 'voluntary euthanasia', where the client ostensibly wishes to die and we are encouraged to debate whether the doctor should be permitted to kill. However, just as significant, but less often discussed, is the situation where a client wishes to have his life prolonged, but where doctors may consider it appropriate to refuse.

2
The development of medical paternalism

Rachael Collins and her little brother Jonathan brush their teeth twice a day ... But sometimes they eat sweets. And that, to their dentist, means they are not worth treating. He has struck the youngsters from his register and accused their mother of failing to provide them with a healthy diet. ... Sharif Khan claimed that treating Rachael, nine, and five-year-old Jonathan was of little value 'if their dietary habits are poor and show no signs of improvement'. ... Mr Khan said that he had warned Mrs Collins 'repeatedly' that the youngsters must stop eating sweets. 'I have 1,000 patients and I do what is in their best interests even if it involves upsetting their mothers.' (*Daily Mail*, 27 June 1994)

Paternalism is defined by the Oxford English Dictionary as the 'attempt to supply the needs or to regulate the life of a nation or community in the same way as a father does those of his children'. In other words, the principle of paternalism is that others should decide what is in a person's best interests, and should act according to their decisions even if this means overriding the person's own wishes. Those others, it is often assumed, will be people who are ostensibly better equipped to make informed judgements about the particular matter in question. However, this need not be the case. When individuals are held to be acting 'irrationally' by comparison with some supposed norm, paternalism may involve interference by those who are not specially qualified in any sense other than being deemed to be more 'rational' than those who are interfered with. Thus it is not only qualified doctors who may feel justified in ignoring client autonomy: medical paternalism can be exercised by health professionals at all levels, from surgeons to junior nursing staff.

Paternalism has tended to present a problem for those wishing to square their belief in allowing people freedom of action with their simultaneous confidence in the virtues of such things as compulsory education, imprisonment of drug users, and so on. Various arguments have been used in the attempt to provide moral justification for paternalism in the areas for which it is regarded as acceptable. Let us consider three of the more important of these.

First, it has been argued that paternalism is acceptable where the person interfered with would like to achieve the end which is brought about by the intervention, but does not have the willpower to bring it about autonomously. Thus, your husband or wife may help you to give up smoking by immediately disposing of any packets of cigarettes which he or she finds in the house, and refusing to give them to you when you ask for them. However, in such a situation, it is typical for the person being helped to have initially requested such assistance, even if subsequently it appears that his immediate wishes (to be given the cigarettes) are ignored. (This type of situation is sometimes compared with the fictional case of Odysseus and the Sirens. Odysseus, it will be recalled, had himself tied to the mast of his ship and ordered his men to disregard any orders on his part to be untied, as he knew he would be unable to resist the song of the Sirens.)

Secondly, paternalism has been held to be permissible on occasions when the person is temporarily behaving or thinking uncharacteristically, so that having been restrained from doing what he seeks to do, he will subsequently say that he approves of the intervention. This is the principle most often used to justify the prevention of suicide.

Thirdly, it may be argued that certain supposedly paternalistic restrictions are really not paternalistic at all, but depend on the majority approving of a particular restriction in their own interests, at the expense of the minority who would *not* choose such a restriction. Thus, if we elect to government a political party whose policy is to outlaw mind-altering drugs, rather than a party with a more liberal policy on drugs, this might be thought to be a choice in favour of paternalism. However, it may simply mean that the majority, who are not tempted to use such drugs, believe it would be better for *them* if the minority, who would use them if they were available, were not allowed to do so.

It is clear that none of these arguments have any relevance to the general situation of medical paternalism. In the typical scenario where a person wants a treatment which he is refused, it is not the case that he would *really* like not to have the treatment, or that he would like to be refused because it would help him to overcome a need he disapproves of. The concept of diminished rationality also does not apply, because we are not typically talking about instantaneous decisions or immediate actions in response to one-off impulses. Finally, and significantly, it can scarcely be argued that the practice of paternalism in medicine is something that the majority has chosen, or consented to. Neither the rule that medical resources can only be obtained via a member of a monopolistic medical guild, nor the principle that those members may exercise their discretion in deciding whether to let a client have a treatment he requests, have been an element in the election manifesto of a major political party or a subject of democratic debate.

As implied above, it is sometimes suggested that intervention against a person's wishes is morally justified if the person subsequently approves of the intervention. However, the fact that a person to whom something has been done against his will no longer expresses an objection to what has happened is not strong evidence for the claim that his views have necessarily changed, or that if he had to make the same decision again, he would make it differently in the light of his experience. The opportunity for implementing his wishes having passed, there is relatively little reason for him to continue expressing disapproval of the intervention. Even if he has genuinely changed his mind, that does not prove that his original view was misconceived. Since the opportunity for preventing the intervention has passed, it may be in the interests of his own peace of mind for him to persuade himself that he is comfortable with what has happened.

Other arguments have been used to try to justify paternalistic intervention. For example, it has been suggested that a client might agree with doctors about what would be in his best interests, but still refuse consent on the basis of certain objections while conceding that these objections are 'irrational'. This is not merely an academic point, since refusal of a recommended option is often followed by attempts to persuade the client that the proposed treatment would be the best thing from his point of view, and no doubt a client can be made to agree that there is no discernible flaw in the doctors' arguments. (In practice, of course, the evaluation that objections to treatment are 'irrational' are more typically made by doctors that by the client himself.) The philosopher Christopher McKnight gives the imaginary example of a Mr Jones who refuses a blood transfusion because of his fear of needles, although he (Mr Jones) admits that a transfusion would be in his own best interests. McKnight argues that if autonomy were equated with 'rational choice' then 'respect for Jones's autonomy requires us to accept his reasoned conclusion that transfusion is the best thing and ignore his refusal of it'. In other words, if the client cannot produce a 'rational' justification for rejecting recommended treatment, then it is not overriding his autonomy to treat him against his wishes. In chapter 11, we shall consider a number of other ways in which philosophers have provided medical authoritarianism with spurious moral legitimacy.

A comparison with legal advice

In the light of the above observations, it becomes pertinent to ask how medical paternalism has succeeded in becoming the norm. How, in an age of ostensible consumer sovereignty, is it possible for a service to exist in which it is the views of the provider that are paramount? In order to answer these questions, I should like to consider the issue of paternalism in relation to another sort of professional, the person offering legal advice.

Each of us is an autonomous legal agent. As far as the law is concerned, we are each responsible for our own actions and their consequences. The law, of course, is highly complex and not always well understood by the layman. In order to ensure that my actions have the consequences I mean them to have, I may decide to obtain the help of someone who has studied the law and who has experience of how it is applied. One's relationship with such an individual (or group of individuals) is typically a contractual one. That is to say, the rights and responsibilities of each of the two parties are determined by agreement. One's role as legal agent vis-à-vis third parties remains unaffected by such a relationship, even if the consultant acts as a proxy. It is no defence in litigation to claim that one was badly advised.

Let us now consider the extent to which the actions of a legal adviser acting as proxy are likely to accord with his client's wishes. First, we can expect that the adviser will consider his only professional duty to be towards his client. There may be certain things he is not prepared to do; for example, telling his client how to exploit loopholes in the criminal code. (In an unregulated market for legal advice, it is of course probable that there will be others who are prepared to do these things.) However, the adviser might not find himself with many clients if it were known that he considered himself to have professional duties to others or to society as a whole, going beyond those laid down in law, which might override those to a client.

Secondly, we can expect the adviser to conceive his duty towards his client in terms of achieving the client's stated objective. Again, if he thought his duty was determined by reference to something different from what his client told him he wanted (assuming his client expresses a wish at all), it is unlikely that he would receive much custom.

Thirdly, we may ask *how* the legal adviser is likely to go about achieving his client's objective, when the client expresses a desire that he tackle the matter in hand *in a particular way*. There are a number of different possibilities here. If the adviser agrees with his client, a problem is unlikely to arise. What happens if the legal adviser considers his client's opinion on how to approach the matter to be mistaken? He may (a) comply with the client's instructions under protest, pointing out the possible bad consequences. If things go contrary to the client's expectations, it is likely that the adviser will be regarded as having fulfilled his duty, since he was simply acting under his client's instructions, and his own advice was being rejected. Or the adviser may (b) follow his own judgement, and go against the client's instruction. If his judgement is wrong, the client may of course be able to sue him for negligence.

Does the client have any claim against the adviser on the ground that the latter ignored his opinions, even if the latter's judgement turned out to have been right? That depends on the terms of their agreement. If the contract (written or verbal) contained an explicit or implied term to the effect that the adviser would not act contrary to the client's wishes, then the client may be able to sue for breach of contract. If there was no such term, however, the client has no remedy against the adviser. He may, however, seek the services of a different adviser in future, and may try to

2. The development of medical paternalism

find one who will respect his opinions absolutely. In an unrestricted market, as long as there are some people who want their legal consultants to do only what they tell them to do, there are likely to be consultants who will provide such a service.

The purpose of the above discussion is to demonstrate the likely presence of mechanisms which ensure that, even where individuals have to rely on the knowledge of others, their wishes – however broadly or specifically they choose to define them – will be complied with. (I am not, of course, suggesting these mechanisms are necessarily perfect.) We certainly need not accept the contention which is sometimes made, that by consulting others for their expert knowledge, we implicitly subscribe to the paternalist thesis that others sometimes know our interests better than we do ourselves.[1] We do not, typically, consult professionals because we think they know more about our interests than we do; rather, we consult them because although we know what our interests are, we do not know the best means of realising them.

The mechanisms tending to produce a correspondence between wants and supplies in the market for intellectual expertise crucially depend, however, on the existence of competition between different agents of the same type. Any given legal adviser has an incentive to act in accordance with his client's wishes, because if he does not, his client is likely to transfer his business to another adviser who will so act.

Let us now consider a situation in which competition between legal advisers has been drastically reduced. Let us imagine that a number of advisers have formed themselves into an association, and have managed to persuade the government to make it impossible for someone who is not a member of this organisation to offer legal advice. Now this organisation starts to make up regulations about what its members may or may not do. If any member breaks any of the rules, he may be ejected from the organisation and hence will have to cease practising.

What are the likely consequences of such a development? In any situation where the majority of legal advisers wish to behave in a certain way, it seems they will be able to behave in that way, regardless of the wishes of their clients. For example, if the majority of advisers think that clients should not be able to obtain advice on a particular subject, perhaps because they think such advice would be used for purposes which they regard as unethical, they can simply invent a rule prohibiting members of the association from offering advice on this topic. This service will then become completely unavailable to members of the public. As a second example, consider a rule which required members always to act according to their own judgement, and never to allow the wishes of the client to overrule that judgement. Such a rule would mean, in effect, that the demand for a non-paternalistic type of legal advice would not be met.

---

[1] See for example Lively 1983.

Incidentally, I am aware that as far as *solicitors* are concerned, such a restricted framework already exists. It is true that you cannot call yourself a solicitor, and cannot offer certain legal services such as representing defendants in the magistrates' courts, unless you are a member of the Law Society. However, it is possible for non-members to offer advice in various areas of the law, even if most legal advisers are in fact also solicitors. This is in contrast with the medical profession, where a practitioner's inability to prescribe medication unless licensed by the General Medical Council makes the possibility of practising without such a licence a somewhat empty one as far as the question of competition is concerned.

Let us consider another way in which the simple competition structure in legal services might be distorted. Let us imagine that advisers started to be paid to provide their services to individuals, not directly by those individuals, but by the government, using money compulsorily collected from those or other individuals, and that this becomes the dominant mode of providing legal advice. Let us further imagine that the government also starts to pay advisers for providing services which are not among those normally requested by individuals, but which are felt to be in the general interest of the community. What would the effects of these developments be?

First, it is likely that legal advisers would feel far less answerable to their individual clients. To the extent that they are remunerated by the state, their dependence on, and hence their answerability towards, their clients will diminish. Secondly, since most advisers are now financially dependent on the same source, i.e. the state, the views of that source are likely to feature very strongly in the way that their trade is practised, creating a service which is highly monolithic. Thirdly, their job now involves duties other than simply helping individuals attain their objectives, and requires them to think in terms of *the public interest*, which may well conflict with particular individual interests. This means that their overall professional outlook is likely to shift to accommodate their new role as agents of the community. The effect on their attitude to their individual clients may well be that they question whether they should necessarily comply with a client's wishes, when these seem to be at odds with the interests of their other master, the 'public good'.

One final likely effect of severing the economic connection between a profession and its clients should be mentioned. While our hypothetical advisers were still dependent on meeting clients' needs sufficiently closely to attract and retain business, the scope for developing a philosophy of legal advice according to abstract principles was minimal. There was no question of advisers asking themselves, 'what is our *moral* duty to our client'; not to any practical effect, at least, since whatever duties they had would have been based on commercial and legal, not moral, considerations. Once our advisers have liberated themselves from the commercial pressure to comply with the wishes of their clients, however, they are free to determine the rules and boundaries of their work among themselves.

We are likely to find them debating such conundrums as, 'should the client's wishes always be respected?', or 'should the client always be told what is going on?', or 'is our responsibility primarily to individual clients or to society as a whole?'. An image of legal advisers is likely to be generated according to which they offer their services from *moral* motives, their self-imposed obligations generating certain justified claims and rights on their part. Thus, questions may be asked such as 'should an adviser be *expected* to provide advice of a particular kind?', or (paradoxically) 'what safeguards should we provide to prevent *advisers* from being exploited by their clients?'

The monopolisation of medicine

It might be thought that a profession which developed in any of the ways outlined above would quickly become unviable. Yet the medical profession has followed precisely these routes.

Monopolisation of the profession was largely achieved in the nineteenth century, as a result of vigorous campaigning on the part of surgeons and general practitioners. As Roy Porter says of the Medical Register created in 1858, '[its significance] lay, of course, in those it excluded. For all ranks of general practitioners now appeared as "insiders" lined up against all "outsiders" – the unqualified homeopaths, medical botanists, quacks, bone setters and the like who are automatically constituted by exclusion into the "fringe".' David Green, in his book *Working-Class Patients and the Medical Establishment*, gives an interesting account of how nineteenth-century medical associations campaigned to monopolise and restrict the profession, and in particular to undermine voluntary medical insurance schemes such as those provided by friendly societies. Green's book provides a number of examples of how doctors regarded competition as inimical and tried as far as possible to avoid it. In 1899, for example, the County of Durham Medical Union passed a resolution 'That when the Qualified Practitioners of any district make a combined effort to raise the standard of their fees, and thereby the status of the profession, it should be deemed infamous conduct [one of the grounds for barring a doctor from practising] for any Registered Practitioner to attempt to frustrate their efforts by opposing them at cheaper rates of payment, and canvassing for clients... .'

Since the time when the profession more or less eliminated competition from conventional medicine, doctors and their supporters have attempted to persuade us of the advantages of a system of medicine free from the squalor of market mechanisms. It may be that we have been spared a certain amount of silly advertising, such as may still be observed to some extent in the United States. But this supposed benefit has been bought at enormous cost in terms of loss of our power as clients to control the medicine we receive, and to promote and maintain its efficiency. In the days of competitive medicine, if a doctor did a bad job, clients had an immediate course of action open to them: they could vote with their feet. In George Eliot's *Middlemarch*, a doctor fails to diagnose that a young man (Fred) has typhoid. Fred's family do not believe that doctors are infallible and decide to call in another doctor for a second opinion. The second doctor correctly diagnoses typhoid, and Fred's father duly shows his dissatisfaction with the first doctor in the strongest possible terms. This should be compared with the modern situation, where, as an NHS client for instance, one needs to get the *permission* of one's GP before one can get a second opinion.

Curiously, some analysts of the health service have suggested that the intrinsic tendency of the medical profession to become monopolistic can only be combated by getting the state to intervene; not to encourage competition, but to run the monopoly itself. While privatisation may not be an automatic cure for all inefficiencies, it is hard to see how the problems of a monopoly are solved by having the government run it. Professor Bosanquet, for example, argues that the NHS is 'a countervailing force to the medical monopoly'. The state *qua* NHS is not, however, an independent third party standing between the medical industry and consumers. It *is*, to all intents and purposes, the medical industry. The fact that some differences of interest remain between itself and practitioners reflects no more than the traditional difference in perspective between employers and employees. While doctors may not be 'employees' of the NHS in strict legal terms, as a group they are without question economically dependent on the NHS.

The move to domination of the medical profession by the state was, at least to begin with, less obviously driven by the wishes of the profession than its monopolisation was. In the UK, attitudes among doctors to the 1946 National Health Service Act were ambivalent, although largely because doctors feared a loss of independence and status. However, promises of financial compensation from the then Labour government succeeded in overcoming resistance. Since then, the profession has shown little sign of being unhappy with its close association to the state, and indeed has been a vociferous supporter of the principle of state medicine.

Paternalism rejected

What, it may be asked, is wrong with paternalism? If doctors really *were* better able to assess what will be best for the client, what would be wrong with them making the decisions? The answer is, nothing, provided the client agrees with this and wishes it. The primary question is not whether doctors' decisions do usually produce better results than clients' decisions would – although we should be suspicious of this claim when it is made by doctors themselves – but whether the choice between paternalism and non-paternalism should be made by clients, by doctors or by society. Some

2. The development of medical paternalism

clients might well opt for paternalism for themselves in specific situations if given the choice. At present, however, it is doctors who make the choice, and the vast majority of them tend towards paternalism. That they do so is often assumed to be because of their preference for 'doing good' over respect for the client's wishes, but it is also possible that it reflects a preference for greater power over their clients. The situation in which it is doctors' preferences that determine the 'first round' of the decision process, i.e. who determines the basic principles of medical practice, has not come about as a result of ethical discussions or democratic choices. How, then, can this situation be legitimate?

Even if it were the case that doctors' decisions produced better results for clients than those which would be made by clients themselves, *on average*, it is not clear that this is a sufficient argument for preventing everyone from determining their own treatment. Nor is it clear that, if universal paternalism were democratically chosen (say, by referendum), this would suffice to legitimise the current situation. If a person judged that his own decisions, perhaps informed by the advice of a doctor, were more likely to lead to optimal results, then it is hard to see how those who preferred paternalism for themselves would have the right to infringe that person's right to autonomy.

It is not only the *legitimacy* of an arrangement in which paternalism is exercised automatically by one group of people over another group which we must question. It is necessary to consider the possibility of exploitation. If a client asks his doctor to make all the decisions for him, and hence to act paternalistically, then it will be clear that he has given his doctor a power which he will expect to be used sensibly and carefully. The doctor will have some incentive to do the best possible thing for the client, as he is unlikely to be granted the same power again if he does a bad job. If, on the other hand, as is largely the case at the moment, doctors feel they have an automatic *right* to act paternalistically, and do not need to be empowered by the client to do so, what incentive do they have not to abuse this 'right'? Perhaps we can rely on a fear on their part that they might lose business if they did so. However, if doctors can decide collectively how they will act, and if – as we shall see – they are generally judged only by the standards of their colleagues, it seems that exploitation is perfectly possible provided only that the form it takes is not too exceptional. Moreover, the professional mystique which surrounds medical practice protects it from scrutiny and criticism, which facilitates the abuse of an automatic power to act paternalistically.

Doctors would perhaps argue that they have a *self-imposed* requirement to act in the best interests of their clients, even under paternalism. Membership of the medical profession imposes a moral duty on them never to abuse their power. But one is perfectly entitled to question whether this is true of all, or even the majority, of practitioners; and whether in any case such a moral duty is always observed even if it is felt. An alternative, less sanguine view of the moral status of medical practitioners might be that many of those who enter the profession are attracted to it by the prospect of gratifying sadistic power urges. The greater the discretion given to such persons to make medical decisions without referring to the wishes of their clients, the more they are likely covertly to exploit their power in order to indulge those urges.

This view, at the opposite end of the spectrum to the view that doctors are noble and saintly creatures, may strike some as extreme. It might be argued that there is insufficient evidence for such a degree of cynicism about the medical profession. However, it is not necessary for our purposes that one should be able to prove that it is applicable to a significant number of doctors. All we need note is that the view may not be immediately rejected, and that it is one to which a client holding it is perfectly entitled. Such a client would rightly object to automatic paternalism, and would rightly refuse to tolerate a model of medical practice which depended crucially upon the premise that doctors are benevolent.

Thus criticisms of medical paternalism which argue that the principle of client autonomy should have priority over the principle of beneficence (doing what is 'best') miss the point. It is rather like arguing over whether a particular slave should be freed, *merely because* autonomy is an important principle; or maintained in his existing state, because his material welfare is likely to be better while he is owned by his master. The argument becomes academic once it is accepted that slavery is not an option, and that one person cannot have an absolute right over another. Similarly, doctors do not have a *right* to impose their values on clients; the question of which moral principle *they* should follow when deciding on treatment is therefore irrelevant in this context. What is wrong with medical practice is not paternalism *per se*, but the fact that it is applied without overriding choice on the part of the client. Moreover, to take the slave analogy further, we may rightly be sceptical of the claim that the slave's welfare is maximised under the ownership of his master when this claim is made by someone other than the slave himself.

As with other medical dilemmas, the one about paternalism versus autonomy is exacerbated by the fact that medicine is not subject to any market pressures. If there were competition between doctors, and some of them were out-and-out paternalists who never took any notice of their clients' wishes, then these doctors might get clients who preferred that approach, but there would no doubt be others who would put their clients' wishes first. It is largely because of the absence of competition, and because doctors more or less decide among themselves as to how in general they will proceed, that it is necessary to argue against medical paternalism at all.

On the other hand, in view of the theoretical possibility that imperfections in a genuine market for medicine might mean that unwanted paternalism was practised even in the complete absence of restrictions, there is a case to be made for having some kind of legal prohibition on doctors refusing a treatment which a client has requested. Withholding an available treatment should, I would suggest, be treated in a similar way to slavery: it is not enough to remove the economic and political structures which encourage its prevalence, it should be absolutely forbidden.

3

Medical professionals: facts and fictions

A woman lay dying from lung cancer in a hospital ward for six days without being visited by a doctor ... Despite repeated requests from her husband, who was constantly at her bedside, the couple were ignored by medical staff ... Nurses had contacted the junior doctor several times but he had found the persistent requests annoying and had tended to 'blank them out'. The couple were fobbed off with excuses such as that the doctor was too busy ... On the sixth day, when the consultant visited the woman on his ward round, he told her husband not to look so worried and that he hoped she would be able to go home in a few days, but said nothing about the diagnosis or treatment. She died that night. (*The Times*, 11 December 1992)

I wouldn't want most of my clients to realise what an ego trip I get from taking care of them, because there's something selfish about the fact that a lot of women are dependent on you. ... I think there are some in the specialty who like to punish women. Some doctors really get a kind of unconscious kick from seeing a woman in labour. There are some doctors who are very sadistic. (American gynaecologist, quoted in Daly 1979, 260)

The desire to believe in the benevolence and wisdom of health care professionals finds support from the iconography of medicine as purveyed by books, films and television drama. Doctors and nurses, as they are usually portrayed, may unintentionally make mistakes, but they are always caring, scrupulous, idealistic, and act from the highest of motives. At worst, they are the victims of a system forcing them to be less considerate to their patients than they would like to be. It has been questioned whether this romantic vision corresponds to the perceptions of the public about real-life medicine.[1] Even if not, there must presumably be a distinct readiness to accept such images, and a strong desire for them, if the entertainment industry finds it profitable to promulgate them.

It seems that in the public imagination the medical profession towers in moral stature above the rest of human society, including other professional groups such as lawyers (unscrupulous), politicians (sleazy) and businessmen (rapacious). The mere fact that a person chooses to occupy a position providing power over other people's lives in the most intimate way

---

[1] See for example Neuberger 1994.

possible is regarded as indicative that he is marked by a kind of moral eminence. So high is our regard for, and expectation about the goodwill of, the medical profession, that even doctors themselves have to remind us gently from time to time that they, too, may occasionally be fallible. 'Doctors are only human ... and are subject to the same temptations as other human beings despite their generally high motivation and extensive training', doctors Bliss and Johnson point out.

Apart from such rare concessions of fallibility, the standard comment about medical practitioners is to express admiration for their selflessness, their dedication, their exalted motivation. On the day Dr Nigel Cox – who administered a lethal injection to his client – was found guilty of attempted murder, a BMA spokesman reminded us of the tenet that 'doctors ... will always put the interest of their clients above their own self-interest'. The idea that this might be a ludicrous exaggeration seems to be ruled out of consideration. In a recent article commenting on the case of a bogus 'doctor', a practitioner is quoted as saying that 'the desire to be a doctor and powerful and influential can be so great that the underlying inadequate personality is well hidden', and that fake doctors may be motivated to satisfy some perversion by practising surgery. Yet it is rarely suggested that the same points may apply to some or even many qualified practitioners.

The taboo against disparaging the motives of the medical profession appears to be a relatively modern phenomenon. In an 1823 issue of *The Lancet*, for example, the editor of the journal referred to the Royal College of Surgeons as 'this sink of infamy and corruption, this receptacle of all that is avaricious, base, worthless, and detestable in the surgical profession'. An editorial in *The Times* in 1856 opined that the President of the Royal College of Physicians 'is so nearly on a par with the meanest herbalist. The result of the longest, most profound medical experience is so often a discussion of the worthlessness of medicine.' Such a level of cynicism about medicine is now almost unimaginable. It helps, of course, that the different sectors of the medical profession nowadays take more care not to air their differences in public. Strenuous efforts appear to be made to maintain the image of the profession as one which speaks with a single authoritative voice.

By the turn of the century, doctors had already begun to take on that image of middle-class professional respectability with which they are now intimately associated. George Bernard Shaw's statement about doctors, made in 1906, is sometimes used to show that criticism of the medical profession has always been with us, but it also serves as an illustration of the way in which the position of doctors as affluent members of the establishment had been legitimised by Shaw's time.

> If you are going to have doctors, you had better have doctors well off; just as if you are going to have a landlord, you had better have a rich landlord.

3. Medical professionals: facts and fictions

Taking all the round of professions and occupations, you will find that every man is the worse for being poor; and the doctor is a specially dangerous man when poor ... . (cited by Neuberger 1994, 377)

Shaw implicitly notes here the potential for exploitation of those in control of essential resources such as housing or medicine. Although there is a tendency nowadays automatically to regard private landlords as morally suspect, the analogous perception about doctors is no longer expressed.

Medical power and its implications

By having absolute control of medical technology, thus being able to make the difference between agony and comfort, or between death and life, doctors have an extraordinary amount of power over us. Yet the implications of this fact are obscured by a certain amount of hypocrisy. Instead of considering the possibility that many doctors enjoy the power they wield, we are frequently regaled with complaints about the difficulties such power creates for them. Commenting on the decision whether to treat a comatose client who is dependent on mechanical life support, for example, the authors of a standard textbook on medical ethics (Mason and McCall Smith) say that the decision relates to the allocation of scarce resources, and comment that making a choice between clients 'may be among the doctor's most agonising moments and the weight to be given to economic and policy considerations can only be judged by the individual physician or surgeon ...'. Statements about the 'agony' of such choices should be viewed with the same scepticism that would be accorded to a teacher's claim that, while he approved of corporal punishment, it was 'agonising' for him when it came to administering it.

The dogma that doctors are virtuous almost by default leads to a certain *naïveté* when it is discussed how much discretion over the fate of their clients they should be given. There are of course phenomena such as the Nazi biological experiments, or contemporary torture practices in South America, in which qualified physicians have played roles ranging from the ambiguous to the abominable. These, and the occasional media report of outrageous medical negligence or malevolence, have made it harder to claim that doctors invariably seek to reduce suffering, and that they invariably do so efficiently. However, the original theory can be maintained by the expedient of mentally splitting the population of health care workers into two quite distinct groups. On the one hand there are those (the vast majority) who are well-intentioned and skilful. On the other hand there are the very few who are intrinsically mad or evil, and who somehow slipped through the net. Thus the philosopher Jonathan Glover, for example, having raised the question of whether doctors should be allowed to switch off the respirators of unconscious clients, dismisses the fear that this power might eventually be abused along the lines of Treblinka and the

Nazi euthanasia programme. 'Pessimism here seems hard to reconcile with any knowledge of the deeply ingrained attitudes of most doctors and nurses. There is a widespread reluctance to kill, and much awareness of the difficulty of knowing that someone's life is not worth living.' The evidence to be considered in the second half of this book, however, suggests that the reluctance to kill may be somewhat less ingrained than Glover imagines.

Interestingly, in the various debates this century between supporters and opponents of euthanasia, the assumption that doctors are the best judges of what should be done has been a remarkably consistent feature on both sides. Glanville Williams, in his book *The Sanctity of Life and the Criminal Law*, describes the arguments employed when the House of Lords debated the 1936 Euthanasia Bill.

> Lord Dawson [who was not against euthanasia on principle] opposed the bill on the ground that he preferred the present position under which everything was left to the discretion of the doctor. The Archbishop of Canterbury seized upon this idea with approval and relief; at the end of his speech he guardedly admitted that 'cases arise in which some means of shortening life may be justified'; but he thought that Parliament should fold its hands because these cases were best left to the medical profession. (Williams 1958, 300)

Williams himself, a supporter of euthanasia, gives as his chief objection to this approach that it leaves the doctor 'unprotected against the (admittedly remote) possibility of a vindictive prosecution, the result of which, if it takes place, and if the defendant is unlucky in his judge and jury, may be professional ruin – loss of reputation, loss of liberty, loss of livelihood for himself and his dependants'. The loss of life to the client who is killed without consent, on the other hand, is not an issue to which Williams makes much reference. Commenting on his own favoured solution, that full discretion to kill their seriously ill clients be given to doctors, and that consent on the part of the client should be presumed in a trial, with the burden of proof resting on the prosecution, he dismisses fears that doctors will be tempted to murder their clients for private reasons as 'irrational'.

A new kind of doctor

It is not only the moral elevation, and hence moral authority, of health care workers which is habitually presumed. Their function itself has changed as the character of medicine has altered. Doctors have begun to take on, through self-advertisement and through legislation which reinforces their propaganda, the role filled at a previous stage of history by the clergy, of being general all-round do-gooders and social arbiters. Indeed, doctors are now sometimes *discouraged* from fulfilling their traditional function of supplying treatment, it being argued for example that what many clients

3. Medical professionals: facts and fictions

want is not a prescription but sympathy and understanding.[2] Indeed, there appears to be a more general trend for doctors to take it upon themselves to guess what is *behind* the statements or requests made by their clients.

The new identity of doctors appears to include acting as community guardians: detecting and reporting child abuse, identifying psychological or social problems, disclosing suspicions of criminal activity, and so on. During the Cleveland child abuse inquiry, for example, it emerged that certain paediatricians were more concerned with the possibility of sexual abuse than with dealing with the specific condition about which they were being consulted.[3] One of the paediatricians was reported as asserting that 'sexual abuse of children occurred and that until recently it had passed largely undetected. She believed that paediatricians *had a responsibility to right this wrong* ...' (my italics). There was no suggestion from the Inquiry that there was something fundamentally flawed about this attitude.

Like priests, doctors demand an attitude of absolute trust, and encourage us to believe that they can solve all manner of problems. Merely talking to a doctor, or being examined by one, is akin to communion or confession, dissolving away one's troubles. The following quote, by a former director of Cleveland County Council's Children's Resource Centre, illustrates this faith in the potency of the physician. 'A lot of abused children feel bad and dirty inside, so the medical examination is part of the therapeutic process because we can show them that we can make it better and affirm the child's body. A lot of older children feel they've got cancer inside, so that something has invaded them, and so a medical examination can help clear that away.' In other words, it is supposed to be good for a young girl who has been raped to have a medical authority figure inspect her anus, irrespective of whether or not she genuinely wants to have such an inspection.

Doctors are encouraged to become involved as protagonists in political debates about health provision. The fact that this is not really part of their job, and that such an approach could lead them to compromise the interests of their individual clients, is disguised by referring to the notion that the role of a doctor is principally a *moral* rather than a commercial one, as the following quotation illustrates.

> Medicine is an individual discipline, but ill-health has a variety of causes, many of them environmental – poor housing, unemployment, poverty and inadequate nutrition, smoking and alcohol. These factors should be of some concern to doctors if they want to remedy ill-health. ... No one is asking a doctor to lay down his or her stethoscope and march off to the housing department to insist on a new flat with an inside lavatory and hot and cold

---

[2] See for example Coleman 1988, 5-6.
[3] Butler-Sloss 1988, 37.

running water for Mr Bloggins (although he could try to persuade him to stop smoking). But it is possible to distinguish between the local and the national scene ... Indeed, it is not only possible, but it would seem entirely appropriate if doctors are to pay attention to the higher ideals of their calling – in short, their ethical duties. For the ideals that doctors have set themselves are among the very highest. (Phillips and Dawson 1985, 149)

The idea that the role of a doctor is merely to comply with the wishes of the client, if necessary after appropriate advice has been given, or even simply to provide the client with the necessary instruments to carry out the treatment he wishes himself, appears to be beneath contempt as far as the majority of doctors are concerned. Thus 'advance directives', which clients could use to determine in advance what treatments they would wish to decline if they became 'incompetent', have been criticised on the ground that they would 'gravely undermine the professional expertise and judgement of doctors. It would make doctors nothing more than slaves of society.'

This attitude to client autonomy explains why the debate on euthanasia, for example, revolves around the question of the rights and responsibilities of *doctors*. 'It would be extremely easy', the BMA has told its members, 'to comply with [a request for euthanasia] and end the lives of individuals unfortunate enough to suffer ... problems which cripple them but leave consciousness and rationality intact. It is *a far more demanding and challenging task* [for doctors] to attempt to discover value in the terrible situation that exists [and] it is more in accord with the ethos of medicine to make that attempt than to kill the client.'

The fact that the essential rationality and decency of the medical profession tends not to be questioned leads to some curiously biased interpretations of medical phenomena. Thus, for example, any reluctance on the part of individuals to present their health problems to their GP tends to be taken as a sign that something is wrong with the attitude of *clients*. It is rarely suggested that the complete powerlessness of the client in the doctor-client relationship might have something to do with the fact that many people have an intense aversion to doctors. For instance, it appears that many people in Britain who develop cancer of the bowel wait six to nine months before consulting a doctor about their symptoms, and that by that time more than half of them are beyond hope. Instead of concluding that the reason why these people do not behave in their apparent best interests might have something to do with a dislike of medical authoritarianism, we are told by an expert on bowel cancer that the solution to the problem is 'to screen everybody above the age of 55'.

Bodies as mechanisms

Several critics of medicine have commented on the way that the hospitalisation of medicine has increased the power of doctors over their clients. The status of the client in a hospital setting has become that of a mechanism, temporarily under the jurisdiction of the technicians, rather like a car in a workshop. With the consent-to-treatment requirement (see chapter 9) reduced to a formulaic ritual, the client's body effectively becomes the property of the professionals. When the client is unconscious or otherwise unable to communicate, the temptation to exercise absolute power over the client becomes particularly strong, as we shall see in chapter 10.

The concern of doctors is generally recognised to be with the mechanics of the body. The client's wishes, feelings, pain, preferences take second place to the question of whether the mechanism can be made to work properly again. To some extent, this is perhaps to be expected. The job of a doctor is to recognise problems of physiology and to take appropriate action. The 'customer satisfaction' aspect of this work is one which, as in any area of commercial life, can be neglected if a positive effort to provide it is not made. The incentive for making this effort would normally come from the commercial motive. If I do a good job, but am rude to my customers or neglectful of their preferences, then my customers may well decamp to my rival whose customer relations are better. Without such competitive pressures, the tendency is to neglect this aspect of the work, and this is undoubtedly one of the reasons why the medical profession, and particularly perhaps that part of it operating in the state sector, performs so badly in the area of courtesy and respect for the individual client.

In this respect, demands that doctors take more account of their clients' psychological state, or that they provide a more 'holistic' service, are misplaced. It is not the role of doctors to assess their clients' personalities or psychological problems. What *is* required, rather, is some sort of incentive system which motivates doctors to be more considerate about their clients' subjective experiences, and to treat them as conscious persons rather than as machines.

The trend to be more aware of patient 'needs' should certainly not be confused with the promotion of autonomy, as it sometimes is. It is more likely to involve a form of paternalism, since it encourages doctors to take non-medical factors into account without the client necessarily being aware of this. Thus Ian Kennedy, criticising the old mechanistic approach of medicine, notes approvingly that changes 'intended to cause doctors to address the social context of a patient's complaint and seek to involve the various social services have been made and this is now reflected somewhat in practice'. If anything, this modern form of paternalism appears to be worse than the old model, according to which paternalism supposedly took the form of being arrogant and commandeering. At least under the old system, you knew when the doctor was being paternalistic. The modern approach may mean that interpretations are being placed on statements made by you during the consultation, or that other professionals are consulted to determine your best interests, without your being aware of this, while your doctor continues to present a sympathetic and ostensibly deferential demeanour.

Once medical professionals regard a client as dead, his freedom from unwanted interference is even more severely threatened. Some doctors would prefer to see the individual's rights over his or her own body terminated at death. Thus it has been proposed that autopsies should be mandatory where this would advance medical knowledge.

The suggestion is often made that a presumption of organ transferability should exist, rebuttable by evidence to the contrary. Thus instead of carrying a donor card to indicate their willingness to have their organs removed after death, people would have to carry a non-donor card or equivalent to avoid having their bodies automatically plundered when pronounced dead. Kennedy, for example, favours such a 'contracting-out' scheme and has little time for the claim that this might represent an invasion of the individual's rights. He comments that this argument 'is patently question-begging, as it depends on which individual is considered, the deceased, his spouse or relative, or the dying patient'. On the other hand, Kennedy is firmly opposed to the idea of individuals choosing to sell one of their kidneys while alive. Again, the wishes of the medical experts – that organs of dead clients be exploited – are intended to prevail, the wishes of the possessors of those organs being at best a secondary consideration.

The historical antecedents of the trend to regard corpses as community property, to be exploited as agents of the community (doctors) see fit, are worth noting. In the eighteenth century, graverobbing was a common source of physiological information for surgeons. Although the practice was unlawful, a surgeon who was caught might well escape punishment. Executed felons automatically lost all right to their bodies: the act of handing over their corpses to the surgeons for public dissection emphasised both the power of doctors over the bodies of the lay public and the alliance between medicine and the state. Symbolically, the first incisions into the bodies of criminals were made in the form of a cross, as if to stress that the surgeon was performing not merely an educational but a retributional exercise.[4]

'Therapeutic' deceit

The assumption that health care workers are benevolent and invariably better-informed than their clients has been used to justify the gradual

---

[4] For an interesting account of the relationship between the medical profession and the public with regard to corpses, see Fissell 1991, chapter 8.

3. Medical professionals: facts and fictions

transfer of decision-making powers from clients to practitioners. It is now more or less taken for granted that one visits one's doctor, not to obtain information about one's condition and possible courses of action, but to accept whatever treatment he considers fit, including no treatment at all. If one is fortunate, one may be told something about the condition and the prescribed treatment, but in some cases one may be given only a minimum of information, or even be told lies about one's condition.

The principle that a doctor does not need to tell his clients more than he thinks is good for them has received legal sanction in a number of court cases. Thus the disclosure of the risks of an operation is, in Lord Scarman's view, properly withheld where 'a reasonable medical assessment of the patient would have indicated to the doctor that disclosure would have posed a serious threat of psychological detriment to the patient'. Lord Denning once indicated that it was entirely for the individual doctor to decide how much to tell his client, and that a 'therapeutic lie' was justifiable if deemed to be in the client's best interests.[5] The difficulty with being able to justify non-disclosure by reference to the psychological well-being of the client is that this criterion is hopelessly subjective.

The medical profession may of course like to believe in the distinction between a therapeutic lie and a lie of mere convenience. Thus Mason and McCall Smith argue that the protection of the client from worry 'is not the same thing as deciding to withhold information which it is thought would lead the client to refuse the treatment'. This latter course of action, they say, is 'hardly acceptable ethically'. If, however, a doctor wishes to proceed with a certain course but thinks that his client would not agree, he may easily avail himself of the 'well-being' argument to achieve precisely this purpose.

The courts have generally encouraged doctors in this paternalistic approach. In a New Zealand Supreme Court case from the early sixties which is still cited, the judge argued that 'complete absence of warnings or even a "soft answer" is justifiable depending on the circumstances. Unless this were so, some clients would be deprived of essential treatments by an unreasoning fear, or doctors deterred from giving them the best chance of survival, because no discussion had been possible in the particular circumstances.' Here we already see a hint of the agenda of medicine in the modern welfare state: the doctor is to promote the health of the client in the way he thinks best, regardless of the client's wishes; if necessary, by manipulating him into consent.

More objectionable still is the common practice of not telling the client when there is something seriously wrong. In Japan, for example, a nation with a strong tradition of professional authoritarianism, this appears to be standard practice. It has been alleged that most Japanese cancer victims never find out why they are dying. It may be appropriate in some cases not

---

[5] *Hatcher v Black* 1954; see Nelson-Jones and Burton 1990, 68.

to force bad news upon a client, but many doctors go well beyond this, concealing the true state of affairs however hard the client presses for information. The following case incidentally provides an illustration of the extraordinary power the doctor holds, not only over his clients, but also their relatives.

> Marion was 39 and had a brain tumour. ... The neurosurgeon could only partially excise the tumour and he told David, her husband, about her prognosis. Without any discussion the neurosurgeon stated that he had decided that she should be told only that she had a cyst and that radiotherapy would cure it. ... She was very glad to hear that she would soon be much better, and although David still wanted to tell her the truth, he was reluctant to spoil her pleasure in the first good weeks.
> Initially she did do well, but soon she stopped improving and began to wonder why her efforts in physiotherapy no longer produced results. When she began to deteriorate, she thought she was not trying hard enough and became depressed, and sometimes suicidal. By then her personality had changed somewhat and David felt she no longer had the resources to cope with the truth. When she came into our care she was frightened, sometimes paranoid and often confused. We could not tell her then because we could not be certain that she was able to concentrate long enough to take in all we said. ... So we had to agree with David that it was now too late to tell. We managed her distress as well as we could with drugs, but she died frightened and isolated. ... Because she did not realise that she had a disease that could account for her deterioration, she had to find another cause, and she blamed us. Later, knowing intuitively that she was dying, she said in her paranoia 'You are killing me'. (Corney 1991, 66-7)

Beyond constraint?

The policy of investing health care workers with more and more discretion seems astonishing when considered in the light of empirical data about their behaviour. We already have evidence about what can happen when individuals whose civil liberties are curtailed, so that the requirement for consent to treatment is weak or non-existent, come under the power of doctors. Horrific occurrences of coercive medical treatment in police stations, prisons and psychiatric hospitals demonstrate the strong likelihood of abuse when people who are assumed to have high technical and ethical standards are given near-absolute power over a person's physiology. The same is true of situations where respect for individual volition is weak for other reasons: in children's homes and in institutions for the elderly or the disabled. For example, a recent report by the Central Council for Nursing, Midwifery and Health Visiting reported that the number of residents of old people's homes who had been mistreated by staff had trebled over the space of five years.[6]

The following is a particularly horrific example of abuse which recently

---

[6] *Sunday Times*, 24 July 1994.

3. Medical professionals: facts and fictions

attracted attention as a result of a Cutting Edge documentary shown on Channel Four. The case also illustrates the folly of supposing that the exploitation of power can be effectively prevented by the mere presence of regulations which prohibit such exploitation, while discretion remains in the hands of the professionals exercising that power. All the activities referred to were in breach of the Mental Health Act 1983, as well as contravening various guidelines issued by the medical and psychiatric professions, yet despite being brought to the attention of the Department of Health by the Mental Health Act Commission (a body set up to protect the rights of psychiatric patients) they continued for a number of years.

> A Broadmoor doctor allowed patients to be given electric shock treatment without anaesthetic or the necessary permission, it was claimed last night. Dr Kypros Loucas also allegedly experimented on sex offenders using a controversial hormone treatment which can have horrific side effects. Despite repeated warnings about his conduct, health ministers failed to take action. Instead the doctor was allowed to continue his job as a senior consultant at the Berkshire maximum security hospital for another two years. He then moved to the Horton Hospital, an NHS psychiatric unit in Epsom, Surrey, where a patient in his care died after a massive drug overdose. Dr Loucas ... now works at Wormwood Scrubs Prison ... (*Sunday Express*, 6 December 1992)

A letter sent to *The Independent* by members of staff at Broadmoor in response to an article about the programme is illuminating about the difficulties some have, particularly health workers themselves, in accepting the idea that not all doctors and nurses are motivated by benevolence.

> Sir: On 7 December you gave a great deal of space to the problems that you perceive to exist in Broadmoor Hospital and printed allegations against Dr Kypros Loucas. Rarely do we, the staff of all disciplines, have any chance to answer the sort of allegations made against us without substantiation. Readers of the tabloid press, of course, believe that we [are all] rapists, child abusers and murderers. Although we, the staff, know so much better, and actually care very much for our patients, we can be somewhat upset that ex-patients seem to be believed absolutely while we have no voice. (letter to the *Independent*, 10 December 1992)

I suggest that what prevents abuses similar to those at Broadmoor Hospital from occurring on a comparable scale in conventional medical settings is only the fact that the balance of power in the case of ordinary doctor-client interactions is not yet totally biased in favour of the professional. Of course, we do not know to what extent the abuse of doctors' powers occurs in ordinary hospitals, any more than we can be sure about the extent of abuse in prisons or police stations. In view of the secrecy of the medical profession, it seems reasonable to suppose that any incidents that come to light are merely the tip of the iceberg.

Nursing staff are not immune from the risk of abuse, as various incidents which have recently come to light involving nurses murdering or mistreating clients confirm. In one striking case which went to trial in 1989, four nurses working on the geriatric wards of a hospital in Austria were convicted for the murders of over 40 clients in their charge, although the true figure was thought to have been in the hundreds.[7] The nurses killed their clients by forcing water down their throats to induce drowning, or by injecting barbiturates or insulin. In Britain, the Beverly Allitt case in which a young nurse was convicted of the murder of four children and the attempted murder of three others, provided an illustration of the ease with which recognisably disturbed individuals are given positions of responsibility within the state medical system. In view of the refusal to hold a public enquiry, the case also indicated a worrying reluctance on the part of the government to exercise visible control over parts of the system where standards have clearly sunk to unacceptable levels. A spokesman for the British Association of Social Workers argued that the call for a public enquiry needed to be resisted so that the organisation under review could 'continue to function and to learn from past mistakes ... enquiries in public put the maximum pressure on witnesses [and] cause the maximum long-term damage to the agency under review'.

It is possible that medical positions in coercive institutions attract those of a particularly dubious mentality among practitioners. If so, then what appeals is presumably the impotence of the client in such situations. It follows that the more the autonomy of the ordinary client is eroded, the more the population of ordinary practitioners is likely to number among its members the sort of people who suffer from sadistic urges, a compulsion to punish, or other unsavoury personality features.

There is little reason to think that the medical profession's own systems of self-regulation are by themselves adequate to the task of keeping out the incompetent and the malevolent from among their number. For example, it was recently revealed that nearly half the doctors barred by the General Medical Council are subsequently reinstated.[8] Relying on the members of a professional guild to criticise one another seems a somewhat unrealistic policy. As Margaret Brazier, for example, points out, colleagues in the same health authority 'simply refuse to testify against each other' in negligence cases.

If we cannot rely on self-regulation, those of us who do not subscribe to the belief that every doctor invariably acts in good faith must look to the law for a minimum of protection. Of course, the law is hardly an ideal instrument for this purpose, considering how difficult it is to recognise, let alone prove, medical negligence. If an investor loses all his money in a conventional investment vehicle, there is a presumption that the fund

---

[7] *The Times*, 10 April 1989.
[8] *Sunday Times*, 25 September 1994.

3. Medical professionals: facts and fictions

manager did not do his job properly. If sued in court, the manager may have to explain why he did so badly. When a medical client dies or suffers, however, it is not easy to determine whether this could reasonably have been avoided, given that the client was usually sick to begin with. Medicine is not an exact science, and even if all the relevant client information is available, and another qualified practitioner prepared to assess it critically, the verdict is likely to be ambiguous. Nevertheless, some legal restraint on the behaviour of medical workers is clearly essential.

Unfortunately, this source of protection turns out to be dangerously weak. The courts, particularly perhaps in this country, are reluctant to censure the behaviour of medical professionals unless supported in this by other medical professionals. They are certainly very unlikely to criticise whatever is generally accepted medical practice. For example, in the Tony Bland case (see chapter 10), the barrister representing the *patient* argued that 'the law should strive to be in accordance with contemporary medical ethics and good medical practice'. The meaning of 'contemporary medical ethics' is itself likely to be based on statements made by the profession. Thus several judges in the Bland case referred to a publication by the BMA's Medical Ethics Committee in making their comments. Yet the BMA is merely a body whose role is to represent doctors' interests, rather like a trade union. There is no reason why its views on *ethics* should carry any more weight than those of, say, a political party.

The law clearly prefers to leave criticism of doctors to the medical profession itself. Judges are loath to consider that a doctor was not acting in good faith. If, however, a doctor is more or less automatically regarded as having tried his best, and some colleagues can be found to support his actions, there is little scope for him to be found guilty of misconduct unless he happens to have departed from conventional medical practice in some obviously identifiable way.

Merely suggesting that a doctor might have been acting malevolently appears to be regarded by the legal profession as dubious. In the 1981 Dr Arthur case, in which a distinguished paediatrician faced trial for the murder of a baby suffering from Down's syndrome, the judge advised the jury to 'think long and hard before deciding that doctors of the eminence we have heard ... have evolved standards which amount to committing crime'.

In the Cleveland Inquiry, the heavy-handed tactics of the two paediatricians at the centre of the controversy were criticised by a police surgeon, Dr Roberts, who argued that a child

> cannot distinguish between an assault carried out in a hospital room by a stranger (a doctor) and a similar experience elsewhere. I am concerned that some children will suffer lasting harm as a result of being subjected to examinations involving the use of force. (Butler-Sloss 1988, 201)

Dr Roberts criticised paediatricians for being 'prepared to countenance, or even commit, outrageous sexual assault of children in the hospital which has occurred in some cases in Cleveland'. The fact that she made clear her strong feelings on the subject was, interestingly, used to invalidate her criticisms. Counsel for the Inquiry advised the Chairman Lord Justice Butler-Sloss that the evidence of Dr Roberts was

> extremely and unnecessarily critical and contentious ... far from passing to planes of increasing authority and moderation it became more and more passionate in character and thus perhaps of less value ... We will not be urging you for a moment to adopt or accept her views, because we seek to stress throughout the vital importance of striving for middle ground, and obviously Dr Roberts does not stand on middle ground in regard to this issue. (*ibid.*, 202)

4
Patients: passive victims

> The treatment of illness is for doctors. A social institution has grown up defined and managed by doctors, the role of which is to persuade us that our preoccupations must be related to them, and them alone (since they alone have competence). We appear, perforce, naked both physically and emotionally. However willing we may be, and however well intentioned the doctor, it is hard to overstate the power which this vests in the doctor. It is hard to overstate how such a social arrangement may undermine the notion of individual responsibility and of course, ultimately, individual liberty. (Kennedy, 1981, 7-8)

As Ian Kennedy points out, it is hard to overstate the inequality of power which obtains in the doctor-client relationship, and the effect this has on the character of the interaction. Needing to be cured of an ailment is a far more dependency-creating situation than, say, needing legal advice. The urgency to be treated is typically much greater than the urgency to be legally advised, and the mystique surrounding medicine makes it harder to think that one could get by without the knowledge of a medical expert than to think the same thing about a lawyer.

What Kennedy fails to mention is that the power which a registered doctor has over a person presenting as a client does not derive only from the doctor's putative position of expertise. More to the point, doctors control the medical resources. To obtain a restricted drug or service which he requires, a client must rely on his doctor both making the correct diagnosis and responding appropriately to that diagnosis. If (which is not impossible) the client knows more than the doctor about his condition, he will only be able to obtain the specific medication he considers necessary if he succeeds in convincing the doctor that his own judgement on the matter is correct.

Patient rights

In view of the power inequality between doctors and their clients, one might expect there to be laws, rules and ethical principles which safeguard the principle of consumer sovereignty from the strains which this inequality imposes. On the contrary, what rules exist in this regard reinforce the doctor's rights over the client. It is true that there are rules ostensibly designed to prevent doctors from exploiting their position for the most obvious kinds of personal gain, e.g. financial or sexual, although their efficacy may be doubted, and clients must rely to a large extent on whatever self-imposed standards the individual doctor happens to possess. However, with regard to the question of whether doctors can use their power to override the wishes of their clients – denying them treatment they want, pressurising them into treatment they do not want – not only are there few rules to prevent it but such behaviour is positively encouraged.

Users of medicine lack one of the most basic powers of commercial intercourse; that of having a significant power to determine the form of the client-supplier interaction. Talk about 'patient rights' merely illustrates the *de facto* impotence of medical clients. Genuine consumer power depends on competition and the possibility of getting a different service from another supplier. These factors are not easily replaced by self-regulatory principles, and certainly not in an industry where the suppliers are as confident of the superiority of their own judgement as doctors are.

In medicine, as in other areas of life, the traditional notion of 'rights', in the sense of justified claims of which no social arrangement can legitimately deprive the individual, is being replaced by that of 'social rights', meaning vaguely defined entitlements to share in the collective resources. Thus there is ostensibly a 'right' of British citizens to free medical services. In practice, however, treatment may be refused where the doctor considers it to be 'futile' – for example, a heart operation for a smoker, or antibiotics to treat pneumonia in an already seriously ill elderly patient.

When 'patient rights' are championed, it is often done in a way which suggests that doctors have already won the battle, and that the only thing left to do is to try to gain a few concessions from them. The basic premise that doctors are entitled to make decisions about their clients is rarely questioned. The 'Patient's Charter' introduced by John Major's government, a document ostensibly aimed at 'putting the patient first', provides a good example of this. Among the ten rights of NHS users listed by the charter, one proclaims the entitlement 'to be referred to a consultant, acceptable to you, *when your GP thinks it necessary*, and to be referred for a second opinion *if you and your GP agree this is desirable*' (my italics). Although the Charter supposedly established three new rights, these notably did not include (for example) the right to information about your health which is being concealed from you by your GP 'in your own interest'. While the Access to Health Records Act 1990 made it possible for a client to apply for access to the records kept by his doctor about him, information may still be withheld where the doctor considers that it would cause 'serious harm to the physical or mental health of the patient or of any other individual'.

It is not clear whether clients of contemporary medicine still have any genuine rights, in the sense of claims which they can expect to be able to

4. Patients: passive victims

defend unconditionally against the intrusions of others. The community may apparently impose its wishes on individuals where it considers the issue at stake to be of sufficient importance to collective interests and it is the community which, it is often suggested, should decide on recurring problems of professional practice. In the context of euthanasia, it is an illustration of the automatic assumption of client subordination that discussions of the topic are capable of taking place in the absence of any reference to the client's wishes. A typical case example provided to stimulate discussion in a handbook on medical ethics tells us about a young man suffering from an incurable tumour whose pain cannot be fully relieved by normal means. Before the issue has been raised of what the client himself thinks, the tendentious question is posed, 'Would it be kinder to give him a large dose of morphine and end it all?'

The supposed right to medical treatment, which is often said to be one of the most important rights of citizens in a Welfare State, turns out to be subject to crippling caveats. Most obviously, where the resources necessary to provide the required treatment do not exist because of underfunding or inefficiency, the right is clearly an empty one. When revenue from taxes and national insurance subscriptions is used to pay salaries to the six people allegedly required, on average, to change a lightbulb in an NHS hospital,[1] this clearly limits the resources which can be used to provide the medical services themselves. The main effect to date of the British Government's recent attempts to make the NHS conform to a more conventional model of business administration has been to swell the NHS's managerial ranks. According to a Labour Party document, nearly 11 per cent of the NHS budget is now spent on administration, compared with 6 per cent 15 years ago.[2]

Even where the resources *are* available, the right to have them used for one's benefit may turn out to be seriously qualified. A Canadian book on medical ethics, for example, discusses the real-life case of Mrs Jones, who was in a state of near-coma and allegedly 'dying with no hope of recovery'. The doctors wished to cease treating her, thus bringing about her death, but her son claimed that for religious reasons she would not want to die in the hospital, and demanded that she be kept alive with a view to her eventual return home. The authors complain that it is

> one thing to respect idiosyncratic *refusals* of potentially life-saving treatment, and quite another to respect *demands* for such treatment based on unreasonable or 'eccentric' beliefs. ... Intensive medical care of the sort required to sustain Mrs Jones is a very scarce and expensive resource. Is it clear that Mrs Jones – or her son – is entitled to a share of that resource, given that it can in no way serve a therapeutic or curative function, but only

---

[1] *Daily Telegraph*, 30 September 1993.
[2] *Health 2000: The Health and Wealth of the Nation in the 21st Century.* Labour Party 1994, 5.

postpone impending death? If we continue to answer affirmatively, then what do we say to the client who can *genuinely* benefit from the [intensive care unit] and who may be denied access because a respirator is being used to sustain Mrs Jones' biological existence? (Thomas and Waluchow 1990, 139)

Submitting to paternalism

One of the most curious things about the paternalism of modern medicine is how little complaint is made about it. If a group of workers was systematically deprived of rights over their personal lives, and forced to comply with the will of their bosses on pain of physical suffering, there would be a tremendous outcry. Yet an analogous position in medicine is accepted by individual clients, and sanctioned by society.

Beatrix Campbell, in her book about the Cleveland child abuse affair, describes a case of a man wrongly accused of abusing his daughter which illustrates the reluctance which many people feel about suggesting, or even contemplating, the possibility that a doctor's opinion may be mistaken. The girl's mother having taken her two daughters to hospital for a check-up, the anus and vagina of each of the two girls were examined by a doctor. The doctor performed the examination without being asked to do so, and without giving any explanation of why this should be necessary. The mother was then bluntly told, 'Your children aren't going home tonight, they've been abused.' The mother asked which one had been abused, and the doctor replied, 'Where have you been all your life? All of them.' After the police had interrogated the father for five days, they formed the view that he might be innocent, and encouraged him to obtain a second medical opinion about his children. The couple's comments on this are illuminating. Father: 'We didn't want a second opinion at first because we believed the diagnosis. We had to because the doctor said they'd been abused, and who can argue with a doctor.' Mother: 'If a doctor says you've got a broken arm you don't say no it isn't, it's a broken leg.'

Ivan Illich's 1976 book *Limits to Medicine* highlighted the relative passivity with which individuals have relinquished control over their own bodies. 'Consumers who band together to force General Motors to produce an acceptable car have begun to feel competent to look under the hood and to develop criteria for estimating the cost of a cleaner exhaust system. When they band together for better health care, they still believe – mistakenly – that they are unqualified to decide what ought to be done for their bowels and kidneys and blindly entrust themselves to the doctor for almost any repair.' Yet Illich's solutions were as collectivist as the ideology which drives current medical authoritarianism. Among other things he favoured the diversion of resources away from individual treatment towards 'the engineering of populations and environments', and argued that the 'nationalisation of health production ought to control the hidden biases of the clinic', ignoring the fact that existing nationalisation has been to a large extent responsible for the increase in power of the medical bureaucracy.

Part of the explanation for the lack of popular resentment of medical paternalism may lie in its having been the norm for so long. It is consequently seen as an essential element of medicine, a perspective which it is presumably in the interests of doctors to perpetuate. A book entitled *Doctors' Dilemmas* (published in 1985), for example, assures us that 'the medical profession, and the state itself, are not entirely paternalistic', supporting this claim by pointing out that 'smoking, for example, is not banned; and most doctors do not refuse to treat clients unless they kick the habit forthwith'. Ironically, of course, this is precisely what has now started to happen.

More significantly perhaps, the power which a doctor has over his client's suffering, actual or potential, appears to create a peculiar childlike dependency in the client. Underlying this phenomenon may be a combination of fear that the doctor may abuse his power, and psychological denial of this possibility. As Talcott Parsons has said, 'the exploitation of the helpless sick is "unthinkable" '. Parsons also pointed to the likelihood of *transference*, by which the client attributes the characteristics of parental figures experienced in childhood to the doctor.[3] The unconscious thought of the client may be, 'If I offend the doctor, he/she will punish me.' This is paternalism in the full sense of the word.

The dread of punishment is not without foundation. The fear of clients that necessary treatment will be withheld if they are not compliant has found support in the recent cases of surgeons refusing to operate on smokers who would not give up their habit in spite of being told to do so. The ability of medical staff to indulge their personal preferences and dislikes is likely to extend well beyond such overt manipulation. It is reputed to be the case that airline staff have ways of discriminating against passengers if they do not like them, for instance by assigning them bad seats. Health professionals may use similar methods of expressing their disapproval of particular clients. Strategies which purport to combat socially unacceptable behaviour may sooner or later be used to suppress anything disliked by doctors or other staff, including any kind of objection on the part of a client.

> Clients who sexually harass or become over-familiar with nurses may have their level of care reduced in one health authority. ... [Guidelines] to be posted in all Swindon Health Authority's hospitals warn: 'If a member of the public is well enough to behave in a manner which constitutes harassment [then the manager] should make it clear that certain behaviour is unacceptable and, if appropriate, threaten that the level of service may be reduced if the behaviour does not improve.' (*Daily Telegraph*, 28 September 1993)

---

[3] Parsons 1951, 453.

Given the variety of uses to which the term 'harassment' may be put in the arena of sexual politics, one may wonder how wide a discretion is being given here for health professionals to deny treatment to their clients. The BMA has this to say on the approved approach to 'challenging behaviour' on the part of a client.

> In some cases, violent or challenging behaviour may be a symptom of the client's illness or a side effect of treatment, beyond the client's control. Therapeutic measures including sedation may be used. ... The *routine* use of behaviour-controlling measures, designed to facilitate ease of management rather than promoting the client's interests, should be avoided. (BMA 1993, 5)

This, it should be noted, is not a guideline for psychiatrists working in hospitals for the criminally insane, but is meant to apply to practitioners in general.

The rejection of patient autonomy

'The Moral Maze':[4] exchange between Professor Stuart Campbell (head of obstetrics and gynaecology at Kings College, London) and Rabbi Hugo Gryn.

Campbell: ... [parents wanting to have a child by artificial means] come to us, and it's their choice; and if they don't want this treatment, they don't have this treatment ...
Gryn: ... Have [people] the absolute right to choice? Is choice, like, the big thing in this – if I want it I gotta get it?
Campbell: *Provided* that we as doctors think in our professional judgement that there is more good than harm in what we do; but, I may say, there are layers of committees now supervising what we as doctors do.

It is occasionally suggested that we live in an era in which individual autonomy is a right that is increasingly being asserted, and won, in all sorts of areas of social life. If this is so, then medical treatment seems to be an area which has largely escaped this process. Although one sometimes reads assertions that clients are insisting on, and getting, more choice and control over their treatment, the evidence adduced is usually rather weak.

For example, a recent article in a local newspaper[5] entitled 'Power to the parents' describes the 'Red Book' scheme which makes parents responsible for keeping a child's health records. This change is described by a child health nurse as 'one of the biggest revolutions in health care since the inception of the NHS' and 'a substantial shift of power to the parent'. The nurse concedes that health professionals have 'tended to act as if they owned other people's children and bodies', but seems to think that the mere possession of a document giving details of a doctor's actions will

---

[4] BBC 2, 15 January 1994.
[5] *Oxford Times*, 23 September 1994.

4. Patients: passive victims

somehow transfer real decision-making power to the client. How precisely this is to happen is not, however, explained.

The House of Lords' 1994 Report of the Select Committee on Medical Ethics made frequent reference to the idea that client autonomy has recently been increasing. Curious about the data on which this contention was based, I asked the Committee's Chairman, Lord Walton of Detchant, in what specific ways he thought that client autonomy had improved. Lord Walton answered that the Report's comments on this topic

> were based upon the advice that we received from professional organisations, including the Conference of Royal Colleges and the BMA. Increasingly over the last few years the BMA in its Handbook of Medical Ethics and in the recent volumes on the rights and responsibilities of doctors has stressed the importance of patient autonomy in decision-making. Similarly, I can confirm that during my Presidency of the General Medical Council from 1982 to 1989, that body in its blue booklet giving ethical advice to members of the medical profession stressed that medical paternalism was a thing of the past and that the practice of medicine was a partnership in which it was up to the doctor to offer advice to the patient, but the decision as to whether or not to accept that advice rested solely with the patient. (personal communication)

In other words, the principal evidence on which the Committee relied in reaching its conclusions about client autonomy appears to have been the fact that bodies representing practitioners are allegedly encouraging their members to behave less paternalistically.

Rather than any genuine surrender of power from doctors to their clients, what seems to be happening is that health professionals are having to adapt to a different ideological climate by making subtle changes in their public relations tactics. There are more information leaflets available, more signposting in hospitals, more 'schemes' ostensibly designed to improve client care. Yet without genuine power on the part of clients to demand greater responsiveness to their wishes, and with doctors continuing to adhere to their belief that the client's preferences are not paramount, such changes are likely to be largely superficial. The chairman of a relatively progressive NHS Trust which had adopted the slogan, 'Putting Patients' Interests First!', and which was supposedly operating a policy of 'positive customer care', recently pretended to be a patient in his own hospital. He reported experiencing treatment at the hands of hospital staff which he says would have left him feeling 'frightened, vulnerable and stripped of all dignity' had he been a genuine patient.[6]

Assertions that doctors have become more aware of the need to involve the client in the consultation process, or are being trained to use a more 'patient-centred' approach, need to be taken with a pinch of salt. According to a study published in 1985, there is little evidence that superficial differences in attitude have a significant impact on the doctor-client

---

[6] *Sunday Times*, 24 April 1994.

relationship. According to Julian Tudor Hart, the material for the study was

> 1,302 tape-recorded consultations by two groups of GPs. The first was a study group of eight, selected because they were recognised trainers responsible for teaching consultation skills [who had attended courses] deliberately aimed at changing doctors' behaviour. ... The comparison group consisted of another eight GPs chosen randomly from lists of NHS GPs in the same area as the study group. ...
> [The researchers'] original intention was to look at expected differences in the way these two groups of GPs (one theoretically convinced of the need for mutually shared information, the other with traditional ideas of active doctors and passive patients) actually behaved. In fact there were virtually no differences. All the doctors in both groups appeared in practice to see transmission of information and ideas as an almost entirely one-way process, and none of them sought patients' ideas about how their problems were caused or defined, or how they might be remedied. (Tudor Hart 1988, 193-4)

The meaning of autonomy

A few comments about the word 'autonomy', a term which is in danger of becoming as politicised as its cognate 'liberty', are called for at this point. I take 'autonomy' to mean the ability of individuals to make decisions about their own lives without reference to others. This definition is based on the *wishes* of individuals, and does not concern itself with the question of whether those wishes are 'rational', or otherwise to be regarded as acceptable.

It should be noted, however, that my usage differs from certain modern interpretations, which see the autonomy of an individual in terms of his conformity to certain supposed 'rational' principles, or alternatively as related to the putative advantages with which his community decides to provide him. Simon Lee, for example, tells us that we can 'help others attain an autonomous life by educating them [or] by providing them with options from which to choose their preferred life-style'; and hence that the government may have to 'take positive steps in order to create the conditions under which citizens can act autonomously'. In other words, according to this paradoxical interpretation, promoting the autonomy of an individual may involve coercing others or even the individual himself.

The idea of autonomy within the confines of one's own territory continues to elicit ambivalent reactions, even if in some areas such as sexuality it has become the accepted view that people should not be prohibited from doing things which the majority find distasteful, provided no harm to others is involved. In other fields, the fear of what individuals might get up to if they were allowed to do what they wanted continues to provoke moral hysteria in some commentators. Thus the Archbishop of Canterbury recently warned that 'The doctrine that everyone may do as they like so long as they do not positively harm another leads us into a moral void and

4. Patients: passive victims

the death of society'. (This remark, incidentally, seems highly reminiscent of comments made by the late Lord Devlin regarding the question of whether homosexuality should be decriminalised. Lord Devlin, it may be recalled, argued that allowing people sexual liberty would seriously disrupt the fabric of society.[7])

Medicine is certainly a field where this fear of autonomy is well entrenched. The very thought that medical practice might be determined solely by the wishes of clients appears to be offensive to some commentators. The theologian Paul Ramsey, for example, reacts with horror to the idea that physicians might be turned 'into "animated tools" ... that simply assist a client to attain anything he wishes'.

There seems to be a feeling prevalent among many doctors, and some medical commentators, that if individuals were given genuine power to implement their wishes in the context of medicine, chaos and anarchy would inevitably follow. This feeling becomes particularly intense where the topic of euthanasia is concerned. Discussing the idea that the client might have full control over the administration of his own euthanasia, Bliss and Johnson argue that if 'the right to determine the time and mode of one's death was ever accepted as a dominant or even supreme aim the results could be catastrophic and *the whole basis of medical practice would be overturned*' (my italics). It is not clear, however, why the ability of a person to end his life by his own hand should have any bearing on medical practice at all.

Although the client's consent is in principle required for any medical treatment, the question of which treatment is *offered* to him is more and more seen as a decision for medical professionals. The views of laymen are allowed little or no place in the decision-making process, on the basis that it is beyond them to assess the technical merits and weaknesses of alternative options. In their report on euthanasia, the BMA justify this approach by referring to the extremes to which client autonomy might conceivably be taken.

> ... there is a difference between the client authorising or not authorising a recommended treatment and a client demanding that a certain therapy is used. To put an absurd case: if a client were to present at a hospital demanding to have brain surgery because of an ingrowing toenail, doctors would not feel any necessity to comply with this demand. We may, of course, advise the client against it but find that he has an elaborate theory which connects his ingrown toenail to dystonic growth and brain dysfunction. This ridiculous example is only meant to highlight the fact that there are limits to what a client can legitimately expect a doctor to do. *Clients have autonomy to the extent of accepting or rejecting medical recommendations (when competent to do so) but cannot demand that any physician act in a way solely determined by what they consider to be in their own best interest.* ... The medical profession has a *right* to limit client autonomy where the client

[7] See Devlin 1965.

demands some 'treatment' or action that runs counter to settled and informed medical opinion. (BMA 1988, 18-19, my italics)

The BMA's example of the man with an ingrowing toenail who wants brain surgery is indeed ridiculous. It is also highly tendentious and serves to divert attention from the real issue. (One might speculate that a client with a mental state of the kind implied by the example is more likely to be *given* brain surgery *against his will* than to demand it.) The real conflict between doctors and their clients is not about deranged patients harassing doctors to assist them in self-mutilation, but about differences of opinion regarding the best course of action in response to a particular medical condition. Doctors are liable to refuse requests for treatment where they consider that they carry side-effects which they regard as unacceptable, even if the client does not. They may also refuse treatment if they consider its cost to outweigh the benefits to the client, taking into account the client's age, health and other circumstances.

The question whether clients should be able to demand 'silly' or even dangerous treatments is a secondary one. It may be necessary to restrict treatments under a state health service, but that does not make it a general principle of medical ethics. There is little justification for extending such a restriction to private medicine, and certainly no convincing case for leaving the power to limit autonomy, in order to prevent harm to foolish or deranged clients, entirely in the hands of the medical profession, let alone individual doctors. What is regarded as 'silly' will vary from practitioner to practitioner, and may include things such as hormone replacement therapy, treatment for ME, vitamin supplements and influenza vaccine.

The sham of 'patient power'

[In 1991] St Thomas's Hospital, in London, hired Kinross & Render, one of the few public relations agencies to specialise in NHS work, to undertake an 'audit' of its communications with GPs, with its own staff and with the media. ... As a result, St Thomas's has appointed a director of public relations to try to bring coherence to the hospital's relationships with its various audiences. (*The Times*, 11 August 1992.)

In the absence of competitive pressures, we may ask how the medical profession is to become more responsive to client wishes. The simple answer may be that, with no economic incentive, it will not. Of course, this view challenges the tenet that health professionals are always benevolent and always strive to do the best for their clients. Thus it is sometimes supposed that with a little recognition of the problem, professionals will spontaneously motivate themselves to provide a better service. Or that they will do so if their business is run by professional managers and accountants. But this is as naïve as supposing that the services provided by a utilities monopoly will necessarily become more efficient and less expensive if it is no longer owned by the state.

Similarly, the medical profession may have become aware of the need to improve its image, and to present a more consumer-sympathetic face. However, there is little sign that the results of any programme of improvement are more than cosmetic, intended primarily to enhance the status of the profession.

It is sometimes claimed that doctors have modified their paternalism and now have more consideration for client autonomy. However, if this is true at all, it is probably not because autonomy now commands more respect as a moral principle, but because it has become more fashionable to regard 'client involvement' as a factor which may contribute to the effectiveness of the treatment. As Gary Weiss puts it, 'medical changes have modified the concept of what is best for a client and have made it necessary actively to enrol the client in his care'. That this has nothing to do with 'rolling back' the power of the medical profession may be gathered from the following further quotations from Professor Weiss's paper on paternalism in the *Journal of Medical Ethics*. For Weiss, it is clearly up to doctors to decide whether they should temper their paternalism with any degree of client autonomy. For example, he thinks that 'well-designed studies are needed to answer the question of whether informing cancer clients of their diagnosis leads to suicide or other serious harm so that the decision to tell them can be based on information rather than speculation'. It is the *experience* of autonomy, rather than autonomy itself, which the physician should engender; hence deception may well be appropriate: 'If the client will do better believing he is in control the physician should encourage this belief and indirectly facilitate the right choice of action.' Where autonomy leads to results which are unacceptable to the physician, he should not shrink from overriding the client's wishes: 'many clients choose immediate gratification over possible long-term benefits, even though they realise that the latter course is better for them. For example, a young man with curable testicular cancer may wish to avoid the temporary but severe nausea produced by chemotherapy. This situation justifies and even requires the physician's encouraging, or if necessary, coercing the client to complete the therapy.'

One has to be very cautious when evaluating claims that client autonomy is being promoted in any particular situation. For example, it has been suggested that a shift in medical practice in favour of withholding treatment from clients in a coma reflects increasing respect for client autonomy.[8]

It is sometimes argued that because individual clients are an integral part of the medical market, they therefore have power to shape that market. This is rather like claiming that citizens have power to determine

---

[8] *Lancet*, 12 January 1991, 97.

public spending in a single-party state. Professor H.T. Engelhardt, for example, believes that because clients and potential clients possess the bulk of the economic resources in any given society, this means that 'they can influence the ways in which health care is delivered by setting standards of disclosure required on the part of the physicians who receive reimbursement through insurance policies, use community-owned hospitals, or receive salaries through community-owned health maintenance organisations'. One might as well say that because the postal service is funded predominantly by private individuals, those individuals should be able to set standards of efficiency required on the part of postal service managers who receive salaries through payment for stamps.

5

The good of society

> Doctors are using an unofficial computerised points system to decide which desperately ill clients are to be given the chance of life-saving treatment in intensive care wards. ... The scoring system, which does not yet have the Department of Health's approval, is being used to ration the number of people in scarce intensive care places. ... Under the computerised system, clients are given points according to their age, medical history and present medical condition. The higher the points, the lower the chance of survival. (*Sunday Times*, 6 May 1990)

In arguing against medical paternalism, we are criticising the programme of the medical profession under which decisions are made in accordance with the doctor's view about the 'good' of the client. Conventions such as the Hippocratic Oath encourage users of medical services to believe that it is indeed the client's welfare which is paramount. In the present chapter, I shall consider to what extent this is in fact true. We may regard paternalism as unacceptable in principle, but feel consoled by the idea that the philosophy of the profession at least requires that doctors and other health workers always do what they think is best for the individual client. But is this assumption justified?

Community medicine

In medicine, as in certain other areas of life, we appear to be moving out of an era in which the individual's expressed wishes are regarded as primary and into one where the 'public interest' is seen as potentially more important. In their 1980 *Handbook of Medical Ethics*, the BMA raise the issue of public interest, albeit cautiously. 'How to balance the needs of the individual against the rights of society is not a new question. With the increasing interdependence of individuals in society and the growth of social care, the balance has been moving away from the individual towards the community and, indeed, towards the State.' In the BMA's 1993 publication *Medical Ethics: Its Practice and Philosophy* this caution is less in evidence. 'The BMA believes that a doctor's ethical duty goes beyond the individual client to all other clients and to society as a whole.'

A century ago, medicine was regarded as no more than one service among many offered to satisfy demand in a commercial context. The

Victorians did not, on the whole, take kindly to having their choices about health made for them. When Edwin Chadwick's attempts to introduce public health legislation were resisted in 1854, *The Times* commented that 'we prefer to take our chance of cholera and the rest, than to be bullied into health'. Nowadays, the fashionable view is that medicine is something provided by collective agreement, which must be shaped according to collective wishes. We are told by Ian Kennedy, for example, that medicine is a political enterprise, that 'health' is a political term, and that doctors are political and social agents.[1]

Whatever other concerns are invoked in debating the sort of medicine *we*, as a society, should have, the simple matter of what individual clients want in individual cases appears to come low down on the list of priorities, if at all. This is particularly so in the case of 'ethically problematic' areas such as euthanasia. Bliss and Johnson, for example, having discussed the ethics of euthanasia in the light of religious beliefs, go on to outline what is in their view apparently the only other possible perspective on the matter, namely that those 'who have no interest in spiritual values must look at the problem in terms of results on the community in general and the client's relatives in particular'.

This development in the way medicine is perceived is in large part attributable to the gradual collectivisation of medical services which has taken place over the last fifty years or so. The fact that most expenditure on medicine is channelled through the state by enforced subscription means that discussions about what directions medicine should take are now habitually framed in terms of 'What should society decide?', rather than 'What should individuals ask for?'. J.K. Page, for example, predicted that 'a sharp distinction between the biologically possible and the achievable will emerge, but the consequent social priorities will have to be achieved by society at large, and not by the biological professions in isolation'. The struggle for power in the decision-making process is clearly expected to be between medical practitioners on the one hand and the community as a whole (represented by politicians and civil servants) on the other. Individual clients do not even rate a mention in this connection.

The idea that medicine is a community issue is, it has to be said, not a particularly recent one. Sidney and Beatrice Webb, writing in 1909, argued in their report on the Poor Laws that it is 'surely the worst of all forms of national waste to allow the ravages of preventable sickness to progress unchecked; and this not merely because it kills thousands of producers prematurely ... but because sickness levies a toll on the living, and leaves even those who survive crippled, debilitated, and less efficient than they would otherwise have been'. Indeed, this view of medicine as essentially a community matter has obvious parallels with primitive tribal

---

[1] Kennedy 1981, ix, x, 17.

life, in which curing ills and evils is an issue that concerns the whole tribe, not merely the afflicted individual.

Resource reallocation

An impoverished Victorian or Edwardian would probably have had few illusions about charity, whether publicly or privately funded. He would have realised that unpaid help had a price: that of having no say over the nature of the help given. This level of realism is perhaps not so common these days; it is arguably more common for users of the Welfare State to expect that their individual needs will automatically be catered for. Nevertheless it is beginning to emerge that a medical service which contains no contractual element between health professionals and users, and no commitment to a specified level of service, is one which is subject to serious limitations from the client's point of view.

When the first National Insurance Act was introduced in Britain in 1911, it was only workers on low wages (and their employers) who were forced to contribute towards their own system of health insurance. Although there was considerable resistance to this paternalistic measure, it did at least target those people who were otherwise likely to have been unable to pay for the services which their contributions financed. Unfortunately the encroachment of the state on the medical sector did not stop with the provision of a safety net for the poor. In the post-war enthusiasm for collectivised services, ideals of equality, efficiency and communitarianism fused to produce a wave of interventionist legislation. The National Insurance and National Health Acts of 1946 essentially nationalised medicine in Britain. Although medical professionals were, to begin with, strongly opposed to the encroachment of government on their territory, they seem to have come round to the view that a state system of health care is not, on the whole, damaging to the profession. Since the sixties, the relationship between the medical sector and the state has arguably been highly co-operative, the only major disturbances to this harmonious alliance occurring whenever the state has tried to cut resources to the NHS or to reorganise its managerial structure. Indeed, doctors' main cause for concern with regard to a state health service had been the fear that they might become employees of the government, and in this respect they have succeeded in preserving the *status quo*.

The original, naïvely optimistic theory behind the UK's National Health Service was that expenditure on it would fall as people's health improved as a result of increased access to medical services. With hindsight, it seems obvious that the pressures on a system not restricted by the resources of individual clients would inexorably increase with the passage of time and with developments in medical technology. Most people do not die of old age, but become fatally ill when a specific part of their physiology fails. It follows that, with appropriate treatment, it may well be possible to redeem the specific part and thus extend the individual's life. There is every reason to think that this process can, with advancing technology, be carried out *ad infinitum*.

When deciding to offer services in exchange for a subscription, one obviously has to be very careful to limit what services are contractually to be provided, otherwise the subscriptions will not finance the cost of the services. This is a problem well known to insurance companies, whose contracts are notorious for the fine detail required to cover every necessary exclusion. National health services, however, have never made any serious attempt to follow this basic principle of insurance. At first this was to some extent based on the assumption that there would be a limit to demand, and that demand would actually fall as the new medical system made people healthier. With increasing supply shortfalls in spite of spiralling health expenditure, this assumption has now been abandoned. There has not, however, been any corresponding attempt to define and limit the services to which citizens shall have an unconditional right in return for their taxes.[2]

If the terms of a subscription-based service are not explicitly defined, it is clear that there will arise situations in which more people demand a right to a given service than the system can support. Situations of this kind generate conflicts, given that the allocation to one individual of a service in short supply may carry the consequence that another individual goes without. Such conflicts of interest are arguably highly damaging to the doctor-client relationship, given the implicit understanding that the doctor's only role is to do the best for his client. One might therefore have expected doctors to revolt at the prospect of making allocation decisions, to refuse to have anything to do with making judgements of this kind, and to demand that the government takes the responsibility of deciding the terms of resource allocation. Yet relatively little protest has been heard from the medical profession in this respect. On the contrary, the profession sometimes suggests that the government should *not* legislate in this area, as the decisions which have to be made involve medical judgements and hence are best left to doctors. Again, we find that doctors' behaviour is consistent with the maximisation of power over their clients.

In 1982 three doctors from Guy's Hospital in London wrote to the *Lancet* to say that a physician would be justified, and indeed obliged, to ignore instructions from government about what services may not be provided under the national health service. The authors of *Doctors' Dilemmas* clearly approve of this attitude, and comment as follows.

> ... suppose the government did take the bull by the horns, and said that it accepted that the consequence of its policies was that clients suffering from

---

[2] The US State of Oregon, which has defined a list of basic medical services which would (in theory) be provided by government without restriction, represents a notable exception to this.

5. The good of society

treatable diseases were going to die through lack of treatment. Suppose it went further than that, and said that as a result of the crisis in health expenditure various categories of clients were henceforth to receive no treatment – say, cancer clients or others suffering from terminal illness; or the chronic sick over the age of 65. As the Guy's doctors point out, it would be quite unacceptable for physicians to go along with such a policy. They would then clearly be in the difficult position where their ethical duties conflicted with the stated policies of the democratically elected government and would have to decide which set of duties had the stronger ethical call. (Phillips and Dawson 1985, 169)

Such attempts on the part of doctors to take the moral high ground with respect to resource allocation are, however, unconvincing. First, the argument is somewhat disingenuous, given that doctors currently make allocation decisions themselves. Not treating the very old, for example, at least for certain ailments, is a common medical practice. It is hard to be impressed by the claim that a doctor puts his client above financial considerations when in practice this principle is applied only selectively. Secondly, there is a strong case for the proposition that doctors should respect government decisions more, not less, than their own allocation judgements where the Welfare State health service is concerned, given that the government is ostensibly representing the population.

The medical profession's own response to the resource dilemma is simply to press continually for an increase in the health service's share of the national product, however much the state medical budget has already increased in real terms per head. The BMA's ethics handbook points out that 'the BMA has consistently argued for a substantial increase in overall funding, which it considers would resolve some of the current problems of rationing'. In terms of the quality of the health service, the profession continually justifies any limitations by reference to resource shortages.

There is little admission by practitioners of the fact that there may be economic limits to the advancement of applied medical technology, and that without formal restrictions on what the state will provide, these limits imply the ever-increasing use of subjective allocation decisions. The BMA has countered the 'bottomless pit' argument by asserting that 'there is no final goal – but always the possibility of more change and a need for further evolution.' In other words, more and more resources should be diverted to medicine, and (implicitly) more and more power should be given to doctors. But why should individuals choose to spend more money on health services than they can and do at present, particularly on services which will not, when the time comes, necessarily regard them as suitable beneficiaries? Why is the possibility not considered that Western nations spend *more* on medicine than their populations wish, and that state spending on health services should therefore be reduced?

One way to make sense of the pressure from the state medical sector for more resources is that it is a demand for *re*allocation: that proportionally more money should be confiscated from those with above average income to finance collectivised medicine. In other words, health care workers may have a *political* aim in demanding more resources.

Clearly, being in a 'medical club' funded by joint subscriptions and not defined on commercial and contractual terms is a quite different matter from financing one's own medical services directly, whether by insurance or on a pay-as-you-go basis. In the latter case, one can expect that the limits to what can be obtained, and the degree of choice and control one has, will be determined by one's personal resources, or, in the case of a medical insurance plan, by the terms of the insurance contract. In the case of a medical club of the kind represented by the British National Health Service, one cannot expect any degree of control over what services will or will not be provided, and what form those services take.

The fact that some clients are being refused treatments by state health services which others are receiving, is therefore only to be expected. Yet this problem is discussed as though it were a moral problem intrinsic to medicine *per se*. For example, the involuntary passive euthanasia which is widely practised by doctors in response to resource shortages is presented as a necessary feature of medicine. We are encouraged to think that it is an unavoidable problem which must be solved as an exercise in moral philosophy. There is no suggestion that the underlying premise, namely that state health services will *inevitably* offer a wider range of services than they can realistically provide to everyone who needs them, might be flawed.

Simon Lee, for example, comments as follows on the case of a mentally dysfunctional kidney client who was eventually taken off dialysis because he was judged by hospital staff to have too poor a quality of life. Interestingly, the staff of the hostel where the client lived disagreed with the hospital's appraisal of his condition. The client's physiological deterioration was not apparently the only cause for discontinuation; hospital staff felt that he was 'disruptive' and 'uncooperative'.[3]

> One could argue that if *society* is paying for kidney dialysis treatment and there is only one machine between two clients then *society* is entitled to prefer the brilliant musician or sportsman to the 'down and out'. ... A variation on the quality of life theme would be the standard of a client's value to *society*. ... If we find these competing standards sufficiently ... conflicting or awful to choose between them, we can always [abdicate] in giving the selection over to a lottery. But yet again raffling kidney dialysis treatment may offend our moral sensibilities. ... There is no simple solution. ... But if we do have a *society* in which we can all contribute to the debate ... by being informed and educated with the help of experts, then our *society* will benefit from such reappraisal of fundamental values and constant refining of predictions about the practical consequences of *society's* decisions. (Lee 1986, 69-70; my italics)

[3] *Lancet*, 19 January 1985, 176-7.

As with other aspects of the ethics of medical practice, one can perceive a gradual shift in attitudes to the question of individual doctors' responsibilities *vis-à-vis* resource allocation. In 1958, the expected stance of the profession was expressed as follows by the Medical Services Review Committee.

> For the doctor the primary concern when confronted by a client physically or mentally sick is to restore that client to health as quickly as possible. The fact that a doctor is working in a service financed and organised by the state should not be allowed to affect that fundamental duty. On the other hand no one – least of all the doctor – can fail to be aware of the many legitimate and competing demands within the service for the money available. (quoted in Phillips and Dawson 1985, 154)

Thirty-five years later, we find the BMA arguing more aggressively that 'doctors should not favour their own clients at the expense of other doctors' clients [and] should be alive to the consequences for other clients of their efforts to do their best for one client'. Given that *any* effort to provide a service for one client which is better than that provided to the average client can be said to be drawing resources away from others, this statement could be interpreted as meaning that doctors should never make special efforts for their own clients.

Confidentiality

The image of the doctor as community agent receives support from philosophers and sociologists. Professor Martin Hollis, for example, says of a doctor who knows his client has AIDS, and knows that the client's wife has not been told,

> [he] is not like a priest upholding the secrecy of the confessional in the face of enquiries from the temporal authorities. He is an agent licensed by that state, akin less to a priest than to a social worker who is explicitly the state's appointee, wielding its authority even in seemingly personal relations with clients. The doctor is answerable to the community at large and, although it is relevant whether or not syphilis and AIDS are legally notifiable diseases, his professional conscience is not fully absolved by this test. (Hollis 1988, 10)

Hollis appears to be hinting that traditional views on doctor-client confidentiality should be modified to allow greater consideration of the public interest.

With the intrusion of the state into medicine, and with doctors being enlisted to co-operate with state agents such as the police or social workers, it is perhaps not surprising that the principle of confidentiality is being softened, and has started to depend for its existence on arguments about 'best interests'. Thus when in 1983 the medical profession argued against the provision proposed by the Police and Criminal Evidence Bill under which the police could demand to see a doctor's information about his clients, the popular line used was that it would damage the doctor-client relationship. The then president of the Royal College of General Practitioners wrote to the government that, 'Were it to become practice for police to examine records on demand the whole basis of medical confidentiality would be threatened. Doctors would feel inhibited from recording information which might be damaging to a client in a court of law, and clients might withhold information from their doctor for the same reason, thus jeopardising their treatment.' There was relatively little attempt to base criticism on the right to privacy of the individual client. The resistance of the profession to legal developments in this area is similar to its resistance to euthanasia. In both cases, its chief concern is the supposed threat to the patient-doctor relationship, rather than the threat to the patient's liberty.

The very language in which discussions about confidentiality take place has altered in response to changes in the way medicine is perceived. When confidentiality was still relatively sacred, revealing information about a client was seen as a positive act which implied potentially suspect motivation on the part of the doctor. Now, at least in certain situations, it seems to be the observance of the principle which calls for justification. Thus a doctor writing in the *New England Journal of Medicine* talks about the dilemma posed for a practitioner 'when the health, well-being and safety of identifiable others or of society in general would be threatened by a failure to reveal information about the client'. Expressing the issue in a way that implies that the doctor has a presumed responsibility to persons other than the client obviously creates an ideological bias in favour of revealing information to third parties.

The shift on confidentiality in favour of social considerations is finding support from the courts. In *W v Egdell* (1990), the court decided that a psychiatrist was justified in passing his report, commissioned by the client in a private capacity, on to a state authority, on grounds of public interest. Interestingly, in the contrasting case of *X v Y* (1988), an injunction was granted against a newspaper to prevent publication of the names of two *doctors* who had been diagnosed as HIV-positive. In the latter case, the judge stressed that confidentiality was an important principle which it was in the public interest to preserve, a principle which was evidently given rather less priority in the other, later case.

On the issue of confidentiality a useful comparison can be made between medicine under a competitive system and medicine as a monopoly under state control. The precept that a doctor should scrupulously respect the privacy of information about his client's health, and anything else he happens to learn about the client, was developed very early in the history of the medical profession, certainly well before there was any significant professional organisation or regulation by the state. It is duly stressed by the Hippocratic Oath, which is believed to have been written in the fifth

5. The good of society

century BC: 'Whatever, in connection with my professional practice, I see or hear, in the life of men, which ought not to be spoken of abroad, I will not divulge, as reckoning that all such should be kept secret.'

It seems that the principle of confidentiality was not originally developed as a result of formal self-regulation by the profession, let alone because of state intervention. If we ask why it became a principle for the profession, the answer which most obviously suggests itself is, because clients desired it. A person who allows a doctor to come into his home, and to see him in a vulnerable position, clearly has to be prepared for the possibility that the doctor will learn various private things about him. Confidence that a doctor will respect his client's privacy, and not reveal information he acquires about him, will obviously be desirable from the point of view of the client, and will make him more ready to use the services of a doctor. Confidentiality, however, is a benefit which the doctor confers (or fails to confer) only after the client has used the doctor's services. The client therefore inevitably takes a risk on whether the doctor will respect confidentiality. If individual doctors wish to persuade potential clients of their observance of confidentiality, they may have to do more than merely promise it. One method of persuasion is by means of reputation. This is likely to work better if the reputation is created for *all* doctors. If each individual doctor repeatedly maintains that doctors in general have high standards of behaviour, this may do his own image more good than if he claims certain characteristics for himself alone.

We can see how a principle such as confidentiality might become a basic tenet of professional practice, under the pressure of client demand. Yet the point that confidentiality, like other medical principles, may have developed in response to commercial pressure is often ignored. Raanan Gillon, for example, asks why doctors from the time of Hippocrates should have promised to keep their clients' secrets, and mentions moral arguments based on welfare maximisation, or respect for autonomy.[4] He fails to mention the possibility that this approach maximises the rewards of practising as a doctor.

What we might expect to see, on the basis of the above argument, is that as consumer pressures on the medical profession abate, principles of professional behaviour become softened. It was suggested in chapter 2 that, without commercial competition, such principles are likely to be discussed in terms of moral obligations, and to be redefined to suit the interests of doctors. This is just what we find happening with regard to confidentiality.

The following two examples[5] may illustrate the sea change in attitudes to confidentiality among the medical profession. In 1954, the president of the Derby Medical Society told his members that in recent years, 'the

---

[4] Gillon 1985, 108.
[5] Taken from Phillips and Dawson 1985.

policy of the Association has been that of complete secrecy under all circumstances, with a sole exception that a doctor might warn others against possible infection of venereal disease in an affected client'. In 1980, the following comments were reported in a medical magazine. 'Dr Alastair Moulds, an Essex GP, sees the problem in a very clear-cut way. "It is fair enough to have confidentiality as a general principle," he says, "but when it comes to serious crime, or when there is a danger of menace, that kind of confidentiality is overridden. I see myself in exactly the same position as any other member of society. I am no different just because I am a doctor."'

Guinea-pigs

Medical research is another area where the good of society is promoted at the expense of the good of the individual. There have been cases where experiments of extremely doubtful benefit to the subjects involved were carried out without their consent.[6] Non-consensual experimentation of this kind is theoretically illegal in most Western countries. Nevertheless, we need to ask ourselves why it should occur at all. This is not a wrong committed by people covertly seeking to exploit weaknesses in law enforcement for their own financial gain, but by experts who believe their actions are professionally and ethically acceptable.

So-called 'therapeutic research' is conducted in a relatively lax ethical atmosphere. In theory, such research is a by-product of actions carried out primarily to benefit the client, which means that it is regarded as less important to ask the client's permission. In fact, however, as the philosopher Richard Hare has pointed out,[7] therapy and research are two entirely separate purposes. If research enters into a therapy at all, then an element is being added which has nothing to do with the cure of the client. Hence it is not clear why this kind of research should be more acceptable without consent than any other.

Certainly there is evidence to show that this potential exemption from the consent requirement is liable to be used in highly questionable circumstances. In 1981, for example, a British woman died from the effects of an experimental drug given to her after an operation for bone cancer.[8] It emerged that she, along with a number of other cancer clients, had been entered in a clinical trial for the drug without her knowledge. This non-consensual experiment had been carried out with the full approval of local research ethics committees. The chairman of one of the committees commented that consent for the trial could only have been obtained 'by explaining to the clients why the drugs were being given and how unfa-

---

[6] See for example Beecher 1966.
[7] Hare 1985.
[8] See Lancet, 1982 (i), 1028-9; (ii), 275.

5. The good of society 61

vourable the prognosis after operation was going to be. We thought this would be an unacceptable psychological trauma for many of the clients ... we felt that the quality of the limited post-operative life of many of these clients would be impaired if, in explaining the trial, the grim prognosis was revealed.' This argument uses one wrong to justify another one. Having withheld from their clients their diagnosis, without any instruction to do so from the clients, the doctors presumably found they could not obtain consent for the experimental treatment, as clients would only have accepted the risk if aware of their existing precarious condition. Therefore a second deception was committed.

It is interesting to note that where minors are concerned, the restrictions on *non-therapeutic* research are also relatively weak. One might think that in the case of a person deemed incapable of giving consent to treatment, the use of such a person for experimentation could never be legitimate. Yet it seems that the approval of a parent is sufficient to enable non-therapeutic experimentation on a child to proceed. The British Paediatric Association considers non-therapeutic research on minors to be acceptable. As Margaret Brazier has pointed out, this would seem to imply a belief that the best interests of the child include the interests of the community, and that the child benefits from serving the community. The idea that someone benefits from an action done to him, simply because it is intended to benefit other people, puts an interesting slant on the concept of doing things for a person's 'own good'.

A similar point applies to those deemed not competent to give valid consent. Surely the assumption that they cannot give consent implies that using them for research purposes cannot be ethical? Yet it seems that this argument is not accepted by health care professionals. The Medical Research Council has declared that non-therapeutic research on the mentally incapacitated is acceptable, provided the risks to the subject are not 'appreciable' and there is no sign that the subject objects to involvement.[9]

The method usually proposed for making it less likely that doctors will override the wishes or interests of clients for experimental purposes is to have their actions controlled by medical ethics committees. In practice, such committees are typically composed predominantly of members of the medical profession. Given that doctors are encouraged to give primacy to their own views over those of their clients, and to believe that they ought to take into account the interests of society in their behaviour, can we really rely on the profession regulating itself with regard to research? It is often supposed that an institutional setting, where doctors are aware of the scrutiny and potential disapproval of their peers, makes the exploitation of medical powers less likely. But paradoxically, an institutional setting may actually facilitate exploitation, by concealing the degree of

---

[9] Medical Research Council 1991, *The Ethical Conduct of Research on the Mentally Incapacitated.*

responsibility for specific acts, and by giving them a spurious legitimacy. Medical workers operating in an institutional setting, such as a hospital, arguably have more respect for one another than for their clients. They work within an elaborate system of routine and bureaucracy which tends to screen them from scrutiny. It is a hypothesis worth considering that the larger the organisation, the *less* likely it is that the occurrence of individual deviations will be adequately controlled.

The Milgram experiments[10] also provide food for thought in this context. In these a series of volunteers were asked to form part of a small research team and were instructed to test the ability of an ostensible subject ('the Learner') to remember lists of words, by giving him an electric shock which got stronger each time the Learner made a mistake. They were told by the lead researcher to raise the voltage of the shocks regardless of the Learner's complaints of increasing intensity, and were informed in passing that the Learner suffered from a mild heart condition.

> ... at 120 volts the Learner cries out that he wants to be released from the experiment, complaining of a heart disturbance ... at 180 volts, the Learner cries out 'I can't stand the pain,' and by 285 volts his response to the shock is an agonised scream. At 300 volts the victim shouts in desperation that he will no longer provide answers to the memory test, and so forth through 450 volts. (Milgram 1964, 139)

A large proportion of the volunteers (in one experiment, 26 out of 40) went to the maximum possible voltage in response to the instructions, in spite of the protests made by the Learner.

The Learner was in fact a fake subject, a fact of which the other members in the 'research team' were aware. The purpose of the experiments was to see how far the volunteers would go under the pressure of a group situation. The results suggested that the authority created by the institutional setting, in which several people were involved in what appeared at first sight to be a legitimate scientific experiment, resulted in volunteers failing to act on any misgivings they experienced about what was taking place. One volunteer was interviewed after the experiment about his attitude to what was happening.

> *I'd like to ask you a few questions. How do you feel?* I feel all right, but I don't like what happened to that fellow in there [the victim]. He's been hollering and we had to keep giving him shocks. I didn't like that one bit. I mean he wanted to get out but he [the lead researcher] just kept going, he kept throwing 450 volts. I didn't like that.
> *Who was actually pushing the switch?* I was, but he kept insisting. I told him 'No,' but he said you got to keep going. I told him it's time we stopped when we get up to 195 or 210 volts.

---

[10] Milgram 1964 and 1965.

5. The good of society

Why didn't you just stop? He wouldn't let me. I wanted to stop. I kept insisting to stop, but he said 'No.' ...

Why didn't you just disregard what the experimenter said? He says it's got to go on, the experiment.

Do you feel a little upset? Well, I mean I feel concerned about the gentleman in there, I do sir ... I was getting ready to walk out ... I couldn't see the point of going on when the guy is suffering in there. I figured he was having a heart attack or something. That's the reason I wanted to stop ... (Milgram 1965, 128-9)

It is worth noting that Milgram found that persons who had not performed in the experiment, but who were provided with a description of the situation and asked to predict their own behaviour as would-be volunteers, almost always believed that they would defy their instructions at some point in the experiment, arguing (for example) that 'I'm not the kind of person who is willing to hurt others even for the cause of science.'

6

The restriction of medical resources

A 58-year-old woman with a long history of manic-depressive psychosis was well when she was receiving lithium therapy, but without this drug she lapsed into severe mood swings that both distressed her and disrupted her family life. Reports that lithium can lead to permanent kidney damage worried the client's physicians; as a consequence, neither her psychiatrist nor her internist was willing to continue the treatment. Attempts by the client and her family to persuade the physicians to reinstitute lithium therapy failed. Moreover, other drugs were ineffective, and the client was left in a miserable state. (Kassirer 1983, 899)

... dilemmas arise from patients insisting on the continuation of a prescription which the doctor feels can no longer be justified. ... Dealing with the situation requires time for doctors to listen to patients' views and for doctors to explain their clinical understanding of the situation. Some doctors have proposed that if counselling fails to convince the patient of the undesirability of the requested treatment, the patient should be asked to sign a document accepting responsibility for insisting upon a prescription. Such a document is unlikely to carry any weight in law. Ethically, it would not justify doctors who make such a prescription, contrary to their own judgement, at the patient's request. (BMA 1993, 186-7)

Monopoly power

The association between requiring medication and visiting a doctor is so automatic that one tends not to notice the legal and economic factors which underlie it. The vast bulk of treatments are available only via a registered practitioner. In other words, the state forbids sick people direct access to the things which they need to make them better, and coerces them into using the services of conventional doctors. This is an extremely serious infringement of individual liberty, and one which is rarely given attention in discussions of medical ethics.

However much sick people may dislike the paternalism implicit in the standard doctor-patient relationship, they will be driven to consult a doctor by their urgent need for drugs or services which are otherwise unavailable. If they seek aspects of medical service which they find that the registered practitioners they have used do not provide – such as tact, sympathy or deference – they will be faced with a choice between two mutually exclusive possibilities: *either* potential access to the most potent techniques by consulting a registered practitioner; *or*, by consulting a so-called 'alternative' practitioner, potential satisfaction of other requirements associated with medical treatment but with relatively low potency of techniques offered.

It is easy to despise the alternative therapies industry for being unable to offer remedies which are genuinely effective, and many doctors appear to regard it in this way. However, the situation in which a more sympathetic, client-subordinated service is only available in a completely emasculated form because of legal restrictions is one for which the conventional medical profession is itself largely responsible.

A standard textbook on pharmacology (by Laurence and Bennett) tells us that 'some medicines are, *by general consent*, available only on prescription by a doctor' (my italics). This assertion is little more than wishful thinking. The ostensible motives for the restriction of pharmaceuticals were, and continue to be, paternalistic rather than democratically self-imposed by the public. It is argued that it is too dangerous to allow the consumer the possibility of obtaining potent pharmaceuticals and medical technology without the involvement of a practitioner. Indeed, even the enforced involvement of a qualified person, to provide appropriate advice about dosage, side-effects and so on, is considered insufficient. The technology is not available at all to an individual unless a qualified practitioner considers it appropriate to dispense it. There is little evidence that these restrictions have received genuine general consent, beyond the fact that there is little public complaint about them.

Restrictions apply not only to drugs but to practically any medical technology beyond the level of first aid. You cannot, for example, have an X-ray taken without the approval of your GP. GPs act as 'gatekeepers', as it is euphemistically expressed, for the whole range of specialist services. A mere client cannot access these services directly. It is clear that this level of prohibition involves overriding client autonomy in favour of, at best, paternalism, and at worst, the maximisation of professional power. Indeed, this is arguably the area where the question of autonomy becomes most relevant. If clients were not dependent on doctors to supply them with drugs and medical technology, they would be in a much stronger position with regard to refusing paternalistic medicine. Yet this is not a point to which the medical profession or their supporters in the field of medical ethics draw much attention. Lord Walton of Detchant, former President of the General Medical Council, for example, argues that denying clients direct access to resources is merely a helpful convention.

> The reasons why it is not possible to obtain certain tests, such as an X-ray, without the approval of one's GP relate to economics and established medical etiquette rather than autonomy. Thus it is a cornerstone of British medical practice that the GP acts as the gate-keeper, referring patients to specialists

such as radiologists, and that it is therefore not customary for a patient to consult a specialist direct. I do not believe that this important principle of British medical practice breaches patient autonomy. (personal communication)

The reference to economics may imply that the gatekeeper mechanism is a way of controlling demand for NHS services. On that interpretation, the GP performs a cost-controlling role by ensuring that only clients who ostensibly most need the specialist service are referred. Perhaps such restrictions on state medicine are to be expected, although users surely ought to be actively informed about their true purpose, rather than deceived into thinking that it is all a matter of 'best interests'. However, clearly no economic argument exists for such restrictions on the provision of private medicine.

The law governing the practice of medicine results in the restriction not only of drugs and other technology, but also of information. Since a doctor will be unable to practise effectually unless registered, there will be little incentive for anyone to become an expert on medical matters while operating outside the medical guild system. Expertise itself is therefore a restricted and monopolised commodity. Like drugs, it is carefully guarded and controlled by practitioners. For example, even basic information is not available to clients about the pharmaceuticals which are prescribed. The UK, it seems, is particularly backward in this area, as indeed it is with regard to other aspects of client autonomy.

> Under section 118 of the Medicines Act, information supplied to the Medicines Division of the Department of Health is strictly confidential, as is the Division's advice to ministers. Consumers are not permitted to know under what circumstances their medicines are licensed. They cannot see any information on adverse drug reactions. They cannot learn why a medicine has been withdrawn from sale. No member of the Medicines Division may divulge the ingredient names in any drug formulation.
> This is in stark contrast to the situation in the United States where the Food and Drug Administration is required to publish a 'Summary Basis of Approval' about a drug, giving information about pre-clinical and clinical studies, indications for use, dosage, pharmacology, side-effects, packaging and labelling details. (National Consumer Council 1991, 76)

Without their command over these potent commodities – drugs, technology, information – the enormous power of practitioners would eventually be eroded by competition from outsiders. This may be one reason why the exclusivity of this command is so fiercely protected.

An analysis of the structure of the medical industry suggests that the prices of pharmaceutical products are likely to be too high. Given that clients have no say over what is prescribed, and that doctors themselves do not bear the cost of the medication, there is likely to be relatively weak price competition among drug producers. If doctors were subject to competition and included the cost of drugs in their bills to clients, pharmaceutical producers might well have to develop a different attitude to pricing. However, the monopoly of the medical profession largely escapes criticism as a source of excess drug prices, and it is the pharmaceutical companies who bear the brunt of public hostility to the market for medicines.

The fear of autonomy revisited

While pharmacological restrictions have their roots in paternalism, and now fulfil the function of maintaining the medical monopoly, their continued existence also derives support from other factors. There is a fear of what individuals might do if allowed to have power over their own physiology, comparable to the fear of suicide, which goes beyond mere concern about what the less intelligent might do to themselves unintentionally. This fear expresses itself most forcefully where control over physiology is used to provide positive effects, as opposed to mere restoration of health. The use of technology to overcome infertility, for example, seems to arouse opposition among many commentators. This opposition is usually rationalised in terms of concern for the effects of such technology on families which make use of it. However, such concern is not always matched by an equivalent interventionist concern for the welfare of families that are economically or psychologically incapable of caring for the children which they produce by purely natural means.

The use of psychoactive drugs arouses similar but somewhat more extreme reactions. Thomas Szasz interprets the persecution of illegal drug users and suppliers as a form of political oppression. He has argued that drug users are seen as individuals who rebel against the prevailing social taboos of chemical recreation which permit only the ritual use of alcohol and tobacco.[1] 'Drug abuse' has of course become one of the *bêtes noirs* of the late twentieth century, comparable to extra-marital sex in the late nineteenth century, and attitudes to it demonstrate similar levels of hysteria and unrealism. Those who supply on the black market drugs on which their customers are dependent are reviled as 'vermin'. Yet doctors are in a similar position, differing only in that their treatment is supposed to do more good than harm, and that their behaviour is legally sanctioned. The possibility that in certain cases *their* position of power over dependent individuals is abused does not elicit comparable critical reactions.

The use of the term 'drug abuse', it should be noted, is not necessarily confined to euphoric and psychedelic drugs. One definition which has been given of it is 'the use, usually by self-administration, of any drug in a manner which deviates *from approved medical or social patterns* within a given culture' (my italics). It is obviously not part of the currently ap-

---

[1] See Szasz 1975.

proved medical pattern that individuals should administer, say, influenza vaccinations to themselves without the involvement of a doctor; hence this could presumably also be classified as abuse.

It is interesting to note that paternalism based on the fear of autonomous use of pharmaceuticals can have effects which are far worse than the dangers which were ostensibly to be avoided. With regard to the thalidomide disaster, for example, it has been pointed out that we owe this tragedy in part to the endeavour to find a substitute for the barbiturates, because of their reputation for being used in suicide attempts.[2]

Frustrating clients

Potent drugs and other medical technology are not available to individuals except with the approval of a member of the medical monopoly. Even this understates the degree of restriction: a particular treatment normally becomes available only when a doctor recommends it, in which case the choice for the client is typically one of yes-or-no, rather than a choice between alternative treatments.

Being forced to go through a registered practitioner in order to obtain medical goods and services is by no means merely a formality. The practitioner is expected by law to exercise his professional judgement in any such matter. He not only does not have to give his consent to a client's request if he considers the desired examination or treatment unnecessary, but is under a duty to withhold it if he regards doing so as being in the client's best interests.

Let us consider the following hypothetical scenarios which this situation makes possible. First, we may have a case in which a client asks for a particular treatment which would relieve his pain or save his life but his doctor simply refuses to provide it. Secondly, we can have a less explicit form of refusal. Since clients know they cannot get treatments simply by demanding them, there is less incentive for them to ask. We may have a case in which client and doctor both know what treatment the client needs, but the client does not ask for it and the doctor does not offer it. Thirdly, the lack of client control means that the client has little incentive to be informed about possible treatments, and is forced to rely on the expertise of the doctor in this respect. On the other hand, the doctor may also have little incentive to find out about possible treatments, given that he is free from the pressures of competition. We may therefore have a situation in which both client and doctor are ignorant about the necessary treatment. In all three cases, the client suffers (or dies) needlessly for reasons which depend on monopolisation. It is true that the second and third cases may also occur without medical restriction; however, the shift of incentives due

---

[2] See Miller 1973, 10.

to the absence of client control clearly makes these outcomes more likely under restriction.

Why should we suppose that a doctor might behave in any of these ways? Simply because if you give a group of people the power to act in a certain undesirable way, it is not advisable to assume that none of them will ever make use of it. In Nazi Germany, doctors were given the power under certain circumstances to dispose of their clients as they saw fit. As a consequence, some of them used this power in ways which they may have thought would benefit the public good but which certainly did not benefit their clients, while others used it in ways which did not serve any purpose except the gratification of destructive impulses. However, we do not need to demonstrate that cases of the kind enumerated actually happen in order to find the restriction of medical resources unacceptable. We need only note that they *can* happen, and refuse to accept any contention to the effect that doctors can be relied upon to exercise the appropriate level of self-restraint.

Our knowledge of events in (*inter alia*) Nazi Germany, revolutionary France and communist Russia suggests that the desire to exercise power over others in unsavoury ways is a feature of human psychology which, if not universal, is certainly not uncommon, and that it is only the illegality of such power which acts as a bar to its use. If it is made possible for individuals to gain positions in which they can torture other people by refusing to provide medication, then it is naïve to think that such positions will never be occupied by people who would want to exercise this power.

Are doctors actually *able* to behave like this? One needs to ask oneself, what is there to stop them? Their only external disincentive is the risk of being found to have acted negligently by either a court or their professional body. They are shielded from this in three ways; first, by the fact that medical decisions are often supposed to involve an element of subjective judgement; secondly, by the reluctance of doctors to criticise one another; and thirdly, by the enormous procedural difficulties of bringing a complaint against a member of the medical profession. While a doctor might hesitate to exercise his power of refusal in a life-or-death situation, where the chances of a complaint are relatively high, there are likely to be numerous less serious instances where he can exercise it without anxiety. He could refuse to prescribe a 'flu vaccine, or a tranquilliser, or hormone replacement therapy, or a barium meal – simply because he does not like his client and enjoys expressing his dislike in this fashion. In that case, of course, he need not reveal his reason for refusal to the client. He can simply say that he has made a clinical decision and does not consider the requested treatment to be in the client's best interests.

It is interesting to note that many commentators see the problem as lying in *over*treatment where doctors' decisions in this area are concerned. The suggestion that we as clients are overmedicalised has to be treated with great caution, since there is often an implicit premise that it is the

6. The restriction of medical resources

misplaced desires of the client which are to blame. Hence, ironically, arguments against the excessive influence of doctors over our lives may be a cover for criticisms of client autonomy which the commentator prefers not to state too openly.

Another factor which has to be considered when discussing the restriction of treatment is the pressure on state-funded health services to cut costs. If medical professionals have to make savings, are they more likely to make them in the area of (a) treatments which they regard as appropriate but which the client would not have agreed to if given a completely free and informed choice, or (b) treatments which the client demands and which are provided in spite of the doctors' disapproval? The prevailing belief that professional judgement is more important than client preference suggests that it is far more likely to be the latter.

The following extract is from a study published in the *British Medical Journal*, commenting on recent government pressures to 'rationalise' prescribing. It appears to convey fairly explicitly the message that doctors need to get tougher about refusing clients' requests for specific treatments.

> A major thrust of governmental and professional efforts to reduce 'irrational prescribing' is directed at educating prescribers. Ignorance is indeed a problem, as is highlighted in this study. Nevertheless, there are clearly many instances where the prescriber is aware – indeed uncomfortably aware – of the problems about appropriateness, safety, efficacy, and cost but these considerations are outweighed by others such as the demand of the client or simply lack of sufficient time to negotiate a different management. Education which fails to tackle these other issues around the prescribing decision may fail to change prescribing behaviour and serve only to increase the level of prescriber discomfort.
>
> In particular, doctors need education in how to avoid prescribing when it is not clinically indicated. This will require the doctor to develop skills in negotiating about whether or not the client's expectation for a prescription should be fulfilled. Changes of treatment, which involve breaking precedents, may also need to be negotiated. ... Based on the scenarios described by the doctors in this study, I have devised an educational exercise called 'learning to say no'. It seeks to address, through an experiential learning technique, many of these issues. (Bradley 1992, 296)

The author goes on to cite a specific case of a doctor who would like to refuse his client's request for medication. It is worth emphasising that the client in question is a fellow health care worker, since it is difficult to believe that a doctor would have as much difficulty refusing a conventional client.

> There is a middle aged, about 40ish, 45, [woman] who ... is a nurse. Looking through the notes ... periodically gets sleeping tablets for no terribly good indication, because she's having difficulties at work or whatever. It was an instance like, 'Dr M always gave those to me.' I just ran into a brick wall when I asked her what particular stress or particular strain she had. We get

a very high level of expectation ... in the negotiations I felt as if I had the underhand and was being dictated to. I was squirming. I suppose it is this feeling of loss of control ... as though I am not in charge. My [previous] practice nurse remarked that she didn't think I was very good with nurses, in particular, because I tended to become too defensive. When I got defensive I used to go perhaps overboard in not playing the sort of paternalistic doctor and too concerned to get their view of things and to get their view of how they should be treated. Perhaps too nervous. I suppose it goes back to being a houseman and being under sister's thumb. (*ibid.*, 296)

Self-medication and client preferences

Clients cannot, it seems, be trusted to use any form of potent medical aid by themselves with sufficient care and consideration. One argument is that they invariably need 'counselling' about the implications of their condition or their treatment. For example, in Britain the contraceptive pill is still only available via doctors or agents of the state such as family planning officers, on the basis that counselling is an essential ancillary service for a person who obtains the pill. This must be regarded as something of an obstacle to those considering contraception, particularly perhaps to girls who are above the age of consent but sufficiently immature to find the prospect of having to confront an authority figure discouraging. Yet access to the pill continues to be restricted in this way, in spite of the fact that the number of abortions performed in Britain on girls in the 16 to 19 age group is currently around thirty thousand per annum.[3]

The desire to self-diagnose is also resisted by the medical profession. Again, it is argued that clients are unable to cope with medical technology without the enforced presence of an adviser. For example, there is some pressure on individuals to have an HIV test if they are in a high-risk group, but relatively little willingness to allow people to carry out such a test in the privacy of their own homes, protected from the embarrassment and scrutiny which a positive result might well generate in a conventional medical setting. Given developments in medical confidentiality (see chapter 5), there is certainly no longer any guarantee that a doctor will necessarily see it as his duty to preserve the secrecy of a positive result. Yet even the representatives of some AIDS charities reject home testing. A spokesman for the National Aids Trust, for example, has argued that screening 'should continue to be done in clinics, otherwise people would never get the support and counselling they need if they get a positive result'.

Within the prescribing system the extent to which individual client needs and preferences are taken into account appears to be less than ideal. Doctors can be reluctant to believe that an adverse report from their client about the medication might be genuinely meaningful. They may assume that it is the fault of the client rather than the fault of the drug. If the client

---

[3] *Social Trends 25*, HMSO, 1995, Table 2.26.

complains, and the condition is not serious, the doctor may simply cease treatment rather than go to the trouble of trying an alternative.

Low sensitivity on the part of doctors to atypical client reactions to the prescribed treatment may mean that clients have only so-called 'non-compliance' (i.e. passive resistance in the form of ceasing to take the treatment) as a response to finding the treatment unsatisfactory. Yet it is clients who are usually blamed for this end result. Non-compliance is almost invariably presented in the medical literature in terms of failure on the part of the client, and the waste of pharmaceuticals which arises through non-compliance as attributable to client misbehaviour.

Highlighting medical repression

Perhaps most people are happy to rest in the belief that their own doctor would accede to any really serious request, except where it was clearly hazardous to their health. Usually a client has in any case no specific idea of what treatment he requires; he merely wants a problem solved and relies on the doctor to determine the appropriate solution. Even where the client has a view on what might be suitable, the doctor is almost always in the position of putative superiority of knowledge, so that the client has difficulty in assessing the doctor's reasons for refusing to comply with his wishes. The resistance of doctors to acting according to their clients' wishes rather than their own is therefore likely to be a largely hidden phenomenon. It may only become visible in cases where each of the following conditions are fulfilled. First, the particular drug or service is widely known about, so that the incidence of request (and of refusal) is high; secondly, some members of the medical profession are prepared to speak out in favour of the treatment; and thirdly, the matter is seen as sufficiently serious to stimulate open dissatisfaction among clients and to merit the attention of the media.

Hormone replacement therapy

One case which seems to have met these criteria is that of hormone replacement therapy (HRT). The symptoms of the female menopause are usually uncomfortable for women, and in some cases extremely unpleasant – although until recently, of course, sufferers simply had to put up with them. HRT in many cases dramatically reduces these symptoms. However, ostensibly because of the alleged risk of cancer from this treatment, it is withheld by many doctors regardless of whether the client considers the balance of risks and benefits to be in favour of the treatment. Only about 10 per cent of British post-menopausal women are thought to receive HRT. By contrast, about 80 per cent of American women with menopausal symtoms receive the treatment.[4]

---

[4] Wilson 1992, 46.

Because of the obvious gender aspect of this issue, it has received a considerable amount of public attention. The justifications used by doctors for their paternalist position are illuminating. One senior gynaecologist, for example, was quoted as being 'horrified at the idea of looking at the menopause as a disease', although he conceded, somewhat inconsistently, that 'if a menopausal woman marries again, she *should* have oestrogen replacement as it keeps the vagina young'.

The argument that restricting medicines means a greater likelihood that the choice of treatment is an informed one also seems to fail with HRT. A survey conducted in 1992 found that clients being prescribed HRT for the first time received an average initial consultation time of only seven minutes. Not surprisingly, 80 per cent of the women in the survey felt that the consultation was not long enough for all their questions about the therapy to be answered. On the other hand, the survey found that in spite of a wide range of forms of HRT, the vast majority of clients taken off HRT because of side-effects were not offered any form other than the one initially recommended.[5]

Other medications

It is perhaps not too farfetched to suggest that some in the medical profession would prefer to see the supply of *all* drugs under the control of doctors. There are two principal indications of this: first, the readiness of the profession to condemn the free availability of pharmaceuticals which carry *any* risk of harm (which in effect means *all* pharmaceuticals); and secondly, the hostility which the medical profession tends to evince towards treatments whose application does not require their involvement.

For example, the contrasting attitudes of the US medical establishment in the seventies to two potential treatments of cancer, interferon (a highly complex drug, not available on the market) and laetrile (vitamin B17, derived from apricot kernels, originally available over the counter) suggests, as Ian Kennedy has pointed out, that home treatments are regarded as a threat to the power of doctors.

> A large number of States, including California, have laws making [the sale of laetrile] unlawful. Some, however, claim it as a valuable aid in the treatment of cancer. The medical establishment and the Federal Government's Food and Drug Administration take another view – that its therapeutic value is unproven, that its ingredients make it potentially dangerous and that a patient may delay or even forgo recourse to other accepted forms of cancer therapy and thus not receive the benefit these could bring. (Kennedy 1981, 39)

As Kennedy says, the difference in response to these two treatments is not

---

[5] *The Times*, 13 October 1992.

attributable to a lack of evidence about the efficacy of laetrile, since interferon was similarly unproven; nor to a difference in toxicity. The apparent prejudice is, however, perfectly understandable if one considers that the free availability of an alternative to a restricted drug threatens the control of resources on which medical monopoly depends.

Similar effects can be seen whenever a new over-the-counter product appears which is claimed to have effects going beyond mere palliation. When nicotine patches were launched in 1992 there was a certain amount of opposition to the idea that people could self-administer them without professional guidance. The Director of Quit, the charity that seeks to help smokers to give up the habit, argued that their use 'should be strictly controlled by general practitioners who know the patient's medical history'. The head of the national addiction centre at London's Maudsley Hospital told the *Sunday Times* that the treatment invariably 'works better if it is given with the guidance and explanation of a GP'.[6] In other words, consumers are encouraged to think that they are incapable of interpreting simple medical information, and making simple treatment judgements, without the aid of a doctor.

Over the last ten years, a few relatively mild drugs, such as ibuprofen, have changed status from being prescription-only to being available over the counter. There is a certain amount of pressure for more drugs to move in this direction, since they are then effectively taken out of the state medical system and cease to form part of government expenditure. On the other hand, there are various ways in which the drugs market is becoming *more* restrictive. Various substances such as medicinal paraffin (used against constipation) are now available only in small quantities from chemists, apparently because one may do oneself harm if one takes them in sufficiently large dosages. If one tries to buy several small bottles, the chemist may consider himself under a professional duty to refuse supply. The same applies to medicines containing small amounts of opiates, such as codeine linctus or kaolin and morphine.

Furthermore, various herbal medicines have been removed from the open market over the last thirty years; for example Ephedra, a mild antasthmatic, and comfrey root, an ulcer treatment. Apart from restricting consumer freedom, this also has the effect of making the herbal medicine industry even more impotent compared with conventional medicine, a development which does no harm to the status and financial rewards of conventional practitioners. Nutritional supplements have been under continuous attack from the medical profession. There are recurring calls for Vitamin C and Vitamin A to be taken off the market. Again, the justification given is that they can do harm if taken in extraordinarily high doses. Of course, so can carrots or oranges if consumed in extraordinarily large quantities.

---

[6] *Sunday Times*, 10 January 1993.

Birthing methods

The observation that restriction is in the interests of doctors applies not only to chemicals but to any kind of medical service. Since medical power only becomes exercisable when clients seek access to restricted medical technology, it is not surprising that we find the profession stressing the benefits or indispensability of that technology.

Giving birth is not in itself a pathological process. While that does not mean it is without risk, or that it should always be done without artificial assistance, it does suggest that this is not an area where we would expect much intervention to be necessary. For millennia women gave birth without the aid of hospital technology, so it is reasonable to suppose that for a significant proportion of them this might still be appropriate. Yet childbirth has become so intensely medicalised that there is now fierce opposition by practitioners to the concept of home birth. For example, a 1993 government report calling for pregnant women to be allowed more choice in how they are cared for was attacked by obstetricians as being dangerous to mothers and babies and impossible to implement without substantial extra resources. The Royal College of Obstetricians argued that it was important to realise that 'pregnancy is a time when underlying diseases may become apparent for the first time in a woman's life. ... We consider the review of every pregnancy by a medically qualified person is essential. ... The college's view is that home confinement is not a safe alternative to delivery in properly equipped surroundings.'

It is of course possible that childbirth represents an illustration of the principle that consumer demand for medical technology is in some respects lower than it might be. Consumers may find that the technology is only available in the unpalatable form of being provided by individuals who are under no legal or professional requirement to give adequate weight to client preferences. Childbirth may well be safer in hospital surroundings since the kinds of complications which can arise are not always predictable from the mother's physiological condition. Given the way modern medical care is delivered, however, the balance of benefits, disadvantages and risks may point towards the older, natural method in most cases. That the natural method is not more extensively practised is, on this interpretation, simply a consequence of there being few practitioners who will offer home birth and the fact that it is illegal for a woman to be assisted in giving birth by anyone other than a registered doctor or midwife.

Alternative artificial aids to birthing which do not involve restricted medical technology are also disliked by practitioners. For example, in 1994 a case was reported of two midwives who were censured for overriding the instructions of their employer, East Hertfordshire Trust Hospital, in favour of their client's wishes. Although the Hospital had agreed that the mother could undergo labour in a birthing pool at home, it insisted that she would have to get out of the pool when it came to giving birth. However, when the time came, the midwives gave in to the mother's wishes and allowed her to remain in the pool.[7]

Professional domination of human reproduction goes beyond mere resistance to non-medical birth. Delivery by Caesarean, which was once regarded as an extreme measure invoked only in extreme circumstances, is now routinely applied to a high proportion of births. In some countries, such as Brazil, the rate of use is over 30 per cent.[8] Although the justification often given for excessive reliance on Caesarean section is doctors' fear of malpractice claims, the evidence for this is limited. Not all countries which have rising Caesarean rates also have rising medical litigation rates.[9] There are other possible explanations for a bias in favour of Caesareans, including the fact that they are easier to schedule for a particular time and therefore more convenient for the medical team.

It is possible to see the Wendy Savage affair[10] as a consequence of the excessive reliance on Caesarean sections now common among obstetricians, a policy which appears to involve giving priority to doctors' preferences over those of clients. Mrs Savage departed from the current fashion of insisting on a Caesarean at the slightest sign of complications, and followed her own principle of letting her clients choose whether they wanted to try for a natural birth first. This, among other things, seems to have led to friction with her colleagues, who accused her of being disruptive and controversial.

Pain relief

One particularly deplorable consequence of the restriction of medical resources is that individuals are not in a position to manage their own pain, but depend on practitioners to provide them with the required medication. Needless to say, what is provided hinges on the judgement of the practitioner rather than on the wishes of the client. Not surprisingly, therefore, pain relief is often under-provided and pain needlessly suffered by individuals; largely because they are not in control, neither directly (of the technology) nor indirectly (of the practitioner). I include the following lengthy extract from an article by journalist Denise Winn, as it rather effectively illustrates the relevant issues.

> In a recent investigation, clients at the City General Hospital in Stoke-on-Trent who had either a hysterectomy or their gall bladder removed said that

---

[7] *Daily Telegraph*, 10 February 1994.
[8] Broadhead and James, in Flamm and Quilligan 1995, 9.
[9] See Ham *et al.* 1988, 14-15.
[10] The Savage case concerned a group of obstetricians who sought to secure the dismissal of their colleague Mrs Savage by making unwarranted charges of incompetence. See Savage 1986. A strikingly similar case occurred in 1988 involving consultant obstetrician Pauline Bousquet.

they had expected little pain relief after their operations – and that reality bore out their expectations. In the first 24 hours after surgery their pain levels were 60 per cent of the maximum possible score on a visual scale, regardless of age, sex or operation, and the pain scores were still high on the *sixth* day after surgery. It was commonplace for clients to have to wait three hours after pain came back before being given more analgesia ...

In another survey, where both nurses and clients were asked to rate the clients' pain, the nurses consistently underestimated what clients were suffering. Often they considered clients who kept asking for pain relief 'wimpish'.

'Most clients muddle through,' says Dr Charles Pither, consultant anaesthetist and pain specialist at St Thomas's Hospital in London. 'But some become very anxious when their requests for pain relief are ignored. So then they feel that they have to exaggerate in order to get listened to and nurses react by thinking the pain couldn't be *that* bad and that the client must be a drug addict. So they withhold the drug altogether.' ...

... clients may lie very quietly in bed because moving causes more pain, and may well be suffering more than those who are sufficiently pain-free to writhe about. ... As a result of misinterpreting the signs, nurses often do not give pain relief as frequently as prescribed: they assume the clients are not in significant pain and don't need it. Even when they know a client needs pain relief, the majority don't give it until the pain has returned, although it is well known that pain control is far more effective if given *before* the previous dose has worn off. (*Sunday Times Magazine*, 24 February 1991. Original study Kuhn *et al.* 1990)

One may wonder whether it is hospitals or concentration camps that are being discussed. Individuals suffering excruciating agonies who are denied the antidote they crave; health care workers looking on while other human beings suffer, secure in the knowledge that they will not be prosecuted for their negligence. Those moral philosophers who believe that intention is irrelevant and that effect is all that matters should be the first to place doctors who fail adequately to relieve pain in the same class as political torturers. Some of the doctors who become involved with the atrocities of repressive regimes at least have the excuse that they are forced to collaborate; health professionals in Western countries have no such justification.

One might assume that efficient pain relief would come high on the list of the medical profession's priorities, second only to saving life. However, the evidence for this is not persuasive. In 1987, for example, a junior anaesthetist was investigated by the General Medical Council because of charges of negligent anaesthesia. 'Four women had complained that during their operations [for Caesarean births] they were in great pain and could feel the surgeon's knife, the babies being lifted out and their wombs being stitched. ... solicitor Ann Alexander, who acted for the women, said that she had received 50 or 60 similar complaints.' The GMC found the doctor guilty of professional misconduct, gave him a stern admonishment, but allowed him to go on practising. By contrast, where professional misconduct involves sexual exploitation of the doctor's position, the GMC has demonstrated a relatively zealous approach in its punishment of offenders.

If doctors ignore pain even in situations where it is clearly present, one should not be surprised if physical suffering in less obvious cases receives relatively little sympathy. The reaction obtained from their GPs by many sufferers from myalgic encephalomyelitis – that they are malingering – is symptomatic of the general resistance many doctors have to accepting statements made by their clients at face value. Not only the *wishes* of clients, but their *assessments* of their own condition, take second place after the judgement of the professionals.

Those who are unfortunate enough to be unable to communicate their pain in unequivocal terms fare even worse. This appears to be particularly true of infants. A study on pain relief in operations on premature babies published in the *Lancet*[11] reported that major surgical procedures were performed commonly with minimal or even no anaesthesia; that half the paediatric anaesthetists who replied to a survey did not use pain relieving supplements in anaesthetics on newborn babies; and that some newborn babies receive no anaesthetic at all during surgery. The authors note that it is 'widely believed that ... newborn babies are not capable of perceiving or localising pain and that they may not be capable of interpreting pain since they do not have a memory of previous painful experiences'.

The failure to administer efficient pain relief has obvious implications for the topic of euthanasia. Unbearable pain is one of the main reasons why terminally ill people may wish to end their lives prematurely, and one of the justifications given for 'mercy killing'. 'Euthanasia' in this context may involve giving a lethal injection, as in the Nigel Cox case (see chapter 7), or it may involve giving pain-relieving drugs in excessively high dosages that accelerate or even bring about the client's death. The latter course, unlike the former, is, as we shall see, not in practice unlawful.

The fear of the market

The insulation of medicine from competitive pressures receives ideological support from an academic literature which has helped to perpetuate the myth that medicine is uniquely unsuitable for a market system, and that doctors are *moral* rather than economic agents. For example, a standard textbook on medical economics (*The Economics of Health Care*) makes the following points about the inappropriateness of a free market in medicine. (I give in italics my 'translation' in plain English of the arguments made,

---

[11] Anand *et al*. 1987.

for the benefit of the reader who is not familiar with the concepts and language of contemporary economics.)

(i) *It is necessary for the consumer to rely on the choices made by the supplier on his behalf.*
The authors assert that the consumer 'is not well placed to judge the utility gains (or losses) to be attached to the consumption of health care ... it is difficult for the consumer to judge quality [of health care] both before *and* after consumption ... the doctor is better placed, through his knowledge, training and experience, to perceive *ex ante* how consumption of health care will affect utility ...'. Hence the consumer has no choice but to depend on the good faith of medical professionals.

Any market for a professional service has an informational problem, in that it is difficult for consumers to assess quality. The same is true of accountancy services, legal advice and management consultancy. Yet arguably consumers do manage to find ways of gauging quality even in these areas. For example, they may extrapolate from the quality of general customer care which they receive, and judge that where this is low, the quality of the expert service itself is also likely to be low. In any case, no one has ever suggested that this difficulty makes a free market for legal advice, or for other intellectual or personal services, an impossible one.

(ii) *Doctors' choices are determined by altruistic rather than economic motives.*
The authors argue that the relationship between supplier and user in health care is not the same as the normal economic relationship posited to hold between a 'principal' (the client) and an 'agent' (the doctor). 'In the usual relationship the utility functions of these actors are separate ... contractual arrangements are arrived at through bargaining to ensure, hopefully, that the interdependent but separate objectives and utility functions of both the principal and agent are maximised. In contrast in health care, the objectives and the utility functions are no longer, or at least ought not to be, distinct or separate and it becomes difficult to distinguish the utility functions of the principal and agent.'

No economic argument is adduced for the claim that doctors are unique in being agents who do not maximise purely their own self-interest. It is no more than wishful thinking to assert that, because clients are trapped in an economic relationship in which they are prevented from exercising informed choices, the interests of the professional 'ought' to include those of the client.

(iii) *Financial motives necessarily operate against the interests of clients.*
'The importance of ethical codes of behaviour may be linked to the assurance that, given the role of the supplier, at the very least if the consumer's best interests are not being maintained, the supplier's conduct is determined by medical rather than economic objectives. In this sense ethical

6. The restriction of medical resources

conduct is, at the minimum, an attempt to abstract away the economic arguments in the supplier's utility function. To the extent that this does not occur there is obvious concern regarding exploitation.'

We are to suppose not only that doctors spontaneously incorporate clients' happiness into their objectives, but also that they suppress their personal preferences. The idea that doctors do not operate as conventional economic agents because they voluntarily eliminate self-interest from their concerns may be seductive to some. However, no adequate argument is given why it should not apply equally to other economic groups, e.g. second-hand car salesmen. Nor is any convincing argument given for why normal economic incentives, which typically operate in favour of consumers, should in this case operate against them.

(iv) *The profession's monopoly power is not exploited because of self-restraint.*

The authors present without criticism their theory that ethical codes of conduct impose constraints upon the use of the medical profession's monopoly power. 'The entry of the patient's welfare into the doctor's utility function and the belief that health care is income elastic are also posited as restrictions on the medical profession from pushing inducement to the limit. ... this is even more likely if doctors' utility functions are held to include status as an argument and status is associated with reasonable pricing policies and ethical conduct.'

The claim that self-imposed ethics are sufficient to prevent the exploitation of a dominant market position stands sorely in need of supporting evidence. Without such evidence, it is merely a fallacious backward induction of the form, 'it cannot be the case that doctors exploit their position, *therefore* (given that there is the opportunity for exploitation) doctors exercise voluntary self-restraint'.

The authors conclude that it is right for the medical profession to be protected from competition. 'Doctors' conduct and right to practise are determined substantially by the medical profession. The existence of these non-market relations, which arise directly from the market failings, are obvious and reinforce the importance of emphasising the need for a non-market-based transactional analysis.' In other words, having proved to their own satisfaction that markets and competition are incompatible with medicine, the authors find, rather conveniently, that medical monopoly is indeed the structure required to deliver adequate health care to the consumer.

If academics bolster the medical profession's claim to be treated differently from other economic agents, clients themselves contribute to the conviction that markets and medicine do not mix. Decades of state medical services have allowed people to cherish a belief that the motivations of health care professionals are untainted by financial self-interest, and that a system which allowed such self-interest to intrude would produce dramatically lower standards of service. Professor Stanley Dennison has pointed to

> the myth that the employees of a state service are dedicated selflessly to serving their fellow citizens, whereas those of private institutions are motivated by ambition and greed. Ambition and a desire for a high income are as much in evidence among 'public' as among private employees. Moreover, because there are no market checks, nor even criteria of performance other than expenditure up to a budget, ambitions in state employment become channelled into growth of the organisation. (Dennison 1984, 47.)

The failure to appreciate that doctors are self-serving individuals just like everyone else is bizarre and extremely worrying. It results not only in the expansion of medical power but also in the diffusion of doctors' responsibilities into other social realms. It is the fallacy which supports the thesis that doctors are suitable agents for general social adjudication.

The politicisation of medicine, urged on us by various critics of medicine, including Illich and Kennedy, is of course highly compatible with a paternalistic approach to pain relief and to treatment preferences in general. If social considerations are to prevail over the client's personal preferences, then clearly the doctor is a much better choice for representing those considerations than the client.

Doctors are encouraged to see themselves not as mere servants of their clients, but as social engineers and even moral arbiters. Just as judges are accused by writers such as John Griffiths of having a political bias because they do not actively support social change, doctors are accused of ignoring social problems if they do not have an agenda beyond that of fulfilling their client's expectations. According to Kennedy, the effect of a doctor prescribing chemical rather than social treatment is that 'the social and economic *status quo* is maintained, through the agency of the doctor. He becomes, once again, an agent of the prevailing social system ensuring that its values persist.'

Part II

Power at the Edge of Life

7

Life-or-death decisions

Prolonging life

Many experiences which are likely to occur naturally to a human being in the course of his or her life, such as the pain of a decaying tooth or the discomfort of childbirth, are now regarded as unacceptable by the majority of people in developed countries. It is usually possible to avoid such experiences by the use of chemical intervention. The prospect of having a tooth extracted without an anaesthetic, for example, would nowadays be unthinkable for most people. But this attitude to such experiences is relatively recent. Only two hundred years ago it was the normal thing to have teeth extracted with no artificial aids other than a pair of pliers. The use of anaesthetics in childbirth was for a long time resisted on the grounds that God must have intended women to suffer.

The doctrine that everything is the product of a benevolent creator has ceased to have much hold over the intellectual world. Yet the related notion that what happens to one in the absence of artificial intervention is natural, and therefore necessarily tolerable, has been abandoned more reluctantly. On the subject of death in particular, the anti-interference ethic is still prevalent. The *Times* columnist William Rees-Mogg, for example, appears to see dying as a sort of obstacle course, with those who succeed in tolerating their condition allegedly reaching a phase of tranquil acceptance. According to Rees-Mogg, this phase can be a period of serenity and joy: those who 'most successfully complete this psychological transition' die in a spirit of hope.

The harsh reality, however, is that death is rarely anything except an extremely unpleasant process. The trouble with dying, biologically speaking, is that it is essentially an extended form of disease. Evolution has arranged for an organism to experience pain in response to disease, since this encourages it to remove itself from the source of the disease, or at least to become temporarily inactive so as to concentrate bodily resources on recuperation. Unfortunately, while pain is of no use when the body finally degenerates irreversibly, there is no evolutionary advantage in being preserved from pain at the final stage of life.

With all our medico-technological expertise, we might have expected to be in the position where dying is no longer painful – at least not physiologically. However, there are two reasons why this is not in practice the case, both related to a relatively low interest on the part of medical professionals (and perhaps human beings in general) in relieving pain in others. The first is that research into pain relief has been neglected in favour of interventionist technology. It is clearly more attractive, both scientifically and clinically, to concentrate on ways of repairing the body rather than on measures which are purely palliative. The second reason why death continues to be unnecessarily unpleasant is the lack of efficiency in applying the pain-relieving technology that is available. As with other inefficiencies in the medical industry, we can point to one likely cause as being the lack of financial incentive for practitioners to comply with their clients' subjective preferences.

Where ageing and dying are concerned, modern medicine is in a paradoxical position. While it is constantly improving its ability to intervene selectively in degenerative processes, it is unable to reverse or even to slow the overall process of decay. Thus we can replace a person's diseased kidney, or provide artificial nutrition, but we cannot return an old person to an earlier physiological quality of life. Medicine has now progressed along this route so far that it can no longer be automatically assumed that a seriously ill person would rather be treated than die. Moreover, what medicine can do to keep such people alive may be very expensive.

Edge-of-life technology highlights the standard problem of medicine, namely that the consumer is not in control. It may be relatively easy to ignore the issue of client-doctor conflict when the condition to be treated is, say, tuberculosis, because the indicated treatment is straightforward and both parties would usually agree that it was appropriate. The same is not true when the condition is an advanced tumour, or a failing heart. A comparison between the benefits of treatment and its costs in terms of the resulting suffering may well vary between doctor and client. Liberalising medicine, in the sense of enabling clients to understand their own problems and make their own choices, might suggest itself as an urgent priority. Yet, although the concept of autonomy is often referred to, most discussions of the problems of edge-of-life technology show a preference for discussing two other issues: the problem of resource allocation, and the question of what is the 'morally correct' thing for doctors to do.

Given that edge-of-life medicine is sometimes administered without considering the client's preferences, it is possible that a culture of increased client autonomy would alleviate at least some of the difficulties currently faced by such medicine. However, what if the elimination of all treatment which people would not freely choose did not completely solve the problem of resource shortages? What if, for example, most of the people with kidney failure want dialysis but the collective health system cannot support the cost of a kidney machine for all who want it? (Indeed, it has been claimed that if the UK spent its entire Gross

National Product on dialysis machines that would still not be sufficient to provide dialysis to every person who needs it.[1])

As was mentioned in chapter 1, out of the three possible options of (a) restricting services to those which can be provided to all who want them, (b) determining eligibility for some treatments on a random basis, and (c) provision on a case-by-case decision basis, it is the third option which is preferred by most doctors and medical ethicists. This option means, in effect, that someone has to choose between two competing individuals who both want life-saving treatment. Many doctors seem to think that interference here with their clinical judgement is intrusive and that the choice of whether or not to treat is best left to them. Other commentators would like to see committees debating each individual choice in detail to ensure that the most sensible decision is reached. Few suggest that a committee might not be the best means of deciding whether someone lives or dies, or indeed that this method might be more obnoxious than allocating treatment by lottery, a course usually rejected as too callous even to contemplate.

Accelerating death

Christian ideology plays little part nowadays in the workings of social policy, and suicide ceased to be illegal in England over thirty years ago. Medical technology certainly exists which makes possible the painless ending of life. One might therefore expect to be in a position where, if one thought it appropriate to end one's own life, one could do so in a relatively comfortable and trouble-free way. Nothing could be further from the truth, however.

The technology which would allow individuals to implement their decisions about the value of their own lives – whether for or against continuing to live – is monopolised by the medical profession. The drugs which would kill quickly and painlessly are not available to private individuals, forcing them to resort to highly unpleasant alternatives. In certain extreme circumstances, some doctors are apparently prepared to make the relevant drugs available to individual clients. However, the context of such cases makes it clear that it is very much the doctor, rather than the client, who controls the technology and on whose ultimate approval its application depends. In any case, this practice of 'voluntary euthanasia' is currently illegal, even if this aspect of the law is not one which is very rigorously enforced.

The reluctance of doctors to provide individuals with the means of bringing about their own death is often justified by reference to the sanctity with which they are expected to regard human life. The Hippocratic Oath is sometimes invoked: 'I will give no deadly medicine to anyone

---

[1] See Coleman 1988, 161.

if asked ...'; or the Declaration of Geneva: 'I will maintain the utmost respect for human life.' More pragmatically, it may be argued that doctors must work by a single, overriding principle – to improve health and prolong life – and that it would place them in difficult positions if they had to compromise this aim. This defence rings somewhat hollow, however, in the face of what actually happens in practice. For we find that doctors do make 'termination' decisions as a matter of course, and without the consent of their victims. We are not speaking here only of the killing of foetuses. As we shall see in the following chapters, there is evidence to suggest that doctors apply involuntary euthanasia to the elderly, to the comatose and to handicapped babies, among others.

As an illustration, consider two recent British cases of doctors wishing to terminate the lives of their clients. The behaviour of Dr Nigel Cox, who administered a lethal injection to his terminally ill client in response to her request that he do so, was condemned by the BMA on the grounds that 'deliberately shortening a patient's life is not the purpose of a doctor'. By way of contrast, in the case of Tony Bland, a young man in a 'persistent vegetative state' (as a result of injuries sustained during the Hillsborough football stadium disaster), the medical experts did not apparently perceive a difficulty, in spite of the fact that the client's explicit consent to his proposed euthanasia was obviously unobtainable. Professor Bryan Jennett, an authority on Bland's condition, expressed surprise that the Home Office might consider ceasing to feed Bland as an act of murder. 'Doctors take decisions like this all the time,' he was quoted as saying. 'We say we are not going to operate on this case, or that we are not going to take this chap to intensive care. It's no more than an extension of that.'

It appears that where medical opinion considers the life of an individual to be valueless, the wishes of the individual may become irrelevant to a consideration of whether or not euthanasia should be administered. On the other hand, where a doctor provides death as a service which the client specifically requests, but which contravenes the self-imposed rules of the medical profession, this is regarded as unethical. This suggests that what is crucial in determining whether doctors end the life of a given client is not the wishes of the client but the opinions of the doctor and the views of society as a whole.

The power of life or death

The medical profession appears to exercise a far wider range of discretion on life-or-death decisions than is formally sanctioned by law. Doctors do not exactly ignore the law, but they seem to feel free to move beyond it, particularly in circumstances which are not clear-cut and where a court would therefore have difficulty obtaining a conviction. It seems reasonable, therefore, to expect that any removal of restraints on doctors would not merely legitimise existing practices, but would allow a shift in the practices themselves. Actions which are currently too clearly beyond the pale to be contemplated by most practitioners might be regarded more equivocally. Ironically, however, the existence of covert unlawful euthanasia is used as an argument to support the claim that legalisation would *not* lead to any decline in moral standards.[2]

Traditionally, the purpose of medicine has been conceived to be that of improving health and hence of saving lives. Medicine in this sense did not spring unbidden into existence, but came about because there was a demand by some people for this service: certain ill individuals *chose* to invoke the aid of trained specialists because they wanted to get better, or wanted not to die. On the other hand, there have always been some people who have chosen not to invoke such aid, either because they consider doctors to be unnecessary or unhelpful, or simply because they do not wish to do anything about their illness. To this group of abstainers we must of course add those individuals who are unable to afford the medical services which they require, or who consider that their resources would better be applied to some other use.

As the character of medicine has changed, however, so the simple model of treatment as client-driven has become less appropriate. This has come about for three main reasons. First, most medicine is nowadays run on a collectivised basis. That is to say, instead of individual clients weighing up their various medical needs against their available resources and deciding whether particular treatments with particular associated costs are worth the necessary sacrifices, all individuals are required to make fixed contributions to a collective health fund. Rather than having an assurance of specified medical services in return for subscriptions – as is the case with most private medical insurance schemes – there are no guarantees attached to this collectivised system, and decisions as to what services will be provided are made by the managers of the fund.

Secondly, in part as a result of the first development, the character of medicine has become more *public*. Rather like education, health is now regarded not simply as something which a lot of people want and which the state must finance for the less well off out of taxation, but as something which is for people's 'own good' and which should therefore to some extent be provided independently of demand. Thus the British government recently set 'health targets' which have nothing to do with the quantity or quality of health services on offer but involve 'educating' people into better habits. These targets include reducing the prevalence of smoking, lowering the average fat content in people's diet, and reducing the suicide rate from 11.1 to below 9.5 per 100,000.[3]

Thirdly, the technology of medicine has advanced to the point where in many cases the breakdown of any particular aspect of the human organ-

---

[2] See for example Institute of Medical Ethics 1990, 611.
[3] Department of Health, *The Health of the Nation ... and You*, HMSO 1992.

ism need no longer be fatal. With sufficient resources it is often possible to extend a person's life span by many years compared with what it would unavoidably have been, say, forty years ago. However, the sort of life which the person has in this extra period is often rather different from that which he was previously able to enjoy. A situation is now very much more likely to arise for a person in which it is not clear that he would wish to undergo treatment offered to him to extend his life, quite apart from the question of whether he would wish to spend his own resources on financing the treatment in question if it were not collectively provided. On the other hand, the situation may also arise in which a person wishes to stay alive by means of technology which is very expensive and which, if offered to all who requested it, would be outside the scope of the collective health fund.

Having explored, in the first half of this book, some of the issues underlying the modern doctor-client relationship, we will now consider the application of medical authoritarianism to life-or-death medicine. We shall find that the decision as to whether life-saving treatment should be applied or withheld in any given case has become increasingly dependent on the choices of doctors, and increasingly independent of the choice of the client. As a result of resource constraints, the collective health fund is not able to supply all medical needs, particularly at the life-extension end of the medical spectrum. However, rather than cease to supply expensive services, or supply them only on a non-discriminatory basis, many doctors and other medical analysts now insist that they be allocated on the basis of 'rational' criteria. Hence it is others, and usually doctors themselves, who are to decide whether someone who wants to live shall be allowed to do so.

Because of the 'public health' agenda which has been adopted by the medical profession working in association with national and local government, it is now not always possible for people to choose *not* to have medical intervention. Here again, it is often doctors who decide whether someone who wants to die passively rather than face severe physiological intervention shall be allowed to do so. For professional and psychological reasons, doctors appear to have an automatic bias in favour of intervention, regardless of the wishes of the client. At least, this is true for those categories of client for which it is deemed to be worth making extreme efforts – those who are young enough, and who have previously had sufficiently conventional lives. For other categories – the elderly, the disabled, those with unhealthy lifestyles – the bias appears to be in the opposite direction.

8

Wanting to die

A doctor [Nigel Cox] who gave a lethal injection to an elderly patient who asked him to help her to die left court sobbing yesterday after being found guilty of attempted murder. (*Sunday Times*, 20 September 1992)

Dr Nigel Cox ... is to be allowed to return to work in the new year, his employers [Wessex Regional Health Authority] said last night. (*The Times*, 21 November 1992)

Every experienced hospital nurse will, I am sure, have assisted a doctor to end the life of a terminally-ill patient, although some may be unwilling to admit it. (letter from hospital nurse to *The Times*, 23 September 1992)

Suicide

The ultimate form of control over one's body is arguably the ability to end one's own life. Suicide has always been achievable after a fashion, and it is notoriously difficult to prevent people from killing themselves if they are really determined. But developments in pharmacology have made it possible for one to end one's life in a painless, if not exactly comfortable, way, while mechanical means are of course highly unpleasant. The question, to what extent painless methods of suicide are available to individuals, is therefore an important one. The answer of course is that they are not, since access to pharmaceuticals is restricted to members of the medical profession.

The act of killing oneself has always been hedged about with moral restrictions. The eighteenth-century jurist William Blackstone wrote that suicide is an offence against the king. After God, it was thought, only the state has the right to take a person's life. Hence the grotesque treatment dispensed in the past to criminals who attempted suicide rather than face the death penalty; first resuscitating them against their will and then, with equal diligence, executing them. Most societies have viewed suicide critically, including those which are sometimes cited as having tolerated it. The Greeks, for example, whose literary references to suicides are sometimes used to suggest a relative indifference to the matter, probably had more ambivalent attitudes than the dramas of Sophocles and Euripides might suggest. Certainly it would be an exaggeration to say they never disapproved of suicide. In Plato's *Phaedo*, for example, Socrates says of those for whom 'death is better than life' that it is 'sinful [for them] to do themselves a good service' and that they must 'wait for someone else to do it for them'. Suicide was considered acceptable in special circumstances, most typically when an individual sought to escape from social disgrace. Similarly, Japanese society has not traditionally approved of suicide except in situations where it was expected according to the prevailing social code. Libertarian considerations have had little influence in any society on attitudes to killing oneself.

Disapproval of suicide is still with us, although it nowadays tends to take the form of censuring suicide victims for having abandoned their responsibilities, upset their relatives, or acted out of questionable motives such as attention-seeking. This modern attitude persists in the face of empirical evidence that undermines its assumptions. Erwin Stengel long ago suggested that the profile of suicide victims should be borne in mind when attempting to make moral evaluations of the phenomenon of suicide. 'Contrary to the popular belief, which associates suicide with frustrated love and "poor moral fibre" ', Stengel wrote, 'the majority of the people who kill themselves are elderly and many of them are physically sick.'

As part of a trend to decriminalise activities which, while not morally sanctioned, are regarded as pathetic rather than dangerous to society, suicide has gradually ceased to be punishable by law. However, we are very far from allowing people complete freedom to choose their own death, in the sense of removing all the legal obstructions. There still exists a good deal of revulsion about suicide. It is an act which some would regard (disapprovingly) as the ultimate expression of a person's autonomy: an apparent rejection of all social conventions and responsibilities, and an assertion of the person's evaluation of his or her own life as being of insufficient value compared with the effort required to continue it. Even among modern rationalists, we find suicide described as 'cowardly', or as 'treason'. Christopher Howse, writing in the *Guardian*, complains that suicide is a betrayal of fellow terminal sufferers – as though the presence of one suffering dying person somehow makes it better for the others.[1]

As things stand, there is clearly too much resistance to the idea that people should be allowed to terminate their lives purely on the basis of their own evaluation to expect a significant liberalisation of the relevant pharmaceutical laws. The Church of England, for example, is surely echoing public opinion rather than Christian doctrine when it argues that if a person 'has dependants who need him, or if he has a positive contribution of a recognisable kind which he could still make to the well-being of others, these could be sufficient grounds for denying him, in the general interest, the exercise of his right to die.' Although Stengel pointed out that restricting the available means of suicide had a negligible impact on the rate at which it occurred in a population, the attitude towards suicide continues to be that it should be made as difficult and repellent as possible.

---

[1] *Guardian*, 19 September 1993.

8. Wanting to die

On the other hand, there is clearly a great deal of public sympathy for cases of terminally ill individuals who would rather end their lives immediately than go through a prolonged period of pain, biological deterioration or other suffering. Polls suggest that between 70 and 80 per cent of people support the idea of euthanasia in principle.

This ambivalence towards autonomy over one's own death is reflected in the law on euthanasia, as we shall see below. There is a desire to end unwanted terminal suffering, but a reluctance to let the suffering individuals themselves have control over the means to do so. The risk of such ambivalence is that it will be resolved by letting someone other than the person concerned make the final decision. Since we cannot trust the individual to be rational about whether or not it is the best thing for him to die, so thinking runs, we must let a supposedly impartial arbiter decide. Given the belief about the objectivity and moral purity of doctors, it is the medical profession which most obviously suggests itself for this role.

Death as a choice

The technology for a painless suicide is not accessible to the layman. The physically healthy individual bent on terminating his life is forced to resort to such agonising and nightmarish methods as self-mutilation or drowning. Unless he raids a chemist shop (and knows precisely what he needs), he will be unable to obtain the drugs which would make his death an easy one. He can certainly expect no assistance from his doctor, who might face prosecution for aiding or abetting suicide, and whose regard for clients' opinions in any case makes such assistance unlikely. 'When unassisted suicide is possible,' Jonathan Glover writes, apparently meaning where the person is in full possession of his faculties, 'there is no need to ask for help. A person's unnecessary request for help would be evidence that his suicide "attempt" was not genuine, but an appeal for support.' In other words, a person who is physically healthy should not require any assistance to commit suicide, beyond the means available in the normal course of events, such as kitchen knives or deep ponds.

There is a great reluctance on the part of many people to accept that the desire for suicide may be a perfectly rational attitude even for someone who has not deteriorated physiologically into a state of constant physical discomfort. There is nothing *a priori* impossible about the idea that a person might find life so psychologically painful that he would prefer not to continue living, nor about the idea that any amount of counselling would not make things sufficiently better for him. Of course someone contemplating such an act is hardly going to be 'well-adjusted' by normal social standards – he must, almost by definition, be extremely unhappy – but that in itself does not invalidate his perspective. Yet the mere fact that such a person will not display normal personality characteristics is taken as proof that his wishes are not in accordance with his interests. For example, a recent NHS report defines 'rational' suicide as 'suicide in the absence of psychological distress'. Contrary to the view of the report's authors, it is hard to see how the act of killing oneself *without* accompanying psychological distress could be regarded as rational.

The unstated assumption in most writing about suicide is that the beliefs and volitions of the suicide are confused or deluded, and that his autonomy need therefore not be respected. What he really needs is not our assistance, but our benevolent obstruction, since with sufficient care his views may be manipulated into more normal directions.

Indeed, *doctors* are once again proposed as suitable agents of intervention. Peter Sainsbury, for example, writes that 'a substantial proportion of suicides could be prevented if their family doctors or hospital physicians were as well trained in the recognition and management of depression, and of other psychiatric conditions known to have high rates of suicide, as they are, say, in the diagnosis and treatment of pneumonia'.

A factor that tends to be left out of account whenever there is discussion of the prohibition or discouragement by the state of a particular activity is the possibility that attempts at suppression actually amplify the demand for that activity. This may not simply be a question of lending the activity the glamour of forbidden fruit. Where suppression is perceived as unreasonable, there may well be a natural and understandable reaction to this in the form of a strong desire that the object of suppression be available. In some cases, this may be all that is wanted: that a choice should be *possible*. After all, it is difficult to make up one's own mind about something if someone else has already decided in advance what can or cannot happen. Making a choice hypothetically may be a very different thing, psychologically, from making it when one knows one will be able to give force to one's decision.

By denying people, especially those who are old or sick, the opportunity of ending their own lives, the law may paradoxically be creating a *perceived need* in certain people who, were the opportunity available, would not in fact take it. Although prohibiting suicide makes no difference to the final outcome for these people, it means that they suffer the frustration of wanting it and being denied it. There are occasional reports of people who urgently clamour for the right not to be treated against their will, or to be allowed access to drugs which would produce a painless death for them, and who, when the law or the doctor finally yields, decide that they actually prefer to do whatever it takes to stay alive. The philosopher James Rachels quotes the case of a young man who sustained horrific burns and other injuries and was kept alive for two years by means of painful treatments, although he seemed to prefer to die and continually demanded to leave the hospital. When, eventually, he was permitted to leave, he decided he wanted to stay alive and continued with the treatments.[2]

---

[2] Rachels 1986, 54.

Such cases should not be interpreted as implying that the person's original belief about what they really wanted was necessarily wrong. Being kept alive regardless of your wishes, and staying alive because *you* decide, autonomously, to carry on the battle against adverse circumstances, are two quite different things.

Assisted suicide

For the hospitalised individual the more dramatic methods of taking one's life do not, for practical purposes, exist. Such a person is therefore utterly dependent on the will of health professionals, not only for conventional analgesia, but for the ultimate relief of death if adequate pain relief is no longer possible. Given the points about pain relief made in chapter 6, one wonders how often it is because a doctor is being less than maximally efficient in his analgesic procedures that a seriously sick person conceives the desire to die.

In connection with the Nigel Cox case, for example, it is not clear that Dr Cox was justified in using a drug the only purpose of which was to kill, when he might simply have continued to increase the dosage of pain-relieving morphine – which, of course, would itself eventually cause death, but as a secondary rather than a primary effect. A practitioner writing to the *British Medical Journal*[3] about the case seemed to think that Dr Cox's assertion about the inability of the client to absorb increased dosages of morphine was inconsistent with his own experience. A consultant anaesthetist commenting in the *Sunday Times* about the case asserted that any client can be rendered pain-free with a sufficiently large dose of narcotic analgesics – provided all the parties involved can accept the probability of fatal side-effects.[4] It is curious that this aspect of the case was not highlighted by the court or by the media.

It is argued by opponents of euthanasia that adequate terminal care is the preferable solution. What those who use this line of reasoning do not explain, however, is how it is to come about that an industry which has no incentive to adapt to demand, and which appears to be relatively immune to accusations of inefficiency, starts to make effective pain relief part of its business. It is true, however, that poor standards of palliative care may well be pushing us in the direction of legalising euthanasia. The reluctance to believe that the modern health industry is appallingly inefficient can easily side-track one to the conclusion that a person's unbearable agony can only be resolved by killing him, as the following case, quoted by James Rachels, illustrates.

> Jack was good-looking, about 28, and brave. He was in constant pain, and his doctor had prescribed an intravenous shot of a synthetic opiate – a

[3] 17 October 1992, p. 952.
[4] Dr George Robertson, *Sunday Times*, 27 September 1992.

pain-killer, or analgesic – every four hours. ... At the prescribed hour, a nurse would give Jack a shot of the synthetic analgesic, and this would control the pain for perhaps two hours or a bit more. Then he would begin to moan, or whimper, very low, as though he didn't want to wake me. Then he would begin to howl, like a dog.

When this happened, either he or I would ring for a nurse, and ask for a pain-killer. She would give him some codeine or the like by mouth, but it never did any real good – it affected him no more than half an aspirin might affect a man who had just broken his arm. Always the nurse would explain as encouragingly as she could that there was not long to go before the next intravenous shot – 'Only about 50 minutes now.' And always poor Jack's whimpers and howls would become more loud and frequent until at last the blessed relief came.

The third night of this routine, the terrible thought occurred to me. 'If Jack were a dog,' I thought, 'what would be done with him?' The answer was obvious: the pound, and chloroform. No human being with a spark of pity could let a living thing suffer so, to no good end. (Rachels 1986, 153-4, quoting from Alsop 1974, 69 and 130)

In commenting on this case, Rachels evades the important question of whether in certain cases euthanasia might be inappropriate because the client is suffering needlessly. He notes that some physicians with whom he discussed this case were indignant that Jack was not given larger doses of the pain-killing drug more frequently. He quickly dismisses this possible interpretation, however, pointing out that the clinic where Jack was staying was 'one of the best-equipped modern facilities we have; it is not as though Jack's suffering was caused by neglect in some backward rural hospital. *Few of us could expect better care*, were we in Jack's position.' (My italics.) As in so many arguments about medical ethics, we are asked to rely on the premise that the average standard of health care achieved by health professionals is an acceptable one.

The idea that doctors should simply comply with their clients' wishes is, as has already been discussed, regarded as discreditable. Assisted suicide (providing someone with the means) and voluntary euthanasia (administering the means) are both illegal, yet curiously the profession appears to regard the former as more shocking than the latter. Mason and McCall Smith have this to say about giving a client the power to decide for himself: 'The occasionally suggested tactic of leaving an obvious means of suicide available to the patient may solve the doctor's legal or ethical conscience but it is such an example of moral cowardice as to be beyond consideration.' By contrast, they assert without equivocation that, for clients regarded by current medical opinion as in an irreversibly vegetative state, it is 'beyond argument' that they 'should not be ventilated when their respiration fails'.

'Voluntary' euthanasia

The importance of the distinction between a person deciding to end his own life prematurely, and someone else deciding this for him, cannot be overstated. They are two entirely different things. Even if one takes the view that the law's response to the latter action should depend to some extent on the motives of the killer, this does not make the latter action more like the former. Yet this distinction is not always adequately signposted. Indeed, on occasion it is not made at all. In order to avoid any possible conflation of the two ideas, I shall use the term 'doctor-assisted suicide' (DAS) for the former type of euthanasia, and retain the term 'killing' for the latter. By referring to *doctor*-assisted suicide, I am merely acknowledging an invariable feature of euthanasia proposals; I certainly do not mean to imply automatic approval of this feature. Nor should the use of the word 'suicide' be taken to imply that, if DAS proposals were put into practice, it would necessarily be the client's wishes which would initiate the euthanasia process.

The law on DAS, in Britain as in most other countries, currently suffers from profound ambiguity. Notionally DAS is illegal, but in fact it appears to be practised extensively. On the rare occasions when a case comes to court, the practitioner in question is usually found not guilty, and at worst is given a suspended sentence. Yet the legal system seems reluctant to condone DAS to the extent of changing the laws. Even in the Netherlands where, it has been claimed, the majority of people who end their lives in a hospital do so as a result of euthanasia, the formal legislation was until recently as prohibitive as that of most other countries.

The tide is clearly changing, however. More and more doctors and clients support the suggestion that a practitioner should be able to end a person's life if requested to do so. This attitude seems to be determined by a vision of DAS as a merciful act, inhibited only by professional or religious injunctions against the taking of life. Recently the House of Lords considered possible changes to the legislation on DAS, and more legal and political debate is no doubt on the way.

If assisted suicide pure and simple is not to be contemplated, we shall have to consider whether we want doctors to have the legally sanctioned power (it is, one should note, a *power* that is usually proposed, not an obligation) to administer lethal injections to clients who express a wish to die. From a certain perspective, this may seem desirable. If one is in an unbearable physical condition, and the only possible form in which life-terminating treatment might be permitted is by the hand and with the consent of a doctor, then perhaps one had better remove the ban on doctors obliging their clients' suicidal wishes. Perhaps granting doctors the power of veto, and the sole power of dispensation, is not too high a price to pay for the possibility of committing suicide in extreme physiological circumstances, compared with no possibility at all.

This line of reasoning is one which many countries are now following in their search for a solution to the problems of dying, problems which are becoming more urgent as the proportion of people who are elderly or permanently ill rises. It is, however, a flawed and dangerous line to follow. It assumes that doctors are neutral agents, with no agenda or vested interests of their own, who will generally oblige their client's wish for death when it is a considered one and would, on the other hand, have no particular incentive to counsel this course of action. This assumption is a highly questionable one in a climate in which medicine and politics are increasingly becoming inextricably linked.

There is a danger in equating suicide with being killed by someone to whom you have given your 'consent'. This danger is increased, not reduced, by the reverence with which doctors are regarded, and by the position of technical and moral superiority which they are believed to occupy. Although Jonathan Glover, for example, thinks that there is an important *practical* difference between the two types of action, he points out that 'it is hard to see why it matters *in principle* who actually puts the pill in the man's mouth. If we were in a position to have no serious doubt about the person's considered and strong preference for death, the fact that I put the pill in his mouth rather than left it at his bedside would be in itself of no moral importance.' Unfortunately, it is easy to imagine the criterion of 'no serious doubt' being gradually redefined to suit the medical profession, especially when 'best interests' arguments may also be invoked as tending towards the conclusion that the client is better off dead.

Most people who advocate 'euthanasia' appear to agree that the consent of the client is crucial, and that *involuntary* euthanasia is ruled right out of court. Yet it is worth considering the proposed development in the light of the current situation. On the one hand, it is currently unlawful to act as assistant to a friend or relative trying to take his own life, and there is no suggestion that this should change. On the other hand, *doctors* killing certain categories of client without their consent, such as the senile or the comatose, by withholding treatment is a regular and apparently not unlawful occurrence. One may ask oneself, on that basis, whether the legalisation of DAS is more likely to be related to respect for autonomy or to respect for the medical profession.

Support for the consent requirement has not been a consistent feature of the DAS movement. In 1950, for example, Lord Chorley had this to say to the House of Lords on the subject of the Voluntary Euthanasia Bill then being debated. '[One objection to the Bill is that it] does not go far enough, because it applies only to adults and does not apply to children who come into the world deaf, dumb and crippled, and who have a much better cause than those for whom the Bill provides. That may be so, but we must go step by step.' At the first annual meeting of the American Euthanasia Society in 1939, at which the Society's Treasurer Charles Nixdorff proposed specific DAS legislation, it was reported in the *New York Times* that

'Infant imbeciles, hopelessly insane persons ... and any person not requesting his own death would not come within the scope of the act. [Nixdorff] explained to some of the members who desired to broaden the scope of the proposed law, that it was limited purposely to voluntary euthanasia because public opinion is not ready to accept the broader principle. He said, however, that the society hoped eventually to legalise the putting to death of nonvolunteers beyond the help of medical science.'

In fact, the supposedly all-important distinction between voluntary and involuntary euthanasia, which it is often assumed will be scrupulously respected, turns out on inspection to be a good deal less secure than is usually thought. We can see some sign of this if we consider the way in which DAS is frequently described as 'mercy-killing', and compared with putting down an injured animal. In many discussions of the subject, the question of whether it is *better* for the client if he is killed is given more prominence than the question of whether he requests this option. This partly reflects the moral ambivalence, discussed above, towards the whole issue of suicide.

It is interesting to note that certain spokesmen aligned with the Protestant faith are among those who imply that voluntariness is not the crucial factor in deciding the ethicality of euthanasia. The Dean of Salisbury, for example, commenting on the Nigel Cox case, describes the case of a man terribly mauled by a lion in the South African bush whose injuries are 'appalling and agonising' and who cannot survive the long journey home. His friend, who has accompanied him, has several options.

> To leave him and ride for help is to abandon him to the lions. To stay with him only a prolongation of his terrible pain. The only kindly solution is quick and merciful oblivion. The bullet in the back of the head was his only option and so he shot his friend. (*Financial Times*, 3 October 1992)

The Dean does not mention any expressed wish on the part of the injured man, so one is led to presume that he did not ask to be shot. If he did, why is this not mentioned – is it not thought to be relevant? Perhaps it could be argued that the man would have found it difficult and painful to consider the options if they had been presented to him. Perhaps, but is this an adequate justification for usurping his right to choose?

There are of course motives for killing people who are visibly suffering which have nothing to do with their own wishes, and there is evidence to suggest that it may be primarily these, rather than the desire of the terminally ill to die, which drive the DAS movement. To justify DAS on *utilitarian* grounds, we do not merely invoke the suffering of the client, but also the suffering of his relatives and the inconvenience caused to medical staff. There are grounds for suspecting that the consent requirement is not regarded as primary, but is rather thrown in as a sop because killing a person against his will, however much it is supposed to be in everyone's best interests, still offends certain old-fashioned moral prejudices. Consider, for example, the following defence of a utilitarian approach to euthanasia by James Rachels, which elegantly evades the question whether the arguments used may legitimise killing people against their will.

> Suppose a person is leading a miserable life – full of more unhappiness than happiness – but does not want to die. This person thinks a miserable life is better than none at all. Now I assume we would all agree that this person should not be killed; that would be plain, unjustifiable murder. Yet it *would* decrease the amount of misery in the world if we killed him – and so it is hard to see, on strictly utilitarian grounds, it could be wrong. ... So, suppose we substitute a better conception of welfare: rather than speaking of maximising *happiness*, let us speak of maximising *interests* – let the principle of utility say that actions are right if they satisfy as many interests as possible. ... the new principle avoids the problems that plagued the old one: if it is in a person's best interests to have freedom of choice in religion, or in choosing to remain alive, then the principle will not countenance taking away that freedom or that life. (Rachels 1986, 155-6)

In other words, a person will be allowed to decide for himself whether to continue living provided we consider it to be generally in people's interests to make such decisions for themselves. It is hard to see how this approach to utility is more sympathetic to autonomy than the maximisation of happiness. It does illustrate, however, how autonomy is seen as something to be *accommodated* rather than something to be given priority in questions of medical practice. The idea that autonomy about one's death will be permitted to the extent that we regard it as good for people to make such decisions is reminiscent of an existing trend in contemporary medicine. This is the practice of letting clients participate more in the decision-making process, on the basis that this is helpful to the treatment process. Or rather, of letting clients *think* they are participating in decision-making, which comes to the same thing in terms of the consequences thought to be of relevance. We can expect a similar effect if DAS is ever legalised in the form usually proposed. Clients will be encouraged to think that their opinion is very important in reaching the decision whether their doctor should treat or kill them. Whether it is in fact important may be irrelevant as far as the doctor is concerned, since what is in their interests is to *experience* freedom of choice.

The interests of the community

If a client who permanently requires intensive medical support and who relies on the state to finance this support decides to end his life, this is clearly in the interests of the rest of the community. The money saved by not having to continue the support will either reduce the taxation levied on others or will be used to fund services which benefit others. To pretend otherwise is a dishonesty. The only question which needs to be settled is, should individuals be killed, with or without their approval, to serve the community's interests? Most people would answer no to this question. Thus there can be no *explicit* policy to kill such ill individuals, whether actively or by withholding treatment. Yet the temptation to engage in such a policy notwithstanding must be enormous.

We have seen how the interests of society are permeating medical practice. In chapter 10, we will consider the possibility that clients are already being killed against their will. For the purpose of considering proposed DAS legislation, we need to ask whose interests would be best served by such legislation. The answer may well be, those of the community as a whole rather than those of the suffering individuals.

Supporters of DAS often cite with approval practices in other cultures that have not been subject to 'over-civilisation'. Derek Humphry and Ann Wickett tell us about Bolivian Indians, among whom the family withholds food and drink until the dying person slips into unconsciousness and dies; and certain tribes of Eskimo, where, when an individual tells his family he is ready to die, the family will 'immediately comply by abandoning the aged person to the ravages of nature or by killing him'. They also quote Pliny's descriptions of 'natives of Amboina in Indonesia, who ate their failing relatives out of charity, and the Congolese who jumped on the tired and old until life was gone'. Humphry and Wickett appear to believe that, at least in the first two of these cases, a person was only killed when he wanted to be. However, primitive cultures are not particularly noted for their respect for individual volition. If a certain tribal custom exists, it is more likely than not to be applied irrespective of a person's wishes. At least there is likely to be a good deal of social pressure to conform with normal practice. If it is customary in a particular tribe for an old person who has reached the end of his useful life to jump off a cliff, what happens when a member of that tribe refuses to observe that custom? Are his family likely to congratulate him on his courage and moral fibre, or to feel disapproval and even outrage that an honoured custom is being breached?

Unfortunately, it is easy to imagine that similar motives enter into the thinking on euthanasia of at least some modern Westerners. If a person's physiology has degenerated to the point where he ceases to be able to partake in the normal social life of the community, his wish to go on living in spite of this may not be regarded very favourably. In any case, we should certainly be wary of the argument that legalising euthanasia represents a return to a more 'natural' attitude to death.

Humphry, incidentally, like other pro-euthanasists, demonstrates remarkable faith in human nature when answering the objection that the euthanasia option might be abused, as it was under the Nazis. Writing from his home in California, Humphry originally noted that

> Medical costs rise in tandem with the expectation of a long and good life. Might there come a point when the younger generation, finding itself in harsher economic times, would turn against the elderly and rule: You are dying; why should we spend our scarce resources on prolonging the inevitable?
>
> This line of argument confuses economic and technological issues with the murderous tactics of the Third Reich. An estimated ten thousand people lie in irreversible comas in American hospitals, mostly the result of traffic accidents, and there would be a justifiable howl of protest at the first person who suggested that they are useless and should be eliminated on grounds of cost. (Humphry and Wickett 1986, 30-1)

However, as Humphry himself commented in a footnote, in March 1986 the Judicial and Ethical Council of the American Medical Association announced that it is ethically permissible for doctors to withhold all life-prolonging treatment, including artificial nutrition and hydration, from patients in irreversible coma, even if death is not imminent. Since then, the Karen Quinlan and Nancy Cruzan cases in the United States, and the Tony Bland case in Britain, have confirmed the feasibility of killing clients who are pronounced by doctors to be irreversibly brain-damaged.

The role of doctors

Let us consider a situation in which suicide has been fully legalised *for a finite set of circumstances*. By 'fully legalised' I mean that not only is it not punishable to kill oneself, but also that the means to do it painlessly are readily available. What must surely be considered as crucial in any such arrangement is that, whatever the conditions which have to be satisfied, it must be *the person himself* who chooses if and when to die, and not someone else. Otherwise it would not be a partial legalisation of suicide but a partial legalisation of murder.

Now if one or more other persons are to be involved in the act of suicide as assistants, it is surely of paramount importance that those persons should be clearly under the control of the would-be suicide. This seems a much more important condition than that they should not stand to benefit from the person's death. The possibility of a pecuniary motive in such cases is so obvious that it is readily suspected by police and judges, and tends to be seized on by juries. On the other hand, gratuitously destructive or ideological motives, which may well arise when the suicide assistant is not fully and genuinely answerable to the suicide, are not something which the law tends to recognise.

Another point is that people who stand to gain financially from the suicide's death usually have at least a relationship of some kind with the person and therefore are likely to have a greater than average psychological resistance to killing them against their will. Strangers having no relation, whether emotional or economic, with the person are unlikely to have as much compunction about failing to respect the person's wishes.

Since doctors are to play the role of assistants under the currently favoured proposals for euthanasia, the crucial question therefore arises, *are doctors under the control of their clients*? The evidence considered in this book suggests that the answer to this must be no, and that doctors are therefore quite unsuitable as suicide assistants, and should certainly not be entrusted with the power to kill.

Even more ominously, it is proposed not only that doctors should add to their armoury of monopolies the power to end human lives, but also that they are to be the arbiters in deciding whether the conditions for permissible 'suicide' are met in any particular case. The world view of the medical profession, both covert and explicit, and in particular their tendency to take into account the interests of *other people* (relatives, the community, society as a whole) in making decisions about clients, makes this possibility an extremely dangerous one.

There is a widespread fear that DAS might lead to sick people being put under pressure to consent to termination by their relatives, to whom they may represent an unwanted burden. Geoffrey Robertson, for example, warns of the danger that the repeal of the restrictions on assisting suicide 'would leave the elderly open to artful persuasion by greedy relatives, and even permit the kind of manipulated hysteria which produced the mass suicides at Jones Town'. It is curious, then, that there is no corresponding alarm about the possible pressures from doctors themselves. Doctors would arguably not only have far greater influence in the death decision than relatives, if DAS were legalised, but their interest in the person's death is potentially both stronger and less subject to the restraining influence of conscience, considering that the 'fair' distribution of medical resources now features on a doctor's list of ostensible priorities.

On the other hand, the legalisation of DAS – rather than of assisted suicide in general – may also mean that those who really do want to die are frustrated by the obstacle of having to convince an obdurate professional. Jonathan Glover argues that a request for DAS would be less worth taking seriously if it depended on a client's 'exaggerated view' of the pain he was suffering. Considered in the light of the observations made in chapter 6 on the attitudes of medical staff to pain, this remark indicates the sort of resistance which might be encountered by a client who was finding his pain unbearable.

The desire to permit DAS without any liberalisation of the attitude to suicide leads to proposals which demonstrate the illogicality of this position. A person in unbearable agony might be required to submit an application to a state body, would then need to be interviewed, and would have to wait patiently for the decision. The following suggestion, made by a medical practitioner (Tim Helme), provides a good illustration of how the whole process could become bogged down in bureaucracy, the client's volition being swamped by a series of formalities in which other people's judgements are decisive.

> ... it would be possible to institute a system of Euthanasia Tribunals to whom patients (and perhaps their next of kin or guardians) could appeal ... Criteria could be specified to ensure that it would only be carried out on those who, for instance:
> a) Understood the nature of the application that they were making;
> b) And had an enduring and a considered wish to die, and were not under any form of external coercion, either for financial or for other reasons;
> c) And were suffering from a condition which was both permanent and incurable, and which was causing them significant distress;
> d) And were not suffering from any distortion of judgement due to temporary or treatable psychiatric illness.
>
> The intention would be to assist patients in the exercise of their present liberty, under the Suicide Act 1961, to choose to die, but only if and when it appeared compassionate to do so, and without in any way converting that liberty into a right which could be acted upon inappropriately or capriciously. ... the Tribunal might comprise five members ...
> 1. A chairman, with a suitable legal qualification and experience.
> 2. A medical practitioner, with a special interest in the illness from which the patient suffers.
> 3. A psychiatrist, in order to exclude the presence of treatable mental illness, and to provide a psychotherapeutic input if required.
> 4. A solicitor or social worker, to examine the social and especially the financial implications of the death being contemplated, in order to minimise the possibility of duress.
> 5. A layperson, to provide a balancing and general perspective. (Helme 1991, 27)

Another danger of legalising DAS under present circumstances stems from the fact that doctors do not consider themselves under an obligation to keep their clients informed. Once one had given consent to euthanasia, especially if conditional upon some particular medical development, one would again have completely lost control of the situation, although now one would be potentially in the position of being unable to go on living, instead of unable to die. Bliss and Johnson refer hypothetically to the awful state of uncertainty of an elderly lady who previously requested euthanasia if her condition should become hopeless, and who now wonders whether the injection the doctor is about to give her is a lethal dose of barbiturate or her monthly Vitamin B12.[5] The same point applies to so-called 'advance directives', or 'living wills'. The principal effect of these appears to be to make it easier for doctors to withdraw treatments when they consider this to be appropriate. Whether they actually fulfil their supposed chief function, that of preventing treatment which the client does not wish, remains to be seen. The BMA, for example, have said that

---

[5] Bliss and Johnson 1975, 83.

8. Wanting to die

they regard stipulations contained in an advance directive as 'helpful', but not binding on doctors.

It is true that the medical profession as a whole tends to oppose the legalisation of DAS. But this opposition does not invoke the dangers of abuse by practitioners as an argument. Instead, one of the most common points made in defending the *status quo* is that it is important for clients to have faith in the judgement and goodwill of their doctors, and that this faith would be jeopardised by the knowledge that doctors sometimes deliberately end clients' lives. In fact, of course, active DAS *is* practised, albeit illicitly and (as far as one can tell) in a minority of cases. In other words, then, the argument is that clients must be preserved in their unjustified conviction that doctors never intentionally kill, so that their more general belief in the dependability of doctors is not threatened. Interestingly, the German legal profession expressed opposition to DAS on the same ground. As late as 1945, after years of involuntary euthanasia under Hitler, German legislators argued against euthanasia on the basis that 'the law must take care not to shatter the confidence of the sick in the medical profession'.

In any case, one has to ask oneself whether doctors oppose DAS because they disapprove of it in principle, or because they prefer the whole matter to be left to their discretion. As long as DAS is unlawful, but in practice no doctor is prosecuted for administering it, health professionals are in the happy situation that they are under no pressure to provide it, nor under much threat if they choose to administer it. It is interesting to note that Lord Dawson of Penn, who opposed the 1936 Voluntary Euthanasia Bill on the grounds that the proposed legislation would interfere with the judgement of the medical professionals, was the physician who (by his own admission) administered a lethal injection to George V in order to hasten his death.

If death becomes something produced by a doctor then, whatever the law may say, it will come to be regarded as a treatment. And treatments are things which are given according to whether doctors consider them medically indicated, subject only to the client's supposed right not to consent. But given how ineffectual the consent principle is in practice – as we shall see in the next chapter – we must doubt whether DAS can be a way of enhancing the autonomy of the client, rather than that of the doctor.

9

Wanting not to be treated

A Nigerian woman expecting triplets, who was taken to hospital in Chicago during the final stages of her pregnancy, repeatedly said she was unwilling to have a caesarean. The hospital obtained a court order once she had gone into labour. When both parents were informed of the decision they objected strenuously. The woman was put in leather restraints and her husband ejected from the hospital. (*The Times*, 27 October 1992)

Society ... has an interest in ensuring that life and health is preserved. It is assumed that doctors propose treatments with patients' interests in mind. The individual who refuses treatment challenges society's expectations and may expect to be called upon to demonstrate a greater grasp of the implications of that decision than a consenting patient. ... Whether any person, adult or minor, has or lacks the capacity to make autonomous decisions must be a question of clinical judgement in each case. (BMA 1993, 4 and 74)

The erosion of medical autonomy

From time to time one hears of cases in which a person has been forced, against his wishes, to receive life-prolonging treatment. A man wishes to be taken off a respirator but hospital personnel refuse to comply. A severely disabled woman suffering incurable pain wants to starve to death but doctors insert a naso-gastric tube to force-feed her. A pregnant woman is forced to have a Caesarean operation against her will. How is it possible for such extraordinary coercion to go on?

In principle, the law supports the right of the individual not to receive medical treatment which he does not want. The interference of a doctor with a person's body, whether by examining, injecting, operating or otherwise, falls under the law on battery. This means that such interference can only be lawful if done with the person's prior agreement. *Prima facie*, then, the law demands that no treatment be administered to an adult without his or her consent.

This sounds like a principle designed to put clients in control of their destiny. Even if they cannot actively end their own lives, or ask their doctor to do so for them, they can at least refuse life-saving treatment urged upon them. They need not stay alive longer than they would without intervention if they do not wish to do so. That, at least, is the theory.

We know, however, that medical practice is strongly informed by the principle of paternalism – 'doctor knows best'. Just as there are no doubt many cases where clients want a particular treatment (or would want it if they knew it was available) but their doctors disagree, there must be many cases where doctors consider a particular treatment appropriate but clients object. We know that a doctor is under no legal or professional obligation to comply with a client's request for a particular treatment. But what happens when a doctor is faced with a *refusal* to be treated in the way he thinks best?

Judging from the comments of some doctors, we may guess that many practitioners would prefer to be relieved of the legal consent requirement altogether, in order to have complete freedom in their clinical judgement. If a doctor considers that a certain level of co-operation from his client would be desirable, he can always inform and obtain notional consent to the extent required for this purpose. Anything more stringent than this is (in some practitioners' view) simply an onerous burden, designed to protect the client from a non-existing danger. The BMA points out that 'some people'

> question the emphasis which is currently placed on patient consent, suggesting it implies that the patient is somehow doing the doctor a favour by signifying his or her agreement to be treated. They feel it would be more appropriate to talk about a 'request for treatment'. (*ibid.*, 1)

Perhaps what is implied here is that it is the doctor who is doing the client a favour, and the client should not expect him to ask permission to impose treatment.

In one sense, of course, the requirement to have a strong emphasis on consent is itself indicative of medical authoritarianism. It arises because medicine involves doctors making decisions about clients, subject (in principle) to refusal on the part of the client; rather than clients making decisions which their doctors must then respect. Claims that consent is becoming more important, based on the observation that the concept is receiving increasing attention, therefore have to be treated with caution. For example, a number of commentators have seized upon remarks made in recent English legal cases which seem to be giving reinforcement to the consent principle. Ironically, however, the decisions themselves in these cases have largely upheld the wishes of physicians rather than of clients. Client autonomy is an area where it is particularly important to distinguish between what happens and what is said. The evidence suggests that, in England at least, autonomy is being eroded in favour of the interests of the medical profession and the state.

The philosophical arguments

The view that the consent principle has been given exaggerated importance by comparison with other considerations is beginning to gain ground. This view is informed by theories of society which are hostile to the idea that an individual knows best about his own interests. There is a modern trend of thought which considers there to be few if any areas of private life into which collective interests do not extend. Already it can happen that, where there is a collective health benefit which can only be achieved at the expense of reducing autonomy, as in the case of water fluoridation, it is autonomy which is surrendered. The American writer Robert Veatch, a relatively anti-paternalistic figure in the arena of medical ethics, gives philosophical support to this form of coercive treatment by arguing that a 'duty of justice calling for welfare to be distributed fairly ... could permit violating the autonomy of individuals in special cases where the person already has an unusually great amount of welfare in comparison to others that it can be said to be unfair'.

It is not just other people's interests, however, which may be invoked to override the consent principle. The value of autonomy itself is beginning to be questioned. Paul Ramsey, for example, has argued that 'there are medically indicated treatments ... that a competent conscious patient *has no moral right to refuse*, just as no one has a moral right deliberately to ruin his health' (my italics). He goes on to propose that, rather than respecting a client's right to refuse treatment, 'we need to emphasise his free and informed participation in medical decisions affecting him when there are alternative treatments'.

Ramsey's remarks, incidentally, serve to highlight an interesting feature of modern medical ethics. Much of the debate is generated by a conflict between two opposing ideologies, each of which has its vociferous supporters. On the one hand there are those who believe in 'rational choice', which means permitting abortion, euthanasia, and so on, subject to a doctor giving approval. This side includes many doctors and the majority of philosophers and ethicists. On the other hand there are those, including Ramsey, who have some respect for the principle of the sanctity of life and who are opposed to abortion and euthanasia. Persons of this persuasion are critical of doctors making decisions about clients' 'quality of life', but also oppose the refusal of treatment by clients. Neither side is in fact particularly in favour of increasing client autonomy. Yet it is out of the debate between these two principal forces – insistence on life preservation, and faith in the 'best interests' approach – that some sort of consensus on controversial medical issues looks likely to be forged. Autonomy, if it is catered for at all, is likely to come a poor third.

The legal position

Where a practitioner effects the physical invasion of a person's body without that person's prior consent, he commits the tort of battery. This is different from negligence, which depends on the treatment given having been inappropriate. If a doctor is found guilty of battery, he will be liable to pay damages to his client, regardless of whether his actions were in the client's best interests.

There have always been certain narrowly defined exceptions to this rule. For example, treatment may be given to an unconscious person in an emergency without his consent. What is somewhat ominous, however, is that the circumstances in which the rule may be set aside seem to be increasing. If the present trend continues, the consent requirement is in danger of ceasing to be a principle and becoming merely a minor consideration.

The following comment from the eminent judge Lord Donaldson, whose views have been decisive in a number of recent medico-legal cases, indicates the current British judicial attitude to the significance of consent.

> There seems to be some confusion in the minds of some as to the purpose of seeking consent from a patient. ... It has two purposes, the one clinical and the other legal. The clinical purpose stems from the fact that in many instances the co-operation of the patient and the patient's faith or at least confidence in the efficiency of the treatment is a major factor contributing to the treatment's success. Failure to obtain such consent ... will usually make it much more difficult to administer the treatment. The legal purpose is quite different. It is to provide those concerned in the treatment with a defence to a criminal charge of assault or battery or a civil claim for damages for trespass to the person. (quoted in BMA 1993, 9)

In other words, the consent principle is there, not to protect clients from being abused by doctors, but to make life easier for the medical profession. This is a radical departure from the traditional idea that the principle is a reflection of the client's right of self-determination.

The new intellectual position on medical autonomy has manifested itself in a number of ways in the context of medical law. For example, legal opinion has shifted in favour of medical practitioners as regards establishing whether or not consent to treatment was in fact given in any particular case. It used to be thought that the onus of proof was on the doctor, who had to establish a defence analogous to *volenti non fit injuria*[1] to rebut the presumption of battery. Recent court cases suggest that the onus is now on the client. In a 1980 case it was held that 'in order to establish trespass to the person a patient had to show that she did not consent to the operation'. This view received approval in a subsequent civil

---

[1] 'No cause of action arises to someone who voluntarily accepted the risk.'

liberties case involving a prisoner who claimed that he had been forcibly injected with tranquillisers.[2] As the plaintiff was unable to prove conclusively that he had *not* consented, his action was dismissed.

Another way in which legal practice is biased against the client in the area of consent is that courts[3] are generally unkeen on finding doctors guilty of battery, and will tend to take the slightest evidence of consent as sufficient to rebut a charge of battery. Thus in an English case in 1978, a woman who was asked to consent to sterilisation while in labour with the birth of her third child, and who signed the consent form while in a state of exhaustion, was held to have given valid consent and her claim for damages under battery failed.[4]

Instead of the traditional criterion of battery as involving *intentional* invasion, there is a trend to make battery conditional upon *hostile* invasion. In 1986, a Court of Appeal judge went so far as to argue that a possible defence to the charge of battery should be that the action in question is 'acceptable in the ordinary conduct of everyday life'. Both of these approaches to the law of battery obviously favour the medical professional's point of view.

Informed consent

One area of difficulty in relation to consent arises from the fact that the treatment proposed is often technically complicated. What exactly is the client consenting to? Clearly, an important component of deciding whether to agree to a course of action is knowing the risks involved. If these are not adequately disclosed then surely one can not meaningfully give consent? Again, however, the prevailing belief in the virtue of medical paternalism means that doctors need only give their clients very little information in order for consent to be regarded as genuine. In *Chatterton v Gerson*, a client (Miss Chatterton) who lost the use of her right leg as a result of unsuccessful operations to treat pain arising from a previous operation failed in her claim for battery, although the surgeon had clearly been somewhat economical in telling her about the possible risks. The judge argued that consent to surgery was valid so long as the client was 'informed in broad terms of the *nature* of the procedure which is intended'.

In a relatively old but still influential New Zealand case, the court went further than this in relieving doctors of a duty to disclose relevant information, allowing them to *manipulate* clients into giving consent, a technique which would be regarded as fraudulent misrepresentation in other contexts. The judge in this case stated that

the paramount consideration is the welfare of the patient and, given good

---

[2] *Freeman v Home Office* 1984.
[3] In England and Canada, although less so in the United States.
[4] *Wells v Surrey Area Health Authority* 1978.

faith on the part of the doctor, I think the exercise of his discretion in the area of advice must depend on *the patient's overall needs*. To be taken into account should be the gravity of the condition to be treated, the importance of the benefits to be expected to flow from the treatment or procedure, *the need to encourage him to accept it*, the relevant significance of its inherent risks, the intellectual and emotional capacity of the patient to accept the information without such distortion as to prevent any rational decision at all, and the extent to which the patient may seem to have placed himself in his doctor's hands with the invitation that the latter accept on his behalf the responsibility for intricate or technical decisions. (*Smith v Auckland Hospital Board*, New Zealand Law Reports 1964, 250, my italics)

English judges in particular have been very resistant to the idea that consent to treatment might be vitiated where important risks are not disclosed. The legal establishment seems uncomfortable with the idea that fellow professionals acting by their own light should be accused of battery, and the consensus opinion is that any action should normally lie in negligence rather than battery.

The trouble with claiming negligence in cases of failure to inform – in England, at any rate – is that the doctor is then judged, not by reference to any objective legal standard such as 'consent' or 'misrepresentation', but simply by comparison with whatever happens to be accepted medical practice. This absurdly undemanding test was established in a 1950s case,[5] and is still the touchstone of English medical negligence law. In other words, if the majority of doctors behave in a certain way, then they cannot be held to be negligent, regardless of the harm their behaviour may be causing.

Moreover, an escape clause is now available to doctors whereby they may be legally justified in withholding information where they deem a client to be unable emotionally to cope with the relevant facts.[6] Clients therefore tend to fare little better with negligence than with battery. Thus, for example, Miss Chatterton's attempt to obtain damages for her injury under negligence also failed.

Even if a client succeeds in proving negligence, it may not get her very far, as she must also establish that any loss for which she is seeking damages was caused by the negligence in question, i.e. the lack of disclosure. If the doctor can convince the court that the client would have agreed to the operation anyway, then the client will fail at this second stage. If battery were proven, on the other hand, the doctor would be liable for *all* the consequences of his action.

It is often said that American and Canadian courts have been more sympathetic to the notion of client autonomy in medical battery cases than their British and Antipodean counterparts. Certainly the North American doctrine of 'informed consent', under which the client ostensibly has an

---

[5] *Bolam v Friern Hospital Management Committee* 1957.
[6] See for example *Chatterton v Gerson* 1981, and the Canadian case *Reibl v Hughes* 1980.

inalienable right to be told as much about the risks of a recommended treatment as a 'reasonable' person might expect to be told, has never been endorsed by a British court. To suggest that the North American position expresses consumer sovereignty, however, would be greatly to exaggerate the significance of the difference. Even in the case which established the doctrine of informed consent,[7] the court held that clients might sometimes become too upset by full disclosure of the risks to reach a rational decision, and that in those situations good medical practice required a degree of concealment.

It could be argued that putting doctors under a compulsion to disclose all significant benefits, risks and side-effects to their clients would itself be a form of paternalism. Should we not simply permit an unregulated market in this respect, and follow the principle of *caveat emptor*? In the leading case of *Sidaway*, the House of Lords implied that, if Mrs Sidaway had wished to be informed about the risks of the operation which left her severely disabled, she should have explicitly asked the surgeon to tell her what they were.

As with euthanasia, however, it seems necessary to adopt an approach which takes account of the realities of medical practice as it stands, in particular the immense power over clients which doctors and surgeons yield. In view of the asymmetry of the client-doctor relationship, and the prevailing belief in the professionalism, integrity and solicitude of doctors, there is a strong case for claiming that there exists an *expectation* among most clients that relevant information *will* be disclosed, and a case for demanding that this expectation be given legal force. In this respect, there is an argument that the law should be consistent with other areas where the expectation of clients is upheld; thus, for example, unqualified practitioners who practise surgery are guilty of assault, regardless of the consent of their clients, on the basis that a client would expect anyone holding himself out as a surgeon to be appropriately qualified.

In any case, the *Sidaway* view that a doctor is obliged to tell his client about the risks of an operation if the client asks about them has not been followed in subsequent cases, and it would not be advisable for a client to rely on it. In 1987, for example, the Court of Appeal held that a health authority who had not given a client all the information she had asked for about a controversial contraceptive drug which was prescribed for her was not guilty of negligence.[8] The judge argued that the proper amount of disclosure, even where the patient had made enquiries, had to be made 'in the light of responsible medical opinion'. In other words, it is up to practitioners to decide what to tell a client, however much the client makes specific efforts to ascertain the available facts.

Such paternalistic attitudes to consent appear to rely on the premise

---

[7] *Canterbury v Spence* 1972.
[8] *Blyth v Bloomsbury Health Authority*, *The Times* Law Reports, 11 February 1987.

that the doctor is invariably in the best position to arrive at an objective judgement about whether to apply a particular treatment. Evidence from the sociology of medicine, however, does not support this premise. As a number of commentators have pointed out, there is likely to be a psychological bias on the part of the practitioner in favour of doing something rather than nothing. Talcott Parsons, for example, discussing the option of surgery, suggested there was clearly 'a bias in favour of operating. After all the surgeon is trained to operate, he feels active, useful, effective when he is operating.' More generally, Parsons commented on the prevalence of 'an "optimistic bias" in favour of the soundness of ideas or efficacy of procedures'.

The medical profession is reluctant to admit that this often results in treatment being proposed which is determined more by the inclinations of the practitioner than by the needs of the client. The BMA in this connection characteristically asks us to rely on the image of the medical professional who can do no wrong. 'Although recognising that in some instances doctors may have a professional disposition to recommend treatment over non-treatment, society takes the view that whatever measures doctors propose will be in the best interests of patients.'

While *legal* professionals may, in forming their views on consent, be relying chiefly on the integrity of medical professionals, we may question whether this reliance is all that goes into the avoidance of the 'informed consent' principle by medical professionals themselves. Apart from the belief that he knows best, a practitioner may dislike the intrusion of the client's judgement into his professional territory for other, more complex reasons. We may expect, for example, a desire to be protected from potential criticism. The more the doctor tells his client, the easier it will be for the client to spot any mistakes which the doctor may make.

There may also be resentment that some clients will be better able than others to make use of any information acquired. Intelligent, scientifically educated or self-confident clients are more likely to benefit from participation in clinical decision-making, and may get better treatment as a result. Here again, it is possible that some doctors take it upon themselves to play a political role, refusing to give more information to such clients on the basis that it might enhance inequalities in health. Thus Margaret Brazier writes that recent pro-doctor court cases are 'understandable', explaining that 'A test that gave the inquisitive patient greater rights than her less vocal neighbour could operate unfairly. Articulate, middle-class patients would be at an advantage.'

Medical philosophers seem happy to accept limited disclosure by doctors as ethically justifiable. H.T. Engelhardt, for example, maintains that

> one can morally defend [the standard of disclosure according to what happens to be accepted medical practice] in terms of the principle of mutual respect. Unless otherwise warned, patients may reasonably expect that

9. Wanting not to be treated

practitioners will give that amount of disclosure customary for members of that profession, school, or group ... To give more [disclosure] than a reasonable medical practitioner would give may presuppose a hierarchy of values different from that endorsed by the profession or school. Such an increased disclosure might require a special warning to the patient ... (Engelhardt 1986, 272)

He concludes that unless individuals have 'taken steps to create special expectations and/or special requirements, the [usual standard of disclosure] meets the principles of autonomy and beneficence'.

Consent in practice

Recent legal developments are in a sense merely reflecting what is already standard practice in hospitals. Theoretically, no one can be treated against his will, but practitioners who do not feel inclined to respect this principle have ways of getting round it. Brian Clark's play *Whose Life Is It Anyway* illustrates one approach available against those who adamantly refuse to give consent to treatment. This is to have them 'sectioned' – i.e. compulsorily hospitalised – on the grounds that their refusal is evidence of their derangement. This particular approach is no longer *legally* available to doctors as a result of revised legislation brought in by the 1983 Mental Health Act. However, medical professionals may more generally be able to argue that the client is not 'competent' either to give or to refuse consent, and that treatment can therefore be given without his agreement. Or the consent requirement may simply be ignored altogether, as illustrated by the following case reported by a nurse.

> When I was working on a bowel surgery ward we had an 82-year-old patient with cancer of the rectum. He knew this and told us that he would prefer to have no further treatment and be allowed to die. He didn't want to have a colostomy.
> But the doctor decided he should have the operation. He got a relative to sign the consent form by saying it was necessary. The nurses couldn't do anything. We're not really able to argue with doctors or stop a person being taken to the theatre. (Age Concern England 1986, 64)

More commonly, there is evidence that the consent requirement is often not taken very seriously by health care workers. The signing of the consent form can be a mere formality that follows once the client has been pressurised into concurring. The following is an example of 'consent' being given by a couple to an operation on their daughter, but is probably not far removed from the typical situation for many adult clients.

> In a not unusual example at the Brompton Hospital, the new house officer (SHO) assured Briony's parents that her operation, a high-risk correction, was very complex, and their child's consultants were among the very few

people in the world to understand it thoroughly. In the darkened babies' room there were no spare chairs to enable adults to sit and talk together with dignity, and hardly enough light to read the form. Briony's mother was sitting on her husband's knee. The SHO briefly stood near them, then left them to sign the form, returning later to collect it. He informed me that it was crucial that parents did not lose their faith in surgery ... He seemed to assume that parents needed reassurance about the excellence of the unit and that information would merely arouse anxiety. (Alderson 1990, 37-8)

There is very little reference to consent in codes of medical ethics. Among the duties owed by doctors to the sick, the International Code of Medical Ethics lists the preservation of life, loyalty, confidentiality and emergency care, but does not mention the need to obtain approval from the client for any treatment. It does, however, state that a physician 'shall act only in the patient's interest when providing medical care which might have the effect of weakening the physical and mental condition of the patient'. The Declaration of Helsinki's code of the ethics of medical research encourages an even more cavalier attitude to the wishes of clients, giving as one of its rules that 'If the physician considers it essential not to obtain informed consent, the specific reasons for this proposal should be stated in the experimental protocol for transmission to the independent committee.' An illustration of the effects this can have in practice is provided by the case described in chapter 5 of the woman who died as a result of being given an experimental drug. The research ethics committees which approved the proposal not to obtain the woman's consent to participating in the experiment apparently drew on the Declaration in reaching their decision.

Unconscious clients

A point of potential weakness in the consent principle arises from the fact that a person who is not conscious cannot be asked whether or not he consents to proposed treatment. This leads to the defence of 'tacit consent' or 'necessity' in situations where emergency surgery has to be applied to an unconscious client. As most people would expect to have life-saving treatment applied in such a situation without first being asked for their consent, it is perhaps reasonable that doctors should assume this to be the case in the absence of evidence to the contrary. On the other hand, it ought to be possible for individuals to make advance arrangements to prevent treatment from being applied when they are unconscious, even where such treatment is life-saving. This right used to exist, in the sense that it was respected by physicians and upheld by the legal system, even where refusal was based on beliefs which diverged significantly from the social norm. It is, however, beginning to be seriously undermined.

In practice, the test point for consent to emergency treatment has most often occurred in connection with Jehovah's Witnesses. People of this

9. Wanting not to be treated

denomination typically have strong religious objections to blood transfusions, and have in the past been allowed discretion to exercise their autonomy in this respect. Medical professionals were required to observe a person's signed declaration that he refused to be given blood even when necessary for his survival. In a recent case involving a Jehovah's Witness,[9] however, this respect for autonomy was seriously qualified by making the right of refusal conditional on the 'capacity' of the client to make the appropriate decision. The client in question was a pregnant woman injured in a road accident, who was admitted to hospital and later given a Caesarean section. Although she twice expressed her wish to hospital staff that she should not be given a blood transfusion, and signed a refusal form, her father (who was not a Jehovah's Witness) succeeded in his application to the court to have her wishes overridden. The judge, Lord Donaldson, held that the twenty-year-old woman had been unduly influenced by her mother in forming her attitude towards blood transfusions, a condition which vitiated her refusal to give consent. In an emergency situation, Lord Donaldson said,

> doctors faced with a refusal of consent had to give careful consideration to what was the patient's capacity to decide at the time the decision was made. It might not be a case of capacity or no capacity, but of reduced capacity. What mattered was that the doctors would consider whether at that time the patient had a capacity commensurate with the gravity of the decision he purported to make. The more serious the decision, the greater the capacity required. ... In some cases doctors would have to consider whether the refusal had been vitiated because it resulted not from the patient's will but from the will of others. ... In that context the relationship of the persuader to the patient, for example, spouse, parent or religious adviser, would be important, because some relationships more readily lent themselves to overbearing the patient's independent will than others did. (*The Times* Law Report, 21 August 1992)

How valid were the court's grounds for holding that the woman's refusal could be disregarded? First, it was argued that she had not reached an independent decision about the question of transfusions, but was acting under the influence of her mother. It seems a strange step to suggest that because an adult of sound mind has been influenced in her decision by the advice of another, this undermines the exercise of her autonomy. Not many decisions made by individuals would pass such a stringent test. The problem with setting aside a client's expressed wishes on this criterion is that it allows doctors to override the wishes of a client whenever these appear unusual, provided only that they can point to someone who may have been influential in determining those wishes. There is, of course, no corresponding suggestion that

---

[9] *In re T* 1992.

consent might be regarded as invalid where *doctors* have placed the client under pressure to agree with *their* preferred course of action.

Secondly, the decision to act against the woman's instructions was justified on the ground that she had not been adequately informed about the possible options. But, as we saw above, there is no recognition on the part of British courts that full information about the available options is necessary for genuine *consent*. It therefore makes little sense to argue that it is essential for valid refusal.

Some observers may fail to find this development disturbing. Does it matter, after all, if social outsiders are not allowed to express their eccentricity in the form of refusing to have their lives saved in the way medical science thinks best? Unfortunately, erosion of the principle of autonomy is unlikely to stop at the point where only the most exceptional refusals are ignored. Once the principle has been established that people can have treatment forced on them against their wishes by reference to received medical wisdom, there is relatively little to stop the principle being applied in other areas of medicine – inoculation, cancer screening, AIDS testing, pregnancy termination, sterilisation, and so on.

Already before this seminal case, there was considerable resistance among the medical and legal establishment to the principle that doctors must concede to client autonomy even when the client's refusal to give consent is irrational from a medical perspective. Margaret Brazier commented in 1987 that the wishes of a competent patient, or of a formerly competent patient who had made his wishes known while competent, should be respected, but immediately proceeded to qualify this by arguing that 'in life-threatening situations patients are not always capable of making rational decisions: they may no longer be "competent".' She concluded that 'superficial and automatic acquiescence to the concepts of patient autonomy and death with dignity threaten sound clinical judgements; and doctors should continue to exercise their professional responsibility for thorough clinical investigation and the exercise of sound professional judgement.'

Once doctors are given a legally sanctioned let-out from the consent requirement which depends only on their subjective judgement that the client's 'capacity' is insufficient to validate a refusal of emergency treatment, perhaps because they have been influenced by someone else, it is hard to see why they should ever have to respect such a refusal. One can no longer speak of autonomy when the right to self-determination becomes conditional on whether you are deemed to have capacity, and that capacity is questioned unless your decision is consistent with the views of others.

The elderly

It is not only the unconscious who may be treated against their wishes. Under Section 47 of the National Assistance Act 1948, an elderly person who is ill or physically incapacitated, and who is living in insanitary conditions, may be forcibly removed to a hospital or other institution if a doctor certifies that it is in the person's interests for this to happen. Once there, he is liable to be given medication or other treatment regardless of consent. It has been argued that Section 47 was introduced with the implicit objective of imposing order and hygiene, not merely as a way of protecting others from disease, but because deviance from social norms of cleanliness offends and disturbs us.[10] Indeed, the use of the section is often triggered by the complaints of neighbours.

In practice, the provision can be used to force people of sound mind into an institution, as was attempted in the following case. There they will often remain for the rest of their lives. According to the organisation Age Concern, only 15 per cent of people institutionalised under this section ever return to their own homes, and the average survival rate of those who have been 'sectioned' is only two years.[11]

> A 70-year-old man who did his own shopping and lived a fairly independent life frequently left the gas tap of his cooker on. Neighbours smelt gas and feared he might one day blow himself or them up. They complained to their local authority who in turn approached his GP. The GP considered that his patient was suffering from dementia and urged the district community physician to undertake a Section 47. ... It transpired that the gentleman had simply not been used to the gas cooker and indeed had shown a preference for electricity. (Age Concern England 1986, 42-3)

Even without invoking this somewhat Draconian piece of legislation, elderly people may be institutionalised against their will. Age Concern comments that some old people have residential care

> forced upon them. Relatives or carers who are unable to cope, or elderly people who have no such close support, could find themselves in a situation where their consent is never directly sought, but taken for granted, being 'the best for all concerned'. ... Elderly people suffering from some form of dementia may be misled or simply not fully informed, on the assumption that they would not be able to understand fully what is happening to them. (*ibid.*, 24)

The same is true for medical treatment. The consent requirement is not

---

[10] Gray 1985, 100.
[11] Age Concern England 1986, 40.

stringently observed with elderly patients, given that a greater effort tends to be required on the part of health care workers in ascertaining their wishes.

> ... in many circumstances, particularly when elderly people are extremely frail, whether mentally or physically, medical treatment may be pressed upon them for reasons that are difficult to justify ...
> ... many elderly people are admitted to hospital as emergency cases and some have surgery without having given informed consent. Obviously many cases are genuine emergencies, such as intestinal obstructions, but many have an elective element. For example a hip replacement operation is not a life-saving procedure for most old people. (*ibid.*, 25 and 26)

Giving birth

We noted in chapter 6 the popularity with doctors of Caesarean sections, and their opposition to more natural ways of giving birth. It seems that many women are put under pressure to agree to a Caesarean birth. Lack of respect for autonomy goes well beyond this, however, since the operation may be carried out even where the mother refuses to give consent. In the United States, this practice has been accepted for some time, and it now appears to be becoming possible in Britain as well.

In 1992, a British woman was given a Caesarean section against her wishes by surgeons at a London hospital, on the ground that the surgeons believed that her baby could not be born alive otherwise. The woman strongly objected to a Caesarean. The surgeons were given permission by the High Court in a hearing at which the woman was not even represented. Judge Sir Stephen Brown broke with the precedent of an earlier British case, in which the idea of sacrificing a mother for the sake of her child was rejected.

This form of non-consensual treatment sheds an interesting light on the much-debated distinction between 'killing' and 'letting die'. The medical profession tends to support the view that letting a client die by withholding treatment is different from, and more acceptable than, administering a lethal injection. In the case of forced Caesareans, however, this moral ordering appears to be inverted. While it is considered acceptable for an unborn child to be killed (aborted) if mother and doctor agree to this, it is not regarded as acceptable that an unborn child be allowed to die if its birth would require medical intervention of a kind unacceptable to the mother. In fact, it appears that the state may go so far as to authorise (in effect) the *killing* of a mother, against her wishes, in order to save her child. In the American case of *Re AC* (1987), a woman dying of cancer was forced to have a Caesarean operation despite it being known that the operation was likely to bring forward her death. In the event, both mother and baby died during the operation.

Minors

Minors also fare badly where involuntary treatment is concerned. In the UK, those under 16 may be treated against their will, on the say-so of either their parents or a doctor. In practice, the views of doctors are increasingly likely to take priority over those of parents in cases of dispute. This is what the BMA have to say about overriding the views of parents (without, of course, implying a deferral to the child's views).

> [Health professionals] retain a duty to intervene if the child appears to be exploited and/or abused, or if decision-making seems seriously awry by the usual standards of what a reasonably prudent person would choose. In cases of decision-making for immature children, there must be a reasonable presumption that the parents have the child's best interests most at heart. Such a presumption cannot be taken for granted, however, and where there seem grounds for doubt it should be contested. (BMA 1993, 71)

Even where the child is competent, medical considerations may be invoked to override the right to self-determination. Two recent court cases involving minors illustrate the alarming development that even where a client is deemed to have decision-making capacity, his wishes may be overridden. In the 1991 case of *Re R (A Minor)*, Lord Donaldson ruled that a competent minor may be overruled by a doctor. In the subsequent case of *Re W* (1992), a 16-year-old girl suffering from anorexia nervosa was allowed to be treated against her will, although there was no suggestion that she lacked competence to consent or refuse.

Children are in a position similar to that of other groups who refuse treatment normally considered unobjectionable, in that they may be unable to refuse in practice, given that refusal is taken as evidence that they lack competence. Thus the BMA writes that children 'sometimes refuse medical treatment because their anxieties are focused on the short-term effects, such as fear of injections, in which case they are not expressing a considered choice in favour of non-treatment'. This may sound reasonable enough, until one realises that fear of 'short-term effects' can mean the desire of a child not to undergo another transplant operation, or further chemotherapy. For example, in 1992 British doctors considered court action to override the wishes of a four-year-old boy who did not want further chemotherapy to treat his otherwise fatal brain tumour. His mother commented that he was 'being made to suffer with needles and drugs and has to stay in bed for days sick each time ... He tells me he wants to die because he just doesn't want to go through it all the time.'

In connection with chemotherapy for children, the BMA have commented that it is

> an example of a treatment which carries particularly unpleasant side-effects. Children who have previously undergone the treatment and there-

fore understand what is involved may be reluctant to accept further treatment. Nevertheless, the chances of successfully treating the condition in children are generally such that some pressure on the child to agree would be justifiable, with the parents' consent, and the child's opinion may be overruled if the anticipated benefits in the individual case are good. (BMA 1993, 77)

On the other hand, where it is the *parents* who are advocating treatment which might be harrowing for the child, but which differs from the preferred strategy of the professionals, the BMA expects doctors to spring to the defence of the child.

> ... for desperate parents to expose fatally ill children to all manner of painful, unproven or essentially futile treatments breaches the child's right to be free from intrusion. ... The bias appears to favour any treatment over non-treatment partly because of the psychological comfort parents derive from knowing that they have tried everything. But this is to put the interests of the carer before those of the patient. (*ibid.*, 76)

10

Wanting to live

Doctors at two of the country's biggest heart centres are refusing to perform life-saving operations on smokers, unless they give up the habit. Surgeons at hospitals in Leicester and Manchester, serving 6.5m people, have introduced the controversial policy because they are unwilling to waste scarce resources on patients who, they say, will die prematurely anyway. ... 'If people don't stop smoking, they don't get the surgery. It's a good way to persuade them to give up,' [one of the Manchester cardiologists] said. Stuart Horner, chairman of the British Medical Association's medical ethics committee ... said that he supported a recent case in which a surgeon discharged a patient hours before a serious heart operation after the man was caught smoking in a lavatory. (*The Times*, 23 May 1993)

Non-treatment in the patient's best interests
... Usually, the preferences of the patient should prevail but if the patient is incompetent, the doctor, together with those close to the patient, must act in his or her best interests. ... the term 'incompetence' covers a wide range of varying or fluctuating abilities and does not simply mean that the patient has no preference or no voice in the choices made. Rather it implies that the importance accorded to those preferences must be individually decided. (BMA 1993, 166)

A duty to maintain life?

Having observed that the wish not to be kept alive against one's will is ceasing to have decisive force in the context of modern medicine, and given that the desire for treatment also carries relatively little weight when it conflicts with the opinions of doctors, it is interesting to consider to what extent health care workers respect a client's desire *not* to die.

Let us begin by considering the position of clients who are, or have been, conscious while suffering from the condition in which they find themselves. When speaking of a 'desire not to die', it should not be necessary to point to an expressed wish on the part of the client to go on living as evidence of such a desire. Where the client is or has been able to communicate, the presumption must be in favour of his wishing to survive as long as possible, in the absence of any communication to the contrary. Such a presumption is consistent with what is known of human psychology. Most people faced with the possibility of death are extremely reluctant to die, however desperate their circumstances. Even if occasionally a person really wants to die but does not express this desire to anyone else, it is surely obvious that the law should never allow such a desire to be merely *inferred* by another person as a justification for committing what would otherwise be an act of violence or negligence. The deliberate termination of the life of such a person without his explicit consent, whether by a positive act or by an omission, should therefore be classified as *involuntary* rather than *non-voluntary* euthanasia. (In the terminology of medical ethics, 'involuntary euthanasia' is used to mean the killing of a person who is competent to request or consent to the act but does not do so, while the term 'non-voluntary euthanasia' is applied when it is not possible to ascertain the wishes of the person who is killed.)

On this basis, a doctor should always make every effort to prolong the life of such a client unless the client has said otherwise. If the client is still able to communicate, then of course he should be consulted about each invasive procedure which the doctor considers it appropriate to perform in pursuing this objective, and asked whether he wishes to proceed. (Ideally, the client should in each instance be presented with the options and asked to choose, rather than given a simple yes-or-no choice about the one treatment which the doctor prefers.) As we shall see, however, the evidence suggests that prolonging life is a goal which is pursued rather more conditionally than this, at least for certain categories of client.

The case of smokers being explicitly refused surgery is a relatively exceptional one, at least at the time of writing. There are more subtle ways for health care workers to limit treatment. As we saw in earlier chapters, a doctor need not tell his client what is wrong with him, he need not tell him about all the options for treatment, he need not necessarily choose the best option for him, and he need not offer any option at all if this would divert resources from another client whom he considers more deserving. It is these which are probably more common forms of refusal, leading in some cases to the unnecessary death of the client concerned, without the client ever being aware of the background to his doctor's decision.

The choice open to doctors is not only between either treating or not treating a given client. Between complete neglect and maximum treatment there is a wide range of discretion available, and there is little doubt that health professionals work harder for some of their clients than others. Sometimes an explicit and concerted policy of 'go slow' is adopted for a particular client.[1] When we are talking about the question of more or less sedulous treatment, rather than of some as compared with none, there is clearly a difficulty about deciding by what standard the doctor's approach should be judged. However, if a doctor strives less officiously for one client than he does for another, purely because he takes into account the client's likely 'quality of life' or remaining age span, he is taking positive action which, if the condition of the client is potentially fatal, could arguably be interpreted as involving the intent to kill.

[1] See Brazier 1992, 459.

Most doctors appear to support the distinction between killing by 'commission' (by means of a positive action) and killing by 'omission' (withholding or removing treatment). A.H. Clough's well-known parody of the sixth commandment – 'Thou shalt not kill; but needs not strive officiously to keep alive' – is often invoked in this connection. The BMA has endorsed this view of the matter, condemning active euthanasia but arguing, for example, that 'it is not always the doctor's duty to resuscitate a patient as this is appropriate only where someone is suffering from a non-terminal or reversible disease process and can be expected to welcome a continuing life'. When a person is at the mercy of his physiology, however, and especially in the authoritarian environment of a hospital, the discrimination between killing him by means of a lethal injection and killing him by depriving him of essential medication may seem somewhat academic from his point of view.

If we take as our standard the medical service which would be provided to (say) a previously healthy thirty-year-old father of two, we can consider the level of service which is typically provided to other categories of client. The evidence suggests that, relative to this standard, treatment is withheld from the elderly, the disabled, the mentally disordered, the chronically ill and those with unhealthy lifestyles. Such withholding of treatment does not typically occur with the knowledge of the client, but is done covertly in the guise of clinical decision-making.

One need not fall into a specific category of client to be the subject of treatment-limiting behaviour on the part of health care workers. A range of considerations including financial ones, and various subjective and arbitrary judgements, may enter into a decision not to offer a particular treatment option.

Involuntary euthanasia for the elderly

The columnist Auberon Waugh, usually associated with relatively libertarian views, recently wrote an article which strongly advocated that industrialised countries 'put down their old people as soon as they became incapable of looking after themselves, if no member of their family is prepared to look after them'. Waugh joked that to maintain the present level of care for the old would, by the end of the century, require that every single school or university leaver become a geriatric nurse. The article contained no suggestion, incidentally, that euthanasia should depend on the consent of the individual, let alone a definite request on his part.

Waugh, one might say, is simply being honest about an issue which others recognise but take care not to express. The fact is that the state medical systems of Western nations are rapidly approaching a demand/supply imbalance of such proportions that severe cutbacks in the extent of service offered will inevitably have to be made. Such cutbacks are most likely to be applied in the area where they will have the least detrimental economic effects, namely the treatment and care of the elderly. No one should be surprised, therefore, to hear that old people are routinely discriminated against in the competition for treatment. What is completely unacceptable, however, is the deception and dishonesty which is being practised on them.

Medical professionals are of course reluctant to admit that elderly clients get a worse level of service. The aim of a health care worker is supposedly to do the best for each individual client. Neglecting someone because of the shortness of their expected remaining life span is inconsistent with this principle. In practice, however, this simply means that an elderly client may not be offered treatment which a younger person would receive, but without being aware of it. Resource allocation based on age appears to be already with us, and it is likely to be practised more and more as budget constraints bite more deeply. Since the profession will not admit it is going on, we may find that clinical arguments will increasingly serve to rationalise allocation decisions.

There is plenty of evidence that *passive* involuntary euthanasia (killing by omission) is indeed practised on elderly clients. According to Bliss and Johnson, an example of passive euthanasia is 'the withholding of antibiotics in an elderly person with cancer who develops pneumonia. It is common practice to allow the natural progression of the condition, formerly called the "old person's friend", which produces a peaceful death preceded by a few hours of unconsciousness.'

Certain clients are not given cardiopulmonary resuscitation (CPR) after suffering cardiac arrest if medical staff consider them to be in a condition which does not justify the effort of resuscitation. The use of 'do not resuscitate' (DNR) orders without the knowledge of either the client or his relatives has become one of the more notorious scandals of the medical industry. If asked to justify a particular case, doctors may refer to the difficulty of discussing the subject with the client, or may give as an excuse the fact that hospital policy on DNR orders is unclear. Neither of these explanations should be regarded as acceptable.

A recent newspaper article reported that clients over 75 years of age hospitalised in the US with heart attacks are six times less likely to be treated with the clot-dissolving drugs that are commonly given to younger clients, despite only limited evidence that the risks of the treatment are any greater for older clients.[2] In a questionnaire study of coronary units in the UK, 19 per cent of the chief consultants who completed the questionnaire said they operated an age-related admissions policy, and a further 34 per cent said they employed age as a criterion when determining the use of expensive but potentially life-saving thrombolytic drugs.[3] This discrimination is practised covertly, however. As has been pointed

---

[2] *Wall Street Journal*, 2 July 1992.
[3] *The Times*, 28 December 1992.

out, for example, few if any UK coronary care units have an explicit policy of not admitting patients over a certain age.[4]

Dr Grimley Evans, Professor of Geriatric Medicine at Oxford University, has remarked that the older age group tends to be given palliative and symptomatic care rather than a proper diagnosis and intervention. Elderly clients at risk of death from influenza are not routinely offered vaccinations. In a study of 800 elderly people, 47 per cent of the 565 who replied had medical conditions that meant they should have been vaccinated, but less than half of these clients were offered the vaccine.[5]

'Poor quality of life'

There are other categories of client who may not be offered treatments that the normal client would receive. Although considerations about quality of life may enter into such decisions when they are made by health care workers, one can only surmise that this is the case, since such decisions are almost invariably made covertly. Even if one practitioner transmits to another the rationale of his decision, the likelihood is that it will be done in such a way that there is no written record of the non-clinical reasons.

The mentally ill are one such category. We referred in chapter 5 to the case of the client with kidney failure who was taken off dialysis partly because he was found a nuisance by medical staff. It may well be that continuing giving dialysis to this client was not viable, given that (according to the hospital offering dialysis) he 'was at times violent, generally uncooperative, dirty, incontinent of urine and faeces, unable to take medication reliably, could not adhere to the prescribed diet, exposed himself, and masturbated while being examined', and that he 'had to be sedated while he was being dialysed to prevent him from removing the blood lines from his arm'. What is alarming, however, is that it was decided that discontinuation of the treatment was justified on the basis that it was in the client's 'best interests'. Since permanent discontinuation would have led to the client's death, doctors were in effect saying that their duty of acting in the client's best interests lay in refusing life-saving treatment.

A case of treatment refusal reported recently concerned a mental health hospital in Hampshire. In the winter of 1993, doctors at the hospital decided not to administer 'flu vaccine to any of the long-stay mentally disturbed clients resident on one particular ward. Nine of the seventeen clients died as a result of catching 'flu.[6]

---

[4] *The Times*, 9 January 1995.
[5] *The Times*, 9 April 1993.
[6] *Sunday Times*, 9 October 1994.

The 'terminally ill'

It is undoubtedly the case that medical professionals are at times over-interventionist, in the sense that drastic life-saving measures are imposed on some clients who would prefer not to have such measures applied. Ironically, this includes clients who have explicitly requested 'do not resuscitate' status, and who have obtained the assurance of their doctor that they would not be given CPR. Certainly this phenomenon is part of what fuels the 'right to die' movement. Yet because the autonomy issue is evaded, the debate has a tendency to turn on the question of whether treatment is 'inappropriate' rather than on whether it is not wanted by the client.

One of the results of this has been the development of a view on the appropriate treatment of clients in a state which has been diagnosed as 'terminal'. This is that life-prolonging measures may well be 'inappropriate' in certain circumstances and therefore may – indeed, should – be withheld. This is a consideration which operates to some extent independently of the wishes of the client. Thus, ironically, arguments about the right to die have so far not resulted in any facilitation of suicide for the terminally ill, but instead have promoted a tendency to deny treatment to those who might wish to prolong their life however poor its apparent 'quality'.

The proposition that the level of medical service should be reduced to those who are diagnosed to be dying receives wide agreement, as the following quotations illustrate. It is to be noted that none of the quotations refers explicitly and unambiguously to the wishes of the client. Rather, they seem to be tacitly concerned with the rights of doctors not to treat. We may also note that when the expression 'permitted to die' (or similar) is used, it may be the medical team, rather than the client, to whom the permission is to be given. Neither of these observations need surprise us. What is at stake is a potential conflict between the patient's desire to live and society's or the doctor's wish not to treat. Honesty about this is unlikely to be forthcoming so long as the issue can be fudged by referring to the client's comfort and dignity.

According to the Catholic Church, when inevitable death is imminent,

> it is permitted in conscience to take the decision to refuse forms of treatment that would only secure a precarious and burdensome prolongation of life, so long as the normal care due to the sick person in similar cases is not interrupted. In such circumstances the doctor has no reason to reproach himself with failing to help the person in danger. (Sacred Congregation 1980, 11)

Note the ambiguity about who is taking 'the decision to refuse' – client or doctor. The Christian Medical Fellowship says that it sees

> no requirement to give all possible treatments to all possible situations just because those treatments exist. It is precisely this sort of meddlesome medicine which does not recognise that the natural end is drawing near that has led to over-treatment of some patients ... a time may come when interventionist treatment need not be started or continued, and the patient should be allowed to die. (cited in House of Lords 1994, vol. 1, 15)

According to the Linacre Centre for Health Care Ethics, the prolongation of life

> has not traditionally been understood as an independent goal of medicine, without reference to the good of health. It has been considered a justifiable aim only in so far as a patient has had some continuing capacity for organic well-functioning sufficient to allow him to share in some of the goods of human life. (*ibid.*, 16)

One way to ensure that the conflict between doctor and client on whether to try to save the client does not become explicit is to avoid telling the client about his condition. This is a strategy that is used more widely than is perhaps suspected. In a study of 22 GPs, fourteen reported using 'denial' as a tactic; that is to say, deliberate deception of the client about his condition. For example, one GP reported that one of his clients

> said he wanted the truth and I said I didn't know exactly what it was, he would have to have an x-ray ... but it would probably be an ulcer. In all probability it was a tumour but I didn't say that ... so during his illness we played it along like this all the time. We talked about how it was going to take a long time to get better because of his age, and he would be tired and weak because of the operation ... and he never knew the truth. (Todd and Still 1993, 271)

Some GPs not only lie to a client about his condition, but pretend they are providing treatment when they have in fact given up on him.

> I have even gone to the stage of lying to patients and saying I've given them treatment for this condition, when what I'm doing is giving them placebos so that they don't think that I've just given up trying to cure them ... I would rather tell a lie to a patient to let them think you are doing something constructive. (*ibid.*)

Delaying death

There are signs of resistance to the idea that a client might insist on being kept alive beyond the point where health care workers consider it appropriate for him to exit gracefully. Bliss and Johnson claim there are examples of *'thoroughly bad medicine* where patients dying of widespread cancer have been repeatedly given cardiac massage when their hearts stopped. ... It is no part of the doctor's job to prolong suffering but it is his job to restore life by every means when there is a hope of a *reasonable quality of life.*' (My italics.) Resistance to autonomy in this context is typically evinced in the form of a mixture of disgust and moral disapproval. The late Professor Henry Miller wrote that most doctors have felt 'uneasiness, if not revulsion, at the spectacle of some stuporous ancient in hospital being maintained in a state of suspended animation by all the sophisticated paraphernalia of modern resuscitation'. What is this revulsion based on, though? Is it concern that the client's wishes are being ignored, or a feeling that the client's physiology has reached the point where it 'ought' not to be preserved? Ian Kennedy refers to the 'unseemly intervention of doctors, flown in from all over the world, in the dying agony of such figures as General Franco, President Tito and the Shah of Iran'. Since there is little evidence (although some speculation) that these clients were being kept alive against their will, the unstated implication appears to be that doctors should not co-operate with clients who want to stretch out their last few days of life.

Another factor which may enter into doctors' aversion to treating clients in advanced stages of illness is the desire to feel powerful and the correlative fear of failure. From a charitable perspective, this means that doctors want to make things better for their clients, and suffer when they are unable to contribute more than damage limitation. More cynically, it can be argued that doctors suffer from an unwillingness to risk having their sense of omnipotence undermined, and rely on the feedback of achievement rather than the desire to help the client for their primary motivation. It is possible, incidentally, that the said aversion has always existed among practitioners. One of the authors of the Hippocratic Corpus includes in his definition of good medicine 'the refusal to undertake to cure cases in which the disease has already won the mastery'. Revealingly, the same author also asserts that 'when the physicians fail, it is the power of the disease which is responsible and not deficiencies in the science of medicine'. This sounds remarkably like modern prescriptions not to go on working to prolong life when death is inevitable. The difference between then and now, however, is that for those living in fourth-century BC Greece who had sufficient economic resources, there might be some practitioner who *was* prepared to work against the perceived odds to prolong life. In the modern environment of a collectivised health monopoly, exceptions to the rule may well be impossible to find.

In the life-extension approach to a fatal condition, as in all other areas of medicine, the responsibility of the doctor is defined primarily in terms of what he thinks fit, not of what the client wishes. According to Kennedy, once a client is 'seen to be dying', the doctor's duty is 'the duty to make what remains of his life comfortable', and to 'desist from measures which are designed to do other than comfort the patient'. Although Kennedy believes that most of the pressure to fight against the inevitable comes from doctors or relatives, he includes in his list of factors contributing to a situation in which patients are 'not easily allowed to die' the occasional pressure from clients themselves. When Kennedy goes on to tell us that the definition of death calls for 'a normative judgement [i.e.] for the selection of a point beyond which we are prepared to say someone is no longer a person', one begins to wonder just how ill one can afford to get before a doctor's duty to prolong one's life begins to evaporate.

Do doctors actively kill people against their will?

Most medical professions are still, on the whole, opposed to *active* euthanasia for conscious clients without their consent. The practice is also unlawful, at least in theory. However, as *voluntary* euthanasia is similarly both unlawful and condemned by the profession, and yet certainly goes on, we cannot be at all sure that clients in the UK or the US are not being deliberately killed against their will on a significant scale.

Administering morphine in large doses is capable of being used as a covert form of euthanasia. This is because, according to the doctrine of 'double effect', which has been endorsed by the courts, administering a drug which shortens life is legally permissible if the primary purpose of the drug was to relieve pain. Since it is up to the individual practitioner to decide on the appropriate dosage, and since this is a clinical decision which is unlikely to be challenged, it is relatively easy for a practitioner to use more morphine than is strictly required to relieve pain, in order to accelerate the dying process. Moreover, it is sometimes suggested that the use of large doses of morphine is not as inevitable a course of action as it is sometimes presented as being, since there are alternative methods of pain relief which do not have this side-effect. For example, the head of the BMA's Ethics Science and Information Division recently commented that relief of pain 'is not, as some of us who have been qualified for a long time like myself may have been brought up to believe, giving continuously increasing doses of opiate drugs, it is very much more sophisticated'.

In this connection, the following remark by Paul Ramsey sheds some light on the possible underlying motives for using morphine.

> Once in an interdisciplinary discussion, a scientist friend of mine, a proponent of euthanasia on utilitarian grounds who believes we should comparatively evaluate human lives in their declining trajectories – slowing some, hastening others – was poking fun at the 'absurd' distinction between the direct and indirect results of pain-relieving drugs. I asked him what he would think if we had drugs to relieve suffering that certainly did *not* shorten lives or hasten death. He replied that he'd oppose funding the research to discover any such way to deal with the suffering of the dying. (Ramsey 1978, 150)

Certainly a practitioner who deliberately brought about the death of a client using a higher-than-necessary dosage of morphine would be unlikely to be found culpable by a court. Morphine is accepted by the courts as something which may lead to the death of a sick person without this constituting a crime. A court would be unlikely to find against a doctor as far as the specific dosage was concerned, given that the precise detail of treatment is regarded as a matter of clinical judgement and that a wide range of dosages of morphine are used with different clients.

In any case, the whole practice of hastening death is not one for which the notes of practitioners can necessarily be relied upon. It is interesting that Sir Douglas Black, former President of the Royal College of Physicians, was relatively frank on this issue when giving evidence to the House of Lords Select Committee on Medical Ethics. Questioned about the Nigel Cox case, he commented that

> there is no doubt in the world that on the present state of the law [Cox] committed a crime. I think he also committed something that I regard as an element of folly. I am not coming forth to support a lack of candour but one does not have to write everything down. (House of Lords 1994, vol. 2, 67)

The speechless client

> With a patient who cannot express a wish, the doctor's duty is to prolong life only if it can be assumed to be such that this would be the patient's wish. (Institute of Medical Ethics 1990a, 613)

Reviewing the literature in favour of euthanasia, it is easy to get the impression that the perceived dilemma about killing people who are in an unfortunate condition consists essentially in a simple conflict between a strong utilitarian attraction and an intuitive but to some extent unwanted aversion. Certainly many of the arguments about euthanasia seem to be designed to undermine the intuitive element, leaving us with the permissibility of 'mercy killing' as the only rational option.

The approach usually adopted when considering cases where the client is unconscious, or otherwise unable to communicate, reinforces this impression. Although we might expect the moral problem to be more acute in such cases, given that the client is not in a position to give or withhold consent to the proposal that he be killed, in fact the reverse seems to apply. Fewer qualms are experienced here than where conscious subjects are concerned. Indeed, the claim that it is morally justifiable to kill a persistently unconscious client whom doctors pronounce to be in a hopeless condition is one of the few opinions in medical ethics for which there exists a high degree of consensus. The moral philosopher Philippa Foot, for example, referring to the question of whether an unconscious client has a right to life, and therefore may not be killed since he cannot give his consent, suggests that 'there is something illogical about the idea that a right has been infringed if someone incapable of saying whether he wants it or not is deprived of something that is doing him harm rather than good'.

Pace Foot, it is not illogical to say that an unconscious person has a right, even if it is one which one might expect the majority of people to waive in the particular circumstances. It may represent an ethical conundrum to have to make a choice on behalf of an unconscious person, but the conundrum is not resolved by ascribing illogicality to one of the options.

The relative ease with which the termination of long-term unconscious clients is embraced is often justified by saying that such clients don't really 'have a life', or don't have a life that has any 'value', or aren't really 'persons'. However, it is worth considering whether there may not be a less rational component that enters into thinking on this matter. Imagine an adult whose brain has been so damaged from birth that we think he has practically no mental life comparable to that of a human being, and who is entirely and permanently dependent on life support machinery. He does, however, show behavioural responses, and when we disconnect the machinery, he reacts to the experiences resulting from this quite vigorously. Now imagine another adult who was previously healthy but whose brain has been damaged in such a way that he is permanently in a deep sleep. Although we think he will never again move or speak or otherwise communicate, we cannot know that he has no mental life. However, when we disconnect the machinery, there will be no way of knowing what the effect on his subjective experience is, whether he is suffering, or whether he minds about what he is going through. Many people would probably find performing the second act of euthanasia less harrowing than the first. It is perhaps this instinctive response which allows discussions about killing comatose clients to proceed relatively uncontroversially.

Another reason why an unconscious client presents fewer difficulties for medical ethicists is that terminating such a person's life is relatively acceptable from a utilitarian perspective. Even if the person has a mental life, he appears not to be aware of external events, and therefore may not notice if he suddenly dies because his life support system is removed (although it must be said that we can never be certain of this). On the criterion of minimising unhappiness, there may appear to be little reason why we should preserve the life of such a person, especially if he is using up resources which could be applied to conscious clients. The philosopher John Harris comments on the analogous, though imaginary, situation in which terminally ill clients who had themselves frozen and for whom a cure is now available are competing with non-frozen people for the same resources. 'Classical Utility will always demand that we favour the contemporary conscious citizens over the frozen and unconscious ones. For this course will save the same number of lives as the alternative, but will have the added advantage of causing much less pain and distress.'

Handicapped infants

To justify terminating the life of a client who is incommunicado, medical and legal professionals resort to attributing to the client interests and even judgements which appear to legitimise their decision. In the case of severely handicapped infants, the standard view of medical practitioners is that 'allowing babies to die ... is in the baby's interest at times'. The question of the infant's potential preferences does not arise, since it is generally assumed that an infant who has not had the idea of 'death' explained to him and formed an understanding of the concept is unable to experience the desire to live. Jonathan Glover argues that 'new-born babies have no conception of death and so cannot have any preference for life over death'. If an infant cries while dying, this is merely because 'in the past those with this behaviour managed to survive better than those without it'.

Currently, it appears that doctors only adopt this approach of passive euthanasia when the parents of the handicapped child give their consent, although in practice we may wonder whether there are not cases where a policy of 'benign neglect' is followed without the parents being made aware of this. But how significant is 'consent' in this context? Clients see doctors as unchallengeable experts, and find it difficult to argue with them. In a situation as fraught as this, it would seem relatively easy for professionals to put pressure on the parents to agree with their viewpoint. It might take a very determined couple, sure of their social and intellectual status vis-à-vis the physician, to challenge the expert opinion that it is in their child's best interest not to attempt to keep it alive.

In any case, there is no reason why, as this practice becomes more accepted and more common, the criterion of parental consent should continue to be seen as a necessary condition for doctors to be allowed to exercise their judgement. In cases where the parents decide it would be better if their child was allowed to die, but doctors disagree, it is the doctors whose view is likely to prevail.[7] The law on edge-of-life medicine now considers that in some cases it is in a person's 'best interests' to die, and the determination of the best interests of a given client is regarded as the prerogative of health professionals.

The 'persistent vegetative' state

The effect of certain kinds of profound brain damage is to leave the client with primitive brain functions intact (sleep-awake cycles, reflex responses), but without any evidence of normal cerebral activity, and minimal behavioural responsiveness. The state of the cerebrum can vary from being completely degenerated, as in the case of Tony Bland, to being intact

---

[7] As, for example, in the 1981 'Baby Alexandra' case.

but with abnormal electrical activity. This condition, which is apparently capable of being permanent, has been called the 'persistent vegetative state' (PVS). Little is understood about PVS, but clients have been known to regain consciousness after periods varying from a few weeks to several years, although if they do they are usually left in a more or less disabled state. It is usually assumed that, since they are showing no normal cortical activity, they therefore can have no mental life of any kind. However, one cannot be sure that this is indeed the case, given our imperfect understanding of the relationship between the brain and consciousness. Amphibians have only a very rudimentary and scanty cortex, while fish have no cortex at all, yet one would not necessarily wish to assume from this that these animals have no mental life.

In any case, PVS is quite different from coma. A PVS patient is by no means without any behavioural life at all, as the following description makes clear.

> Such patients may have long periods of 'wakefulness' with open eyes that alternate with 'sleep'. ... When awake the eyes may briefly follow a moving object by reflex, or be attracted in the direction of loud sounds. All four limbs are spastic but can withdraw from painful stimuli, and the hands show reflex groping and grasping. The face can grimace, small amounts of food or fluid put in the mouth may be swallowed, and groans and cries occur but no words are uttered. (Institute of Medical Ethics 1990b, 96-7)

What seems clear about PVS is that it is impossible ever to be certain that a particular client will not regain a more normal state of consciousness. It may become increasingly unlikely, as the months pass, based on the statistics of past cases, but there is no evidence to suggest that beyond a certain point in time, the condition becomes definitely irreversible. Yet doctors do diagnose irreversibility, and their verdict of irreversibility should, it is suggested, be used to decide when it is appropriate to withdraw life-support treatment from a PVS patient. Ethical debates on this issue seem conveniently to forget that it is impossible to diagnose a *permanent* vegetative state. It is rather like the cases of people being told, 'you have three months to live', and then surviving twenty years. It may well be that these people represent the exceptions to the rule, and that on average doctors' predictions of remaining life span are close to the mark. But few conscious clients would refuse treatment for a condition simply because of a strong likelihood that they would die within a short time from something else.

The fact that diagnoses of the irreversibility PVS are not infallible is illustrated by the following case.

> A brain-damaged man has been discharged from hospital six months after doctors told his parents his life support machine may have to be turned off. Mr Brett Johnson, 32, who went into a three-month coma after a motorcycle

accident last summer, can read, write and is beginning to talk clearly. [His mother] said that two senior doctors at Guy's Hospital had said her son was in a permanent [sic] vegetative state and nothing could be done. (*Daily Telegraph*, 11 March 1994)

Ethicists nevertheless assume that a reliable diagnosis of irreversible PVS is something which can be made. Thus the Institute of Medical Ethics argues that it can be morally justified to withdraw artificial nutrition and hydration from PVS patients, provided only that the diagnosis and prognosis of irreversible PVS is 'beyond doubt', and is agreed by 'more than one experienced doctor'. A contrary desire on the part of the next-of-kin, it would appear, may have to be discouraged: 'Whilst the wishes of relatives should be respected ... it is unfair and unkind to allow unrealistic optimism to be sustained.'

PVS provides a useful test case for medical ethics, for the following reasons. First, it is a condition which normally rules out the possibility of discovering the client's wishes, unless he left an advance directive on this point. Secondly, the likelihood of recovery after a certain period becomes small. Thirdly, the client's quality of life while in this state is arguably poor or even non-existent. Fourthly, it is expensive in terms of resources to sustain a PVS patient by means of artificial respiration and feeding over a period of years. Fifthly, it could be said that no persons benefit from the existence of the client since it is impossible to communicate with him; indeed, it may well be that his existence causes only suffering in that his relatives are continually reminded of his unfortunate existence.

The medical and legal establishment is moving towards a particular resolution of this problem, and it is very important to understand its implications. Briefly, the approach which is being taken is that (a) doctors should judge at which point the client's condition becomes 'permanent' rather than just 'persistent'; (b) once that stage has been reached, doctors should decide what is medically in the client's 'best interests'; (c) it is legitimate to find that it is in the client's best interests to die.

In the case of Tony Bland, it was eventually decided by the High Court, and confirmed by the House of Lords, that doctors were entitled to disconnect his feeding tubes, bringing about his death, as this was held to be in his best interest. Mr Bland's parents had in fact consented to this action – indeed, the way the case was presented to the media suggested that it was they who were most concerned that his equipment should be disconnected. It might be thought that this case merely established that doctors could perform euthanasia under the instructions of the next-of-kin, where the client was unable to give consent personally. However, as with newborn infants, it is likely that the consent of relatives is not crucial in this respect, or that if it is, it will not remain so for long. After the judge's decision was announced, Dr McCall Smith commented that the case showed the importance of 'consulting' the relatives of the client in such situations.[8] Subsequently, the BMA produced a paper on PVS which stressed that legally the views of relatives are not decisive.[9]

'In your best interests to die'

That Tony Bland's treatment was terminated, leading directly to his death, was consistent with the view that long-term care of the kind Bland needed was too expensive for the NHS to finance, given the likelihood that it would be required for the rest of his life. In fact, however, the decision to withdraw feeding was based not on the economic argument, but on a number of highly questionable premises. It was assumed that there was no conceivable hope of recovery for Bland. It was assumed that it was out of the question that Bland could have any kind of mental life. These premises were readily accepted by the courts on the say-so of experts from the medical profession.

What is particularly ominous, however, is the admission of the argument that death might be clinically indicated for some clients. This clearly follows from the claim that death was in Bland's 'best interests', and that these interests were best judged by doctors. Yet the 'treatment' which Bland was receiving was hardly of the invasive, painful kind. Indeed, consisting as it did largely of the provision of nutrition, it is not clear that it should be described as treatment at all. Moreover, since the court's judgement hinged on the assumption that Bland had no mental life, the court cannot have supposed that Bland was suffering in any way. How, then, could it have been in his best interests to be extinguished? How could the choice between an unconscious life and death have been made, on his behalf, in favour of death?

Here again, the courts seem to have had little trouble relying completely on the judgement of medical professionals. According to Dr Cartlidge FRCP, consultant neurologist to the Newcastle Health Authority and senior lecturer in neurology at the University of Newcastle-upon-Tyne, 'it was not in Bland's best interests to prolong survival'. According to Bland's own physician, 'it would be in the best interests of Anthony Bland for [the] artificial feeding regime to be withdrawn at this stage'. Judge Sir Stephen Brown commented approvingly that such a decision 'is one for the clinical judgement of responsible medical practitioners'. Lord Keith of Kinkel concurred, asserting that the decision 'whether or not the continued treatment and care of a PVS patient confers any benefit on him is essentially one for the practitioners in charge of his case'. Lord Goff of Chieveley put the matter even more forcefully, revealing the underlying assumptions of the decision, and also making explicit how conflicts of opinion between relatives and doctors would be regarded by the courts.

---

[8] Channel Four News, 19 November 1992.
[9] See House of Lords 1994, vol. 2, 56-8.

> ... the views expressed by the [BMA's Medical Ethics Committee] on the subject of consultation with the relatives of PVS patients are consistent with the opinion expressed by your Lordship's House in *In re F.* (1990) that it is good practice for the doctor to consult relatives. ... But the committee is firmly of the opinion that the relatives' views cannot be determinative of the treatment. Indeed, if that were not so, the relatives would be able to dictate to the doctors what is in the best interests of the patient, which cannot be right.
>
> ...
>
> The truth is that, in the course of their work, doctors frequently have to make decisions which may affect the continued survival of their patients, and are in reality far more experienced in matters of this kind than are the judges. (*Airedale NHS Trust v Bland*, Weekly Law Reports 1993/1, 373-4)

Lord Goff went on to say how the relationship between the medical and legal professions should be based on mutual respect, almost as if he regarded the former as carrying out some of the functions of the latter.

> It is nevertheless the function of the judges to state the legal principles upon which the lawfulness of the actions of doctors depend; but in the end the decisions to be made in individual cases must rest with the doctors themselves. In these circumstances, what is required is a sensitive understanding by both the judges and the doctors of each other's respective functions, and in particular a determination by the judges *not merely to understand the problems facing the medical profession in cases of this kind, but also to regard their professional standards with respect*. Mutual understanding between the doctors and the judges is the best way to ensure the evolution of a sensitive and sensible legal framework for the treatment and care of patients, with a sound ethical base, in the interest of the patients themselves. (*ibid.*, 374, my italics)

Lord Mustill was alone among the judges in the House of Lords appeal case in striking a note of caution. As he pointed out, a doctor 'who kills his patient even with the consent of the patient is guilty of murder. Plainly a second doctor who kills his patient in circumstances where the obtaining of consent is impracticable cannot be in a better position than the first. ...' Mustill, indeed, hinted at the true motives behind the decision by referring to the interests of the family, the medical staff and the paying community. Yet, in spite of having felt 'profound misgivings about almost every aspect' of the case, he too agreed to dismiss the appeal against the decision.

As we noted in the chapter on wanting to die, some people would choose death over life for themselves. Does this mean it is 'in their best interests' to die? One possible answer to this is that it cannot possibly be in someone's interests to die, on the basis that, after a person has died, he no longer exists and hence cannot be said to be 'better off', or indeed to *be* anything at all. However, let us allow for a moment the possibility that *being dead* could, in some circumstances and for some people, genuinely be somehow preferable to living. Should the decision as to whether it is, or whether that person would think so if asked, ever be made by someone other than the person himself? Surely one has to be very wary before making choices of this kind on another person's behalf. If a choice does have to be made, it is clearly not a clinical one. There seems no justification for giving doctors the power to make the decision.

Explicit refusals

This chapter began with an extract from a newspaper article about the case of smokers being refused heart surgery. It may be worth considering the implications of this explicit form of withholding treatment, which appears to be a relatively recent and alarming development.

In an unrestricted market for services, everyone is free to offer whatever they wish at whatever price they choose, although not every offer will be taken up. In an unrestricted market for services, everyone is also free *not* to offer any particular service. But the health service is not an unrestricted market. It is a sector which has been stringently regulated, with much of the regulation having been promoted by its suppliers, the medical profession. Moreover, its customers do not necessarily have the option of doing without whatever service they happen to require. This means they may be forced into a relationship with a supplier on terms over which they have no control. In such a situation, it becomes relevant to ask whether, or to what extent, it is appropriate for individual suppliers to be free not to offer their services.

There is another way to make this point. I am forced to contribute, by way of taxation, towards a collective health fund, but am restricted in my choice of health professional in deriving benefits from this fund. The terms on which the service is offered are determined by the medical monopoly, which does not have to take client preferences into account. Should those on whom I am forced to depend, then, be able to choose not to treat me?

Traditionally, the medical profession has regarded itself as being to some extent under a *duty* to provide treatment. Thus some codes of medical ethics place a doctor under an obligation to provide emergency care when there is no one else able to provide it. These duties were assumed to supplement the normal commercial relationship under which a doctor is expected to do the best for any individual whom he accepted as a client. How, then, has it been possible for a reverse situation to come about in which doctors feel free to *refuse* their clients life-saving treatment which they are capable of providing, on the basis of their own value judgements?

Allocation decisions in response to resource shortages are no doubt one of the reasons for such refusals, although they are likely to be applied covertly. The 1992 Appleton International Conference on medical ethics reported that

> the US and many European systems now inappropriately disguise the problem of scarcity and, in effect, purchase social stability at the price of justice. ... explicit decisions are made within [European] systems by physicians and administrators within these systems to allocate funds for some sorts of care and not for others. The failure of honesty arises when the reasons for such allocation decisions are not made explicit in public, so that individual patients cannot know when treatment is withheld because of lack of benefit and when for primarily economic reasons. This is exacerbated when doctors and administrators in different regions make quite different decisions in similar cases, so that which patients get care may depend as much on geography as on diagnosis. (Stanley 1992, 19)

It is not clear, however, that resource allocation is the only reason for refusing treatment. It is possible that refusal may in some cases be motivated by a desire on the part of suppliers to impose their views and preferences on the way services are provided. This motive is not unique to health professionals. It is arguably a characteristic of all groups, professional and otherwise, that they seek to maximise their influence over events in which they are involved. One of the useful features of a competitive market is that it generally provides a restraining effect on these forces while nevertheless allowing successful economic interactions to take place. Where, however, market restraints such as competitive forces are removed, the tendency of the more powerful groups to increase their influence over interactions with others is often held in check (if at all) only by more subtle social factors such as expectations.

In the absence of an efficient market to provide aggregate power to individual consumer decisions, the imposition of preferences requires the organisation of individuals into groups. The better organised a group of consumers or suppliers are, the more strongly they will be able to impose their preferences. In the case of doctors and their clients the contrast in this respect is immense. While the medical professions of most countries are dominated by highly influential associations with close connections to the state apparatus, clients as a group are weakly organised if at all. Even in countries where clients have something analogous to a consumer association, the organisation is likely to be dedicated to helping clients make the best of the conditions imposed by the medical profession rather than campaigning for change.

To the extent that the provision of medical services has not yet become wholly dominated by the preferences of doctors, we have to reckon that this is due to social rather than economic forces. As such, however, this situation is relatively unstable. So long as the traditional model of doctors as professionals who serve individual clients held sway, public expectations had some effect in maintaining the status quo with regard to doctor compliance. Once there begin to be commonly-used arguments which purport to *legitimise* dominance on the part of suppliers, however, even this weak form of restraint becomes ineffectual. As we shall see in the next chapter, the role of recent moral philosophy and medical ethics has been to generate and defend arguments of this kind, thus providing medical authoritarianism with spurious intellectual support.

11

Moral syllogisms

We noted in chapter 9 the fact that modern debates on medical ethics tend to consist in a struggle between two opposing forces, one authoritarian and prohibitive, the other utilitarian and prescriptive, but neither giving much weight to the principle that individuals should be allowed access to whatever medical services are available. Modern academic philosophy has predominantly placed itself on the side of the latter of these two movements. Indeed, one of the principal contributions of recent moral philosophy to life-and-death controversies has been to promote the idea that, whatever may be the moral rules which we should apply in deciding such issues, it is *not* those which have traditionally operated as inhibitions against doing harm to others.

The fact that academic philosophy has aligned itself with the more progressive and utopist strand, rather than with what might be described as a reactionary position, is perhaps not surprising. The appeal of philosophy lies in the possibility of inventing new perspectives for viewing the world. The notion that killing people might, contrary to received wisdom, be morally acceptable in certain circumstances appears a radical one and hence is likely to be attractive to those who consider themselves forward-thinking.

What *is* intriguing, on the other hand, is that moral philosophy has adopted any position at all, considering that at one point earlier this century it looked as if it were about to argue itself out of existence. A.J. Ayer, for example, wrote in his influential 1936 book *Language, Truth and Logic* that, 'as ethical judgements are mere expressions of feeling, there can be no way of determining the validity of any ethical system ... All that one may legitimately enquire in this connection is, What are the moral habits of a given person or group of people, and what causes them to have precisely those habits and feelings?' The influence of the later Wittgenstein, who believed that the primary task of philosophy is to show that many of the traditional philosophical problems arise out of linguistic confusions, also contributed to a feeling that ethics was a fruitless exercise.

Such nihilism, however, seems not to have retained its appeal to professional philosophers for very long, perhaps because it was realised that it undermined their claim to contribute usefully to solving the problems of society. By the seventies and eighties, philosophers were firmly back in the business of evaluating competing moral viewpoints, contributing guidelines for behaviour such as: killing the permanently comatose is all right because they are unable to appreciate the difference between life and death; or, overriding a person's wishes may promote his autonomy.[1] Indeed, the logical and definitional purity which in other contexts characterises academic philosophy is noticeably missing from much of modern ethics. To give an illustration, the Australian philosopher Peter Singer, a noted supporter of euthanasia, has no philosophical qualms about using the term 'consent' in a novel way when it suits his purpose.

> Euthanasia can be voluntary even if a person is not able ... to indicate the wish to die right up to the moment the tablets are swallowed or the trigger pulled. A person may, while in good health, make a written request for euthanasia if, through accident or illness, she should come to be ... in pain ... and there is no reasonable hope of recovery. In killing a person who has made such a request, has re-affirmed it from time to time [and who is now in pain] one could truly claim to be acting with her consent. (Singer 1979, 129)

Sanctity of life

Much recent philosophical writing on euthanasia is concerned with showing that the principles behind the inhibition against intentional killing are naïve and based on questionable premises. Jonathan Glover, for example, dismisses the concept of the sanctity of life, arguing *inter alia* that, since we do not make much fuss about killing a cow, it cannot be the intrinsic value of life itself that makes killing a human being wrong. However, the fact that in practice we kill cows with equanimity may not have very much bearing on the question of whether we ought to regard human life, or indeed life in general, as sacred.

One way of making the traditional Western attitude towards killing seem outmoded is to claim, as James Rachels does, that it is 'largely the product of Christian teaching'. Rachels contrasts the Christian ethos concerning life and death with that of other societies. Athens, for example, 'one of the world's great civilisations', approved the destruction of unformed or unhealthy babies. The motives of those who proposed our traditional ethical ideas are presented as suspect. 'The early Christians had decided for reasons of political expediency that the line between acceptable and unacceptable killing should be drawn [to permit killing in war, in individual self-defence, and as punishment, but not on any other grounds].' Rachels's cynicism about motives, however, is applied in a way which is highly tendentious. An alternative reading of the historical facts is certainly possible. It is questionable, for example, whether the idea that

---

[1] These examples are taken from Glover 1977 and Dworkin 1972, respectively.

all life is sacred is a particularly Christian one. Respect for life is certainly found in the Old Testament, although not perhaps in quite so intellectual a form as was later promulgated by Augustine and other Latin Church fathers. As a former Bishop of Sheffield has pointed out, the Old Testament 'presents physical life as the creation of God, who alone has the source of life, and man has no independent right to shed blood and take life. If he does so, he will be accountable to God for what he has done and his own life will be forfeit ... Animal life as well as human life was considered to belong to God and could only be taken by divine permission.' It is true that, as Christianity became more influential and sought full absorption into social life, modifications to the originally strict principle of the sanctity of life were more or less forced on the Church. To call this a *political* move may be something of an exaggeration. In any case, even if, as Rachels implies, the ruling officials of the Church decided to advance their own political influence by diluting the sanctity-of-life principle, this does not in itself invalidate the strong form of the principle.

Another device used by contemporary philosophers in the attempt to provide euthanasia with an ethical basis is to retain traditional principles such as 'sanctity of life' and 'respect for persons', but to argue for substitute definitions of the terms 'life' or 'person'. Rachels, for example, suggests that people whose lives have become unbearable as a result of physiological deterioration 'do not have lives, even though they are alive; and so killing *them* is a morally different matter [from killing other people]'. He goes on to explain that 'there is nothing important about being alive except that it enables one to *have a life*'.

What is in favour of 'being alive' as a criterion, rather than 'having a life', however, is that the former is ascertainable in a relatively objective way. Whether someone can be said to be having a life, on the other hand, is a question which is open to a considerable variation of opinion, and which carries with it the implicit suggestion that someone other than the subject should determine the answer. The evaluation of someone as 'not having a life' might be applied only where the person is permanently unconscious. On the other hand, it is possible to argue that someone who is conscious, but unable to enter into the life of the community, should be regarded as lacking 'a life'. The theologian Richard McCormick, for example, has asserted that 'life is a value to be preserved only insofar as it contains some potentiality for human relationships'. On that basis, if you are unable to communicate then – however intelligent you may be – your life can be said to be valueless.

Some extremely dubious arguments are marshalled in favour of the proposition that killing people is permissible in some circumstances. Rachels, for example, thinks that the 'sanctity of life' principle is undermined by the observation that all lives do not have equal value. Even the subjects of those lives, he says, would readily concede this point.

> Consider a life in which there is no possibility of satisfying one's desires or aspirations; or a life in which friendships are impossible; or one filled only with pain, from which the possibility of enjoyment has been eliminated. Such a life will not have the value which it otherwise might have had. This judgement is not an attempt to impose some 'outside' perspective on the person's situation. The point is that such a 'life' will not have as much value *for the subject of that life*. (Rachels 1986, 65)

The implication for Rachels is that some lives will be completely valueless. But this argument is just as absurd as saying that because some people are shorter than others, and would readily admit this, it follows that there is a minimum height below which a person ceases to be a human being.

Some modern philosophers positively *exhort* us to abandon any old-fashioned moral preferences we may have regarding the ethics of life, death and suffering. It would be 'quite irrational', argues the philosopher and neurosurgeon Grant Gillett, 'to sustain our intuitive response toward a human body once we became aware that the body had become a shell perpetuating the sometimes cruel illusion that the person whose body it was is still alive'. Comparing not feeding those dying of hunger in underdeveloped countries with committing murder, James Rachels concedes that he *feels* there must be a difference, but argues that 'on reflection I can find no reason to think that there really is a difference, and much reason to think otherwise; so I conclude that the intuition is mistaken'. Making this dubious analogy may seem like a shock tactic designed to make people take the problems of underdeveloped countries seriously. Its psychological effect is more likely to be to undermine the inhibition about killing. Given that his comments occur in a book about euthanasia, perhaps Rachels is saying, 'we already allow people to starve so it is hypocritical to resist euthanasia on the ground that it constitutes murder'.

Autonomy

If 'sanctity of life' is philosophically unfashionable, then perhaps one can look for support from philosophers for the principle of autonomy as a defence against medical authoritarianism. It is true that the term 'autonomy' has recently been enjoying a relatively high degree of usage in the ethical literature. It would be wrong to conclude from this, however, that respect for liberty and individual volition is particularly strong. Rather, as collectivist views of medicine, together with the increasing power of doctors, have made treatment more authoritarian, the issue of autonomy has become much more starkly defined. It is now no longer possible to evade the point that medicine is capable of being extremely coercive. The fact that practically all commentators now have to acknowledge the significance of a certain degree of autonomy – that there must be limits to coercion at *some* point – does not mean that autonomy commands widespread support. Indeed, there are plenty of examples of writers who

11. Moral syllogisms

comment adversely on the idea of client autonomy, and argue that it takes medicine away from the ideal of doctor benevolence and the trusting submission of clients.[2]

Although the philosophical notion of liberty is not entirely dead, it receives its principal support in a somewhat distorted form. Mill's original, relatively pure brand of libertarianism has been subject to a certain amount of reconstruction. For example, to the extent that the importance of autonomy is acknowledged, the class of circumstances which are regarded as exceptions to the rule and which call for intervention has grown well beyond the few isolated instances that Mill identified. The basic libertarian premise, according to which it is wrong to interfere with people's freedom of action, except where others are directly harmed by it, has of course itself been subjected to a good deal of criticism.[3]

Certainly autonomy is not the crucial issue for most philosophers who favour euthanasia. Philippa Foot, for example, has criticised the view that 'it is a man's desire for life that makes us call life a good'. She argues that someone may wish to stay alive 'where we would say confidently that it would be better for him if he died, and he may admit it too'. Foot quotes Dmitri Panin's observation about life in Stalin's prison camps, that 'The more that life became desperate, the more a prisoner seemed determined to hold onto it.' Rather than concluding that being alive has intrinsic value, and is defended harder as it becomes more threatened, she interprets this as evidence that a man may 'cling to life though he knew those facts about his future which would make any *charitable* man wish that he might die'.

Fortunately, Foot also recognises a limited 'right to life' in the sense that we may not interfere with a person's life against his wishes, even if we thought it otherwise morally appropriate to do so. This obligation does not extend, however, to giving positive help to someone who requests it if this is not considered to be in his best interests.

> Suppose, for example, that a retreating army has to leave behind wounded or exhausted soldiers in the wastes of an arid or snowbound land where the only prospect is death by starvation or at the hands of an enemy notoriously cruel. It has often been the practice to accord a merciful bullet to men in such desperate straits. But suppose one of them demands that he should be left alive? It seems clear that his comrades have no right to kill him, though it is a quite different question as to whether they should give him a life-prolonging drug. The right to life can sometimes give a duty of positive service, but does not do so here. What it does give is the right to be left alone. (Foot 1978, 48)

Foot concludes that it is possible that a person 'wants to live where it would

---

[2] See for example E.A. Shinebourne and A. Bush, 'For paternalism in the doctor-patient relationship', in Gillon 1994.
[3] See for example Phillips Griffiths 1983, especially the essays by Martin Hollis and Alan Ryan.

be better for him to die: perhaps he does not realise the desperate situation he is in, or perhaps he is afraid of dying. So ... someone might justifiably refuse to prolong the life even of someone who asked him to prolong it ... And it is even more obvious that charity does not always dictate that life should be prolonged where a man's own wishes, hypothetical or actual, are not known.'

Foot also thinks, and here she is being relatively conservative by the standards of her profession, that a *doctor* has some obligation to provide active assistance to his clients even where he deems this not to be in their best interests. But this obligation is limited to what is generally done under normal medical practice. Thus we fall back on the moral views of the medical profession: if the profession as a whole considers it unethical to keep people alive in certain circumstances, then normal practice will shift to reflect this view, and the obligation will, apparently, vanish.

More recently, Margaret Pabst Battin has used the principle of autonomy to argue in favour of euthanasia. Like others who adopt this strategy, however, her support for autonomy is limited to permitting fulfilment of the wish to die when outside observers agree that permission is appropriate in the circumstances. These outsiders seem to be regarded by her as considerably more reliable than the ill person when it comes to having a view about the value of his life.

> When there is no evidence of suffering or pain, mental or physical, and no evidence of factors like depression, psychoactive drugs, or affect-altering disease that might impair cognitive functioning, an external observer usually can accurately determine whether life is a benefit ... Conversely, when there is every evidence of pain and little or no evidence of factors that might outweigh pain, such as cognitive capacities that might give rise to other valuable experience, then an external observer generally can also accurately determine the value of this person's life: it is a disbenefit, a burden, to him. (Pabst Battin 1987, 71)

On the matter of clients being refused treatment, Battin is relatively unusual among philosophers in noting that much current euthanasia-like practice is not autonomy-promoting at all but often turns on convenience or resource considerations. Nevertheless, her support for the principle that clients should receive treatment if they desire it is, as in the case of other philosophers who claim to support autonomy, qualified by reference to what can be regarded as reasonable and consistent with overall resource considerations. For example, she argues that continuous sedation as a solution to a painful terminal condition

> is *not* an option the patient may choose, nor is it a defensible general solution to the problem of euthanasia. The patient's autonomous requests must still conform to the demands of justice ... It is true that continuous sedation may satisfy both the principles of mercy and autonomy, but because there is no ongoing experience or sentient end state to which the treatment leads, the

patient cannot realistically desire the treatment that would maintain him. ... even the patient who articulates his or her choices in advance is not entitled to request *permanent* sedation, since the principle of realistic desire prohibits him or her, like the proverbial dog in the manger, from laying claims to resources he or she cannot possibly enjoy ... the patient must choose death or periodically sentient life ... (*ibid.*, 86-7)

Doing what is 'best' for people

One problem with the principle of autonomy, of course, is that it does not have the same 'do-gooding' appeal as the principle of maximising 'welfare'. If faced with a choice between fulfilling someone's wishes and doing what is 'best' for him, assuming the two options are different but equally easily realised, many people would probably tend towards the latter alternative (only for someone else, of course; not, *ex hypothesi*, for themselves). With the choice expressed in this simplistic way, the temptation is strong to do what one thinks is best overall for the person, rather than satisfy his desires. Otherwise is one not doing the person *harm*, by denying him the option which would really be in his interests?

This partly explains why moral philosophers find it relatively easy to override considerations about autonomy in favour of considerations about happiness and interests, and why libertarianism is readily displaced by utilitarianism. The principle of utility is of course just as unprovable an axiom as the principle of liberty. There is no demonstrable reason why acting morally should be based on the promotion of welfare, any more than there is a demonstrable reason why it should be based on a respect for volition. This point is often evaded, however, because there seems to be something intuitively obvious about the idea that we should always do what is 'best' for someone. Thus Rachels argues persuasively that his approach to ethics 'sees being moral, not as a matter of faithfulness to abstract rules or divine laws, but as a matter of doing what is best for those who are affected by our conduct'.

It is interesting to note, incidentally, that it is nowadays *welfare* which has become the key concept of utilitarianism, rather than the more old-fashioned notion of *happiness*. This has taken us even further away from a respect for liberty, and gives further encouragement to those who would like to be able to override the wishes of others. For while it is generally assumed that an individual is usually the best judge of what makes him happy, this is not always thought to apply in the case of his 'welfare'.

Rachels's interpretation of his own position as value-neutral turns out on analysis to be fallacious. If he thinks that we should always do for someone 'what is best' in the sense of 'the most good thing', this amounts to saying that in order to do the morally desirable thing, we must do the morally desirable thing. This is merely a circularity and hence of no use as a guideline for behaviour. If, on the other hand, the concept of 'best for X' is to be taken as having a more specific meaning than this, e.g. 'that which is thought by the majority of people to be most likely to lead to a maximum amount of welfare for X in the long run,' then the principle that we should always do what is best for a person *in that sense* stands in need of justification. The appeal of the paternalist principle therefore seems to arise partly from a conflation between 'best' in the sense of 'ethically most appropriate' and 'best' in the sense of what is considered to be in someone's interests.

On a more practical level a morality based on doing what is 'best for someone' suffers from irredeemable flaws. Discussions which assume this principle as the basis for ethical behaviour ignore the problems that (a) we have no way of knowing what eventual outcomes are to count as 'good' or 'best' for any given person, and (b) even if we knew the answer to point (a), we do not necessarily know how to achieve those outcomes. On the other hand, we do usually know relatively unambiguously what a particular person *wants* to have happen to him. It appears, however, that acting simply on the basis of what another person wants is in some ways less appealing, psychologically, than working out their best interests. Perhaps this is because it provides less scope for satisfying the desire for power over others.

Slippery slopes

An argument often used against euthanasia, or other controversial developments in medicine, is that such a development takes us onto a 'slippery slope' leading to further, undesirable developments. This type of argument is often disputed by philosophers. Bernard Williams, for example, attacks the use of slippery slope arguments, which he believes are illogical. He claims that such arguments assume 'that there is no point at which one can non-arbitrarily get off the slope once one has got onto it – this is what makes the slope slippery'. In other words, the reference by a person to a 'slippery slope' implies a belief on the part of the person that allowing one thing in a progression of possible developments partially *commits* us to later things in that progression, at least more so than if we had not allowed the first thing. If Williams's interpretation is correct, then of course the use of the slippery slope argument depends on a fallacy. Just because one development in medicine forms part of a sequence which one imagines might follow does not mean that it really takes us any 'nearer' to the next step in the imagined sequence.

The flaw in Williams's analysis, however, is that sequences envisaged by those who invoke slippery slopes are not always merely imagined. More typically, there are connections of social convention or even of law between them. Particularly where the removal of legal restraints is concerned, it is hard to maintain that we are not nearer to taking a second step in a sequence by taking the first. If development B depends on something which is currently prohibited, and on which development A also depends,

11. Moral syllogisms

then clearly acceptance of A requires the removal of one of the obstacles to B. Thus if legalising voluntary euthanasia requires legalising homicide of patients by doctors in some circumstances – given that at present it is (theoretically at least) legal in no circumstances – such legalisation will have removed one of the obstacles to *in*voluntary euthanasia.

A philosophical rejection of slippery slopes is inconsistent with the frequent use which philosophers themselves make of comparisons and analogies in arguing for their preferred positions. Thus the argument is often used that because we allow passive euthanasia, it is illogical (and occasionally cruel) to prevent active euthanasia. Other arguments of this kind include: we allow abortion, so why not infanticide; we stop people taking drugs, so why not stop them smoking or restrict their consumption of alcohol; we perform mercy-killing on animals, so why not on human beings. Given the frequent use of such tendentious comparisons, it is unrealistic to think that the acceptance of, say, doctors killing their clients will not affect what other things people are prepared to contemplate as being potentially acceptable.

Slippery slope considerations are not of course necessarily sufficient to decide any given issue. We may conclude that there are other factors, outweighing the increased likelihood of undesirable developments, which favour a proposal such as euthanasia. What we cannot do is pretend that the slippery slope argument is not relevant. Any given development increases the likelihood of other developments that appear related or similar – regardless of whether professional philosophers are able to 'prove' that there ought not to be a connection between them.

Medicine as a moral enterprise

Modern philosophers like to pose the question, 'what *ought* a doctor to do, morally speaking?' This generates absorbing dilemmas, since what is morally indicated may differ from what the patient is wanting. The problem with proposing that medical services are somehow founded on *moral*, rather than *economic*, considerations – quite apart from the absurdity of thinking that doctors uniquely act out of altruism rather than self-interest – is that the supposed moral duties which doctors, or society, have towards the patient are subject to serious limitations. Grant Gillett, for example, asserts that 'there are certain states in which there is no presumption that we have a moral obligation to keep human beings alive', and that 'there are standards of care and concern that should only apply to creatures within a certain range of capacities'. Gillett adds hopefully that this does not 'amount to a licence for barbarism outside that range because it is very difficult for integrated moral agents such as human beings to be barbarians and sadists in limited areas of their lives and otherwise compassionate souls'. Given our knowledge of the way in which, for example, Nazi prison camp wardens were able to return to their families to be loving fathers, after spending their working day subjecting prisoners to torture and degradation, this seems an astoundingly naïve pronouncement.

In this way a morality-based service, having taken over from one based on contract and exchange, ironically becomes one which *refuses* people that which they would previously have been able to obtain. As Gillett says about patients in a persistent vegetative state, for example, such an individual 'clearly falls below what I have outlined as a minimal state in which our moral concern becomes engaged with the experiences of another creature ... we are not justified in expending the medical effort which we lavish on human beings under the impulse of our moral concern'. Perhaps Gillett is talking only about the principles which should guide resource allocation for the *public* health system. But he does not say that his considerations are confined to non-private medicine. What if an individual had a contractual agreement which provided that, if he were in a vegetative state, he should continue indefinitely to get whatever treatment was necessary to keep him alive? It seems that Gillett might well regard this as immoral, and perhaps he would consider it appropriate for the courts to enforce this moral viewpoint and override the individual's arrangement.

Interestingly, Gillett seems prepared to rely to a large extent on the gut reactions of *doctors*, and assumes that they take everything into account that we would want them to take into account, and more efficiently than we could: '[The] intuitions of doctors and nurses are a very important component of the data to be considered in coming to a good decision about a given ethical problem.' It may be relevant, of course, that Gillett is a doctor himself.

The legitimisation of medical power

One of the chief functions of philosophy is to subject preconceptions to thorough criticism, and to consider alternative viewpoints. British philosophy in particular has a strong tradition of scepticism, and it was this questioning of common sense which, starting with Hume's recognition that the concepts of 'is' and 'ought' are incommensurable, eventually led to the development of the 'emotivist' theory of ethics by philosophers such as A.J. Ayer. We might therefore expect modern philosophy to throw a critical and illuminating searchlight on the ideology which informs current medical practice. In fact, however, most modern moral philosophy does little more than reinforce the prevailing 'rationalist' perspective that everything should be left to those who know best, i.e. those trained in medicine. Rachels, for example, produces all the utilitarian arguments in favour of killing someone in a hopeless and painful condition, merely noting as a final point that if the person himself 'requested to be killed, the act would not have violated his rights'. He goes on to stress that he does not mean that euthanasia is justified *whenever* a patient says he can no

11. Moral syllogisms

longer endure pain, relying once again on the wisdom and benevolence of the medical professionals.

> Suppose the doctor, or the family, knows that the painful condition can be cured, and that the patient's request to die is only a temporary irrational reaction, which he will later repudiate. It is entirely reasonable for them to take this into account, and to refuse the irrational request. The argument from mercy does not say otherwise; in such circumstances euthanasia would not promote his best interests and would hardly be 'merciful' at all. (Rachels 1986, 157-8)

Philosophers seem to share the puzzlement of other commentators over the appropriate attitude to adopt towards practitioners, when confronted with unpalatable facts about the coerciveness of much of modern medicine. Surely, the tacit reasoning seems to run, we cannot regard qualified professional persons who occupy respected social positions as being morally questionable? If there is something wrong with the way modern medicine is delivered, surely we must look for the blame elsewhere, perhaps in ourselves?

> A somewhat natural tendency ... is to think that if murder is an evil, those who murder are evil and blameworthy. [However,] ignorance and compulsion tend to exculpate agents from responsibility for such acts. ... In the absence of any substantive exculpating conditions, we readily would agree that anyone who poisoned the local water supply is blameworthy; however, that is an act that conscientious, reasonable, 'good-hearted' persons would not find morally perplexing. In contrast, many if not all of the disputes in biomedical ethics are perplexing, and there is frequently little or no reason to conclude that practitioners of disputed practices are 'moral monsters' ... the genuine difficulty of reaching a reasonable view about the permissibility of certain practices goes some significant way toward exonerating practitioners of the blame that usually attaches to unjustified practices. (VanDeVeer and Regan 1987, 52-3)

Unfortunately, an aversion to criticising a class which behaves exploitatively or coercively, because of a principle that the class in question has unquestionable moral credentials, results in a tendency to tolerate politely whatever practices the class chooses to adopt. Indeed, the reluctance to criticise doctors, or to question their motives, generates a curious feedback effect. The implied confidence in their moral standards is sometimes taken as *evidence* that those standards are indeed beyond reproach. Peter Singer, for example, invokes this argument to support the proposal that the power of euthanasia should be restricted to doctors.

> If acts of euthanasia could only be carried out by a member of the medical profession, with the concurrence of a second doctor, it is not likely that the propensity to kill would spread unchecked throughout the community. Doctors already have a good deal of power over life and death, through their

ability to withhold treatment. *There has been no suggestion* that doctors who begin by allowing grossly defective infants to die from pneumonia will move on to withhold antibiotics from racial minorities or political extremists. (Singer 1979, 156-7, my italics)

The rejection of old-fashioned principles, and the embracing of the paternalist medical model, are not unique to secular philosophy. Indeed, it is becoming increasingly difficult to find support from *any* source for the idea that human health is *not* a collective commodity to be manipulated by social agents in the interests of the community. Anyone expecting contemporary Christian philosophy to make a case on behalf of patient autonomy, in opposition to the reductionism of modern ethical theory, is liable to be disappointed. In fact, Christian writers include some of the most vociferous supporters of collectivism in the health field. The following quotation may read like an extract from a communist handbook, but it is actually taken from an article by the theologian R.A. Lambourne, published in a Christian journal.

Our whole present medical understanding ... requires that we spend great sums for the treatment of one person, whereas if we could re-apply the expenditure you could save many lives. The real, the new, the excellent men of tomorrow, will at a certain point be required to say, 'No, this cannot be done', and 'This particular person has to be sacrificed'. ... many of the major ethical decisions confronting the Christian doctor are not those involved in the choice between different acts towards the one patient in front of us, such as when to pull out the intravenous tube or stop artificial respiration, but a kind of political decision involved in health care planning which decides quite literally whether thousands of people would live or die. (quoted in Wilson 1975, 24)

12

Conclusions

I shall now outline a model of modern nationalised medicine, in the light of which I believe it is possible to understand some of the dynamics behind the various life-or-death controversies which we have discussed.

There are three types of agent involved in nationalised medicine. First, there are the politicians and bureaucrats whose job is to manage the Welfare State. These individuals are under pressure to provide the minimum possible service compatible with public expectations, at the lowest possible cost, and in a way that arouses the least possible criticism.

Secondly, there are the practitioners of medicine themselves. Their objectives will, notwithstanding any wishful thinking to the contrary, be driven by the usual economic incentives. They are also likely to have non-financial motives for practising medicine. These are conventionally supposed to involve a desire to help people. Less romantically, we may postulate that what attracts people to this profession is the opportunity to have power over other people. In some cases, the practitioner's desire for power will mean that he derives gratification from feeling that he has improved his client's position – although this does not imply that the client necessarily agrees that his position has improved. In other cases, the practitioner may derive gratification simply from exercising authority over his client's state of health, or from frustrating or even harming his client.

Thirdly, there are the consumers of medicine. Clients are characterised by an extraordinary lack of power. They are unable to obtain a medical service or substance simply because they want it. Their legal rights are limited to *refusing* treatment, although as we have seen, this right of refusal is, in the cases where it really matters, somewhat shaky. Clients' ability to enforce quality in the services they receive is also severely limited by the fact that there is practically no competition between practitioners, and by the considerable difficulties of establishing medical negligence.

Let us now consider what kind of a system of medicine an interaction between these three groups of agents is likely to produce. First, is it likely to engender respect for autonomy? The answer is surely no. The only group that has a genuine interest in promoting autonomy is clients; however, as they have little legal or economic power, they have no leverage for getting their way. The interest of bureaucrats certainly does not lie in the direction of increasing autonomy. Permitting autonomy creates complications, delays, higher costs. Nor should we expect any support for autonomy from the medical profession. Their interests are, as we have seen, likely to make them favour the idea that they be given more, rather than less, discretion. Their philosophy, according to which everything is best left to the experts, also suggests that pressure for more client control is unlikely to come from them.

If this model is correct, it has alarming implications for the question of autonomy. It suggests that to the extent client autonomy in medicine still exists, it is likely to be subject to constant erosion. It suggests that there may well be complaints on the part of the client group but that these complaints will have little practical effect. The one effect we might expect is that that the other two groups will make a certain amount of effort to reassure clients that their autonomy is not threatened, or even to pretend that it is being given increasing weight.

Social medicine

Medicine is a field which appears to have immense appeal to collectivists and socialists. It is not merely that basic medical provision is regarded as a natural element of the Welfare State, a safety net analogous to unemployment benefit. Because health is supposed to be a basic human good for which needs and preferences do not vary substantially between individuals, it is often seen as appropriate for it to be organised on a national, or even international, basis. The issue of health arouses utopianist and interventionist tendencies. Perhaps this is because the idea that health might be *imposed* attracts those who enjoy power over other people, given that medicine is one of the most supreme and intimate forms of power — for good or bad. Unfortunately, health care is also an area where the price of collectivisation is extremely high.

It is sporadically revealed that nationalised health services are characterised by widespread inefficiency. Yet those of us in countries with such health services are so habituated to a system of medicine for which we do not make *voluntary* sacrifices that we find it hard to imagine any alternative. The prospect of having to reduce consumption in other areas, simply because we fall ill, usually for no fault of our own, may strike us with horror. However, it is beginning to emerge that the alternative may be equally dreadful. What we get by surrendering autonomy over medical contracting is poor in quality, rudely delivered, often not available, and may be imposed against our wishes.

Moreover, a system of medicine which has been collectivised does not stop at the point where essentially the same transactions are being carried out in a different economic form, albeit inefficiently. As discussed in chapters 2 and 5, the whole character of such a system is likely to change

12. Conclusions

as it becomes a means to other social goals than the mere provision of what is wanted by clients. The public character of nationalised medicine is already apparent, in that considerable resources are devoted to the 'education' of clients, and allocation decisions are made by reference to community interests. However, there is constant pressure to expand the public element of medicine at the expense of the individualistic element, particularly where the two sets of interests conflict. The issues of confidentiality and organ donation are two examples where it is being increasingly argued that private interests should give way to wider social interests.

Finally, and perhaps most worryingly, a state which provides a public system of medicine will be subject to enormous temptation to interfere with people's lifestyles. Since an individual's actions will influence the amount of healthcare he will subsequently call on the state to provide him with, the state has an interest in (and excuse for) influencing those actions. There are essentially three possible ways for a provider to respond to the fact that he will bear the cost of his customer's behaviour: (i) prescribe rules of behaviour and refuse to supply non-compliers, (ii) charge a higher price for costly actions, or (iii) prescribe rules of behaviour and punish non-compliers directly. Thus, to take the example of smoking, a state which provides a collective medical service might issue a no-smoking rule and refuse to contract with those who did not comply; it might levy higher charges on smokers; or it might simply outlaw smoking.

Option (ii), which would be the typical response of a commercial service, is perhaps not politically viable in the case of a system that is supposedly based only on need, not on ability to pay. Option (i) is beginning to be used openly, most notably in the case of smokers. It appears likely that this option is already being used covertly, under the guise of 'best interests' arguments. Both overt and covert forms of this option run the risk, however, that consumers will complain about prejudicial treatment.

Option (iii) therefore suggests itself. This entails forcing citizens of a Welfare State to behave in ways which reduce their subsequent likely health care costs. They will be forced to wear seat-belts, since this is believed to reduce the amount of health care required after an automobile accident. They will be forced to take fluoride in their tap water, since this is believed to reduce dental care required in later life. They will not necessarily be able to refuse what doctors consider to be the most cost-efficient emergency medical treatment, since they might otherwise have to be given alternative, more expensive treatment. If they are mentally handicapped, they may have to be sterilised since the state cannot afford to care for their offspring.

On a less coercive level, there is likely to be great pressure placed on individuals – at least, economically productive individuals – to reduce their risks of disease. There will be resources expended on persuading them to be screened for common ailments; to be inoculated against common infections; to moderate alcohol consumption; to terminate a pregnancy where the survival of the child would call for state support; and so on. There will also be pressure to accept treatment in the most cost-effective, rather than the most comfortable, way.

With regard to euthanasia, it is worth asking oneself whether it is in the state's interest for any given ill client to die or to continue living. In the case of the terminally ill, it might be helpful to the state if a proportion of such individuals consented to premature termination. Claims that there are large numbers of sick people in hospitals craving a merciful release should be considered in the light of this observation.

To the extent that the state seems reluctant to legalise euthanasia, we need to bear in mind two points. First, it may be preferable from the state's point of view if euthanasia takes place covertly. That approach may well be politically and legally less fraught. Secondly, the idea of euthanasia carries – rightly or wrongly – connotations of autonomy. Formally allowing euthanasia might (or so bureaucrats may fear) encourage users of the public medical system to become more demanding with respect to other areas of health care.

Life or death

Many of the so-called 'ethical dilemmas' of medicine arise because the right of individuals to control their own bodies is not respected. A person's wish as to what should be done to his body must nowadays pass the scrutiny of others before it is given due weighting. First, a person must demonstrate that his wish conforms to prevailing ideas of what is rational. Where that wish departs from the majority viewpoint, as in the case of Jehovah's Witnesses, society may or may not allow it to have force, depending on the degree of tolerance prevalent, and probably also on the size and political significance of the class of people who share the deviant viewpoint.

Secondly, if a person's wish has passed the test of reasonableness, modern medicine then regards itself at liberty to weigh it against all other considerations: the 'welfare' of the individual, the wishes of his family, the preferences of the medical profession, and the public interest. The weighting which is given to autonomy relative to these other factors varies according to the opinion of the legal and medical professions of different jurisdictions. While there is talk among these professions to the effect that the individual's wishes are 'important', the evidence suggests that respect for medical autonomy is highly selective, and depends on the degree of consistency between the individual's wishes and the interests of the community.

As far as euthanasia is concerned, we must recognise that the root of the issue is that individuals are denied access to the chemicals which would provide a painless death. Because medical paternalism has progressed to a highly advanced stage, practically all pharmaceuticals are out of bounds to the layman. Moreover, it is plausible to suppose that, even if drugs such as antibiotics or oral contraceptives were available over the counter, the supply of those drugs which lent themselves readily to suicide would none the less be controlled. Society is currently not prepared to countenance that people should be able to kill themselves painlessly simply by buying something from the chemist.

What then of the proposal that doctors should be permitted to kill a client suffering from a suitably horrific illness, subject to the client's consent? Those who advocate this are saying, in effect, that having denied the person the right to control his body, society will give it back to him under certain conditions. We should be very suspicious of such a conditional liberty. Whose interests does it serve if this apparent concession is made? Ostensibly the decision of death will become one of *partnership* between society, the client and the medical professionals, in the sense that all three must give their consent for the act of killing to go ahead. Society will give its consent in the form of procedural rules; the doctors concerned by deciding whether the client's condition warrants euthanasia; and the client himself by signing a form. However, it is questionable whether the balance of power is evenly enough distributed to make each of those acts of consent equally meaningful.

One must ask why mercy-killing is discussed in preference to suicide for clients with painful conditions. It is true that clients sometimes get into a condition where it would be impossible for them to ingest without aid a lethal drug placed in front of them. On the other hand, many seriously ill people who would prefer to die are perfectly able to perform the necessary bodily actions which would place responsibility for ending their life solely on them. Indeed, one wonders how many of the former type of client passed through a stage of being the latter type, during which they would have ended their lives if they had been allowed access to the means. Why, then, is it almost invariably the image of the doctor administering a lethal injection that is invoked in discussions of euthanasia? This alone should make one wary of the assumption that it is the client's autonomy which is primarily at stake in the euthanasia controversy, rather than the wishes of observers such as doctors, nurses and relatives.

Once we allow doctors to kill their clients with their clients' consent, as opposed to letting clients have direct access to the means of death, we are unquestionably closer to the possibility of involuntary euthanasia. Even if this step did not mean that we found it easier to *contemplate* killing conscious clients without their consent – an optimistic assumption – we will nevertheless have *legitimised* one of the factors required for involuntary euthanasia, namely homicide, and thereby eliminated one of the safeguards against it.

It is dangerously naïve to assume that doctors are invariably benevolent and that they operate only on the basis of our best interests, notwithstanding the fact that the profession behaves as if this attitude of submissive veneration were *de rigueur*. The modern presumption in favour of doctor benevolence has meant that the powers of the medical profession have grown to intolerable levels. The correct response to the apparent dilemmas which this development has generated is to reduce these powers, not to consider ways of increasing them still further.

Treating and not treating

One way in which the aims of the euthanasia lobby could be partly advanced, without involving us in the dangers of expanding doctor power, is to strengthen the consent requirement for treatment. Although nominally a practitioner must obtain the consent of a competent client before he can carry out medical intervention, in practice this principle is only weakly observed.

The requirement that a client must agree to treatment should not be imagined to mean that doctors necessarily sit down with a client and discuss carefully, and without putting any pressure on him, the options available, including non-intervention. What typically happens if a person is found to have a life-threatening tumour (for example) is that he is rushed off to hospital for an operation and is expected to sign a standard form when he gets there. Of course he is theoretically entitled to 'get off the bus' at any point, but how easy is it in a situation like this to think things through, arrive at a decision, and then argue with the professionals, all the time being under pressure to accept the experts' recommended course of action? This is obviously not made any easier if a client is deprived of information about his condition, or about the possible courses of action and associated risks and benefits.

Who should decide whether risky or traumatic treatment should be given or withheld from a client who is considered to be incompetent to decide for himself, or to express an opinion? The modern tendency is to allow the courts to override the choices of the person's relatives whenever these are in conflict with expert opinion. The notion of a 'health care proxy' – an agent appointed by the client to make medical decisions on his behalf – receives only muted support. It is not clear, however, that courts or ethical committees are very efficient means for determining the interests of a specific individual in a particular situation.

Of course letting the next-of-kin, or a proxy appointed by the client, make the decisions is not going to produce ideal results. The match between the actions of the client's agent and the client's wishes will not be perfect. The agent will not know exactly how the client would decide for himself if able to do so. And the agent may have preferences and interests of his own which will enter into the decisions he makes on behalf of the client. The question has to be posed, however, whether one or more doctors, or representatives of the judicial system, are likely to score better in these two areas. It is unlikely that they are better at guessing the preferences of the client than the client's appointed representative. As far as agents' own personal preferences are concerned, doctors and employees of the state are, as we have argued earlier, certainly not immune from conflicts of interest.

The allocation game

There can no longer be any doubt that *killing* clients – under which rubric I include letting them die while under medical care – is on the agenda as a possible response to resource pressures. So far, it is largely being done covertly, but we may well see increasing use of the argument that the resources needed for one client's care would be better spent elsewhere, particularly where the client is in some way 'blameworthy'. With medicine regarded as a matter for collective control, the claim that society has a right to allocate medical resources in the way which best furthers the public interest will become harder to resist.

In this connection, the following points are relevant. First, in any discussion about what medicine should or should not do, it is necessary to keep clearly in mind the distinction between private and collectivised medicine. Where private medicine is concerned, there should not be any question of discussing 'morality' on a public level. Medicine should be regarded as a contractual arrangement between an individual and one or more practitioners. Treatment should extend as far as is consistent with the client's requests and his ability to finance the services he requires. Individual doctors are of course free to examine their own moral beliefs and to refuse certain services if they feel they contravene these beliefs. Doctors might even form into groups for the collective discussion of such questions, and perhaps for collectively deciding on the answer. What is not acceptable, however, is that such groups should be able to legislate, either directly or by means of a 'closed shop', against any particular service that is demanded.

In a purely private arrangement, people may die because they lack the financial resources to pay for what is available, resources which others (who may not need them) *are* able to muster. It is a curious feature of the modern ideological landscape that many people find the possibility of this asymmetry more disturbing than the mere fact that some unfortunate individuals will die. Indeed, some would perhaps feel more comfortable with a state of affairs in which *everyone* who suffers from a particular condition dies than with the idea that a few, whose selection does not depend on collective preferences, will be able to save themselves.

Clearly there are many who find something deeply objectionable in the idea that preservation of health will generally be better for those with more resources. However, such a state of affairs should always be considered, not by comparison with some fantastic utopia in which everyone receives the treatment they need, as far as the prevailing technology will stretch, but rather by comparison with a situation in which allocation decisions are made by appointed representatives who weigh up the worthiness of competing invalids, or (as currently) by doctors. In a system of collectivised medicine, there will inevitably be problems of resource allocation, and these will sometimes – perhaps even frequently, as technology advances further – lead to people being denied life-saving treatment.

When the question of resource allocation is debated, therefore, it should be made clear that it is *collectivised* medicine which is being discussed and that the problems that arise do not apply to private medicine. Otherwise it should be openly stated that the institution of private medicine *per se* is being questioned as part of the discussion. What is not acceptable is that the problem of resource allocation should tacitly be applied to medicine *in toto*, so that (in effect) private medicine is covertly attacked without this being made explicit.

Considering now collectivised medicine, the question confronting those who are in favour of it, but who do not wish to impose limits on the range of services provided, is how allocation decisions should be made. Here there is one crucial choice. Either such decisions can be made on such bases as first-come first-served or random selection. Or we arrange for someone else to play the role of arbiter, deciding on some 'rational' basis such as 'quality of life', or likelihood of success of the treatment, or usefulness to the community. According to Simon Lee, *efficiency* could be our standard. 'In which case, we might reject those who, because of their advanced age were prone to other health problems so that society might not get many hours of life from however many hours of treatment were provided.'

The option of 'blind' allocation is usually rejected by those who prefer life to be run on the basis of justifiable principles, and who regard random distributions as intolerable. Such people demand that we should always seek the best way of organising something and should then determinedly enforce the preferred solution, rather than remain agnostically passive. Arguably, however, the idea of other people refereeing about whether a person should live or die, by whatever system, is deeply offensive. Some might prefer to be subject to a random system, however arbitrary its results.

What is certain is that the arbitration option will generate endless discussion of who is to make the decisions, how they will be appointed, to whom they will be answerable, and what principles they are to apply in deciding. As Lee says, 'we can all contribute to the debate [about resource allocation] by being informed and educated with the help of experts'. Of course, once the principles of allocation have been collectively decided, it is likely that individual clients will have no further say in individual decisions.

Surely all users of such a service, including the most unsophisticated, should be clearly and unequivocally warned that they may find themselves in a situation where their wish to live is being weighed up by a committee.

12. Conclusions

It is one thing for a person to be told (truthfully), 'we are sorry, our resources do not stretch to providing the treatment you urgently require'; it is quite another for that person to be refused an available resource because he is considered unsuitable, whether or not he is told the reason for refusal.

Clients have a right to be warned that they may be denied available life-saving treatment, and that this may happen for reasons that have nothing even notionally to do with their best interests. A large sign in front of all NHS hospitals, pointing out the serious dangers of relying on state medicine, might do for a start. If people are to be warned incessantly, at the taxpayer's expense, of the risks of smoking cigarettes, they should certainly be educated about the more invisible risks of relying on a medical system which may choose whether or not to accept any given client.

The myth of doctor benevolence

Finally, let us return to a recurrent theme of this book. That doctors are typically virtuous, responsible, caring people has become one of society's basic tenets, sharing centre stage with such other social clichés as warm, loving parent figures, and innocent, trusting children. Curiously, while the conventional family stereotypes have come under severe strain in the last few decades, the positive image of doctors continues to flourish, apparently unaffected by evidence to the contrary. Many people will readily express a high degree of cynicism about the supposed virtues of traditional family and class structures, yet appear to find it much harder to consider the possibility that their faith in doctors may have little basis in fact.

Without serious popular scepticism about the true interests and motives of doctors, and given a basic assumption that doctors are always better than clients at making the relevant decisions, we would expect the democratic machinery to respond to the medical monopoly by acquiescing in the latter's expansion of power over individuals' bodies. This is just what we have seen.

We observe that, with a collectivised medical service, power of the most intimate kind over individuals is capable of being given to others simply on the basis of majority preference. Like most other problems of authoritarian medicine, this issue is concealed. If the majority decided to deprive a minority social group of the franchise, this would be regarded by many as an unacceptable use of democratic power. Yet if the majority decide that their medical interests are best served by allowing agents of the medical monopoly to exercise paternalistic authority, the fact that a minority may have their medical preferences overridden by those agents goes largely unnoticed.

It should be regarded as *the primary ethical principle of medicine* that, since medical relationships are intrinsically exploitative, *a doctor may never override the wishes of a client*. This should come well ahead of tenets about doing good, avoiding harm, keeping confidence, and so on. A client may of course *choose* that his doctors should act as they see fit without consulting him.

That we now urgently need such a principle, while it appears not to have been required at the time of the Hippocratic Corpus, is a consequence of the monopolisation and collectivisation of medicine. Ethics do not arise spontaneously but, like most other things in commercial life, in response to economic pressures. Medical professionals are no longer under any economic pressure and consequently have no incentive, either collectively or individually, to respond to client wishes.

The full definition of this principle appears preferable to the term 'autonomy', which has now become debased and is used to mean (among other things) 'the experience of exercising rational choice'. How precisely the principle is to be interpreted is to some extent a question of economics. Clearly it can never be ethical to treat someone against their expressed wishes.

The extent to which clients have the right to demand particular treatments is more complex. The distinction between privately-funded and state-funded medicine, which is absent from many discussions, needs to be emphasised. There is a strong argument that privately paying clients should be able to obtain whatever service is potentially available, in the sense that technology and knowledge (enabling those individuals to make their own decisions about appropriate treatment) should not be restricted by the profession. On this basis, resource considerations do not belong to this realm, and there is no ground for allowing doctors to decide what constitute reasonable or acceptable requests for treatment.

What those relying on a *state* health service should be able to demand is obviously more debatable. Individuals should however be given full (and reliable) information about what they may or may not expect such a service to provide under various circumstances, and they should be told this early on in their lives, to enable them to make appropriate planning arrangements and also to exercise what democratic power they have in determining what the rules will be for future generations. Clients *must* be warned about any limitations of the service, and in time for them to respond. Explaining to someone with a fatal condition that the NHS does not supply smokers is obviously not an example of a warning given in adequate time.

If the principle of the primacy of client volition is to be subject to exceptions, for example that parents should decide for children under sixteen, these exceptions should be defined by law in such a way as to leave no room for doubt. The fact that giving primacy to individuals' wishes may seem problematic in some circumstances – say when an elderly person suffering dementia refuses to be attached to a drip feed – does not imply that the principle is not in fact still appropriate even in those circumstances. It *certainly* cannot be used, as it currently is, as a vague justification for allowing departures in general whenever doctors consider a refusal or request unreasonable.

If the coercive application of medicine (or its coercive refusal) is not acceptable in ordinary circumstances, it is completely intolerable in situations of life or death. The individual's right to his own life is supreme; it is the one basic right which even the most primitive societies tend to guarantee. It is barbaric to allow doctors to kill a client, or to keep a client alive against his expressed wishes. This is a road down which we have already travelled too far, and along which we must not move any further.

Bibliography

Age Concern England (1986) *The Law and Vulnerable Elderly People*. Age Concern England.
Age Concern Institute of Gerontology and Centre of Medical Law and Ethics (1988) *The Living Will: Consent to Treatment at the End of Life*. Edward Arnold.
Alderson, Priscilla (1990) *Choosing for Children*. Oxford University Press.
Alsop, Stewart (1974) 'The right to die with dignity'. *Good Housekeeping*, August.
Amnesty International (1991) *Doctors and Torture: Resistance or Collaboration?* Bellow.
Anand, K. *et al.* (1987) 'Randomised trial of fentanyl anaesthesia', *Lancet*, 31 January 1987, 243-8.
Ayer, A.J. (1964) *Language, Truth and Logic*. Gollancz.
Beauchamp, T.L. and Childress, J.F. (1994) *Principles of Biomedical Ethics* (4th ed.). Oxford University Press.
Beecher, H.K. (1966) 'Ethics and clinical research', *New England Journal of Medicine*, **274**, 1354-60.
Bell, J.M. and Mendus, Susan (1988) *Philosophy and Medical Welfare*. Cambridge University Press.
Bliss, Brian and Johnson, Alan (1975) *Aims and Motives in Clinical Medicine*. Pitman Medical.
BMA (1980) *Handbook of Medical Ethics*. British Medical Association.
BMA (1988) *Euthanasia*. British Medical Association.
BMA (1993) *Medical Ethics Today*. British Medical Association.
Bosanquet, N. (1984) 'How to save the nation's health: the social market view', *Economic Affairs*, **4**, 49-50.
Bradley, Colin P. (1992) 'Uncomfortable prescribing decisions: a critical incident study', *British Medical Journal*, **304**, 294-6.
Brazier, Margaret (1987) *Medicine, Patients and the Law*. Penguin Books.
Brazier, Margaret (1992) *Medicine, Patients and the Law* (2nd ed.). Penguin Books.
Butler-Sloss, Elizabeth (1988) *Report of the Inquiry into Child Abuse in Cleveland 1987*. HMSO.
Campbell, Beatrix (1988) *Unofficial Secrets*. Virago Press.
Church of England General Synod (1975) *On Dying Well*. Church Information Office.
Coleman, Vernon (1988) *The Health Scandal*. Sidgwick & Jackson.
Cooper, Wendy (1976) *No Change*. Arrow Books.
Corney, R. (1991) *Developing Communication and Counselling Skills in Medicine*. Routledge.
Daly, Mary (1979) *Gyn/Ecology*. The Women's Press.
Dennison, Stanley (1984) 'How to save the nation's health: 1. The classical liberal view', *Economic Affairs*, **4(iii)**, 45-9.

Devlin, Patrick (1965) 'Morals and the criminal law', in *The Enforcement of Morals*, Oxford University Press.
Downing, A.B. and Smoker, Barbara (1986), *Voluntary Euthanasia*. Peter Owen.
Dworkin, Gerald (1972) 'Paternalism', *Monist*, **56**, 64-84.
Engelhardt, H.T. (1986) *The Foundations of Bioethics*. Oxford University Press.
Fissell, Mary E. (1991) *Patients, Power, and the Poor in Eighteenth-Century Bristol*. Cambridge University Press.
Flamm, B.L. and Quilligan, E.J. (1995), *Cesarean Section: Guidelines for Appropriate Utilisation*. Springer.
Foot, Philippa (1978) *Virtues and Vices*. Blackwell.
Freeman, M.D.A. (1988) *Medicine, Ethics and Law*. Stevens.
Gillett, Grant (1989) *Reasonable Care*. Bristol Press.
Gillon, Raanan (1985) *Philosophical Medical Ethics*. John Wiley & Sons.
Gillon, Raanan (1994) *Principles of Health Care*. John Wiley & Sons.
Glover, Jonathan (1977) *Causing Death and Saving Lives*. Penguin Books.
Gray, J.A. Muir (1985) 'The ethics of compulsory removal', in Lockwood (1985), 92-110.
Green, David G. (1985) *Working-Class Patients and the Medical Establishment*. Gower/Temple Smith.
Ham, C., et al. (1988) *Medical Negligence: Compensation and Accountability*. King's Fund Institute and Centre for Socio-Legal Studies, Oxford.
Hare, R.M. (1985) 'Little human guinea-pigs?', in Lockwood (1985), 76-91.
Harris, John (1985) *The Value of Life*. Routledge.
Health Service Commissioner (1994) *Annual Report for 1993-94*. HMSO.
Helme, Tim (1991) 'The Voluntary Euthanasia (Legislation) Bill (1936) revisited', *Journal of Medical Ethics*, **17**, 25-9.
Hollis, Martin (1988) 'A death of one's own', in Bell and Mendus (1988), 1-15.
House of Lords (1994) *Report of the Select Committee on Medical Ethics*. HMSO.
Humphry, Derek and Wickett, Ann (1986) *The Right to Die*. Bodley Head.
Illich, Ivan (1977) *Limits to Medicine*. Penguin Books.
Institute of Medical Ethics Working Party on the Ethics of Prolonging Life and Assisting Death (1990a), 'Assisted death', *Lancet*, **336**, 610-13.
Institute of Medical Ethics Working Party on the Ethics of Prolonging Life and Assisting Death (1990b), 'Withdrawal of life-support from patients in a persistent vegetative state', *Lancet*, **337**, 96-8.
Ivy, A.C. (1949) 'Nazi war crimes of a medical nature', *Journal of the American Medical Association*, **139**, 131-5.
Kamisar, Yale (1986) 'Euthanasia legislation: some non-religious objections', in Downing and Smoker (1986).
Kassirer, Jerome P. (1983) 'Adding insult to injury: usurping patients' prerogatives', *New England Journal of Medicine*, **308**, 898-901.
Kennedy, Ian (1981) *The Unmasking of Medicine*. George Allen & Unwin.
Kennedy, Ian (1991) *Treat Me Right*. Oxford University Press.
Klein, Rudolf (1989) *The Politics of the NHS*. Longman.
Kuhn, Sandra et al. (1990) 'Perceptions of pain relief after surgery', *British Medical Journal*, **300**, 1687-90.
Laurence, D.R. and Bennett, P.N. (1980) *Clinical Pharmacology* (5th ed.). Churchill Livingstone.
Lee, Simon (1986) *Law and Morals*. Oxford University Press.
Lively, Jack (1983) 'Paternalism', in Phillips Griffiths (1983), 147-65.
Lloyd, G.E.R. (1978) *Hippocratic Writings*. Pelican Books.

Bibliography 169

Lockwood, Michael (1985) *Moral Dilemmas in Modern Medicine*. Oxford University Press.
Marston, Maurice (1925) *Sir Edwin Chadwick (1800-1890)*. Parsons.
McCormick, Richard A. (1974) 'To save or let die', *Journal of the American Medical Association*, **229**, 172-6.
McGuire, Alistair, Henderson, John and Mooney, Gavin (1988) *The Economics of Health Care: An Introductory Text*. Routledge.
McKnight (1993) 'Autonomy and the akratic patient', *Journal of Medical Ethics*, **19**, 206-10.
Mason, J.K. and McCall Smith, R.A. (1983) *Law and Medical Ethics*. Butterworth.
Mason, J.K. and McCall Smith, R.A. (1994) *Law and Medical Ethics* (4th ed.). Butterworth.
Milgram, S. (1964) 'Group pressure and action against a person', *Journal of Abnormal and Social Psychology*, **69**, 137-43.
Milgram, S. (1965) 'Liberating effects of group pressure', *Journal of Personal and Social Psychology*, **1**, 127-34.
Miller, Henry (1967) 'Economic and ethical considerations', *Proceedings of the Royal Society of Medicine*, **60**, 1216-19.
Miller, Henry (1973) *Medicine and Society*. Oxford University Press.
National Consumer Council (1991) *Pharmaceuticals: A Consumer Prescription*. National Consumer Council.
Nelson-Jones, Rodney and Burton, Frank (1990) *Medical Negligence Case Law*. Fourmat Publishing.
Neuberger, Julia (1994) 'The patient's view of the patient-health care worker relationship', in Gillon (1994), 377-86.
Open University (1985) *Medical Knowledge: Doubt and Certainty*. Open University Press.
Pabst Battin, Margaret (1987) 'Euthanasia', in VanDeVeer and Regan (1987), 58-97.
Parsons, Talcott (1951) *The Social System*. Routledge & Kegan Paul.
Phillips Griffiths, A. (1983) *Of Liberty*. Cambridge University Press.
Phillips, Melanie and Dawson, John (1985) *Doctors' Dilemmas*. Harvester Press.
Porter, Roy (1987) *Disease, Medicine and Society in England 1550-1860*, Macmillan.
Rachels, James (1986) *The End of Life*. Oxford University Press.
Ramsey, Paul (1978) *Ethics at the Edge of Life*. Yale University Press.
Robertson, Geoffrey (1989) *Freedom, the Individual and the Law*. Penguin Books.
Russell, William (1983) 'Police and Criminal Evidence Bill and the BMA', *British Medical Journal*, **286**, 571.
Sacred Congregation for the Doctrine of the Faith (1980) *Declaration on Euthanasia*. Catholic Truth Society.
Sainsbury, P (1973) 'Suicide: opinions and facts', *Proceedings of the Royal Society of Medicine*, **66**, 579-89.
St John-Stevas, Norman (1961) *Life, Death and the Law*. Eyre & Spottiswoode.
Savage, Wendy (1986) *A Savage Enquiry*. Virago Press.
Searle, G.R. (1971) *The Quest for National Efficiency*. Blackwell.
Seward, Jack (1968) *Hara-Kiri: Japanese Ritual Suicide*. Tuttle.
Siegler, Mark (1982) 'Confidentiality in medicine – a decrepit concept', *New England Journal of Medicine*, **307**, 1518-21.
Singer, Peter (1979) *Practical Ethics*. Cambridge University Press.
Stanley, John M. (1992) 'The Appleton International Conference: developing

guidelines for decisions to forgo life-prolonging medical treatment', *Journal of Medical Ethics*, **18** (Supplement).
Stengel, Erwin (1964) *Suicide and Attempted Suicide*. Penguin Books.
Szasz, Thomas (1975) *Ceremonial Chemistry*. Routledge & Kegan Paul.
Thomas, J.E. and Waluchow, W.J. (1990) *Well and Good*. Broadview Press.
Todd, Chris and Still, Arthur (1993) 'General practitioners' strategies and tactics of communication with the terminally ill', *Family Practice*, **10**, 268-76.
Tudor Hart, Julian (1988) *A New Kind of Doctor*. Merlin Press.
VanDeVeer, Donald and Regan, Tom (1987) *Health Care Ethics: An Introduction*. Temple University Press.
Veatch, Robert (1989) *Death, Dying and the Biological Revolution*. Yale University Press.
Weiss, Gary (1985) 'Paternalism modernised', *Journal of Medical Ethics*, **11**, 184-7.
Williams, Glanville (1958) *The Sanctity of Life and the Criminal Law*. Faber & Faber.
Williams, R. and Gethin Morgan, H. (1994) *Suicide Prevention: The Challenge Confronted*. HMSO.
Wilson, Michael (1974) *Health is for People*. Darton, Longman & Todd.
Wilson, Robert C.D. (1992) *Understanding HRT and the Menopause*. Hodder & Stoughton.

Sources of quotations

p. 8, line 39: BMA 1993, 309.
p. 15, lines 25-7: McKnight 1993, 210.
p. 19, lines 18-22: Porter 1987, 51.
p. 19, lines 29-35: quoted in Green 1985.
p. 20, lines 17-18: Bosanquet 1984, 49.
p. 26, lines 5-7: Bliss and Johnson 1975, 85.
p. 26, lines 12-14: Dr Fleur Fisher speaking on BBC News, 19 September 1992.
p. 26, lines 16-18: *The Times*, 8 October 1992.
p. 26, lines 25-7; 28-30: Open University 1985, 17.
p. 27, lines 19-22: Mason and McCall Smith 1983, 186.
p. 28, lines 1-4: Glover 1977, 201.
p. 28, lines 22-6: Williams 1958, 301.
p. 28, line 35: ibid., 303.
p. 29, lines 12-14: Butler-Sloss 1988, 143.
p. 29, lines 22-7: quoted in Campbell 1988, 147-8.
p. 30, lines 14-16: House of Lords 1994, 41.
p. 30, lines 19-25: BMA 1988, 15
p. 30, line 40: *The Times*, 19 November 1992.
p. 31, lines 37-40: Kennedy 1981, 27.
p. 32, lines 18-20: Kennedy 1991, 252.
p. 33, lines 11-13: *Sidaway v Governors of Bethlem Royal Hospital*, Weekly Law Reports 1985/2, 493.
p. 33, lines 21-4: Mason and McCall Smith 1983, 121.
p. 33, lines 30-5: *Smith v Auckland Hospital Board*, New Zealand Law Reports 1964, 250.
p. 36, lines 18-20: Letter to *The Times*, 3 June 1993.
p. 36, line 35: Brazier 1992, 153.
p. 37, lines 15-16: *Airedale NHS Trust v Bland*, Weekly Law Reports 1993/1, 329.
p. 37, lines 34-5: quoted in Brazier 1992, 317.
pp. 37-8: Butler-Sloss 1988, 201.
p. 40, lines 33-5: *The Patient's Charter*, HMSO 51-1003, October 1991, 9.
p. 40, lines 40-3: *Access to Health Records Act 1990*, section 5(1)(a).
p. 41, lines 12-13: Bliss and Johnson 1975, 77.
p. 42, lines 21-4: Campbell 1988, 178.
p. 42, lines 27-30: ibid., 181.
p. 42, lines 33-9: Illich 1977, 234.
pp. 42-3: ibid., 232.
p. 43, lines 8-12: Phillips and Dawson 1985, 13.
p. 43, lines 18-19: Parsons 1951, 445.

Sources of quotations

p. 46, lines 29-31; 32-3: Lee 1986, 18.
pp. 46-7: *The Times*, 6 October 1992.
p. 47, lines 10-11: Ramsey 1978, 158.
p. 47, lines 18-21: Bliss and Johnson 1975, 81.
p. 49, lines 13-15: Weiss 1985, 185.
p. 49, lines 20-3: ibid., 185.
p. 49, lines 25-7; 29-35: ibid., 186.
p. 50, lines 3-8: Engelhardt 1986, 279.
p. 51, lines 24-8: BMA 1980, 20.
p. 51, lines 30-1: BMA 1993, 308.
p. 52, line 4: Marston 1925, 119.
p. 52, lines 17-19: Bliss and Johnson 1975, 80.
p. 52, lines 27-30: quoted in ibid., 29.
p. 52, lines 36-41: quoted in Searle 1971, 241.
p. 55, lines 26-8; 34-6: BMA 1993, 302.
p. 57, lines 14-16: BMA 1993, 309.
p. 58, lines 4-9: Russell 1983, 571.
p. 58, lines 22-4: Siegler 1982, 1519.
pp. 59-60: quoted in Phillips and Dawson 1985, 121.
p. 60, lines 4-10: ibid., 121.
pp. 60-1: *Lancet*, 1982 (ii), 275.
p. 63, lines 14-15: Milgram 1965, 130.
p. 66, lines 12-16: Laurence and Bennett 1980, 84.
p. 68, lines 39-41: J.H. Jaffe in Goodman and Gilman, *The Pharmacological Basis of Therapeutics* (8th ed.), Pergamon Press, 1990.
p. 72, lines 36-7: *Sunday Times*, 10 April 1994.
p. 74, lines 4-5; 6-7: quoted in Cooper 1976, 66-7.
p. 76, lines 19-23: *Guardian*, 9 August 1993.
p. 78, lines 41-5: *Daily Mail*, 21 March 1987.
p. 79, lines 20-3: Anand et al. 1987, 247.
p. 80, lines 5-10; 25-32: McGuire et al. 1988. 155-6.
pp. 80-1: ibid., 160.
p. 81, lines 17-22: ibid., 163.
p. 81, lines 30-4: ibid., 195.
p. 82, lines 28-31: Kennedy 1981, 12.
p. 85, lines 21-2: *The Times*, 25 January 1993.
p. 88, line 16: *Sunday Times*, 20 September 1992.
p. 88, lines 23-6: *Sunday Times*, 27 September 1992.
pp. 91-2: R. Hackforth, *Plato's Phaedo*, Cambridge University Press, 1955.
p. 92, lines 15-17: Stengel 1964, 23.
p. 92, lines 37-40: Church of England 1975, 6-7.
p. 93, lines 24-8: Glover 1977, 183.
p. 94, lines 1-2: Williams and Gethin Morgan 1994, 10.
p. 94, lines 11-15: Sainsbury 1973, 588.
p. 96, lines 25-7: Rachels 1986, 153-4.
p. 96, lines 37-40; 42-3: Mason and McCall Smith 1983, 182-5.
p. 98, lines 16-21: Glover 1977, 185.
p. 98, lines 39-43: quoted in Kamisar 1986, 131-2.
p. 99, lines 1-7: ibid.
p. 101, lines 18-19; 21-3: Humphry and Wickett 1986, 2.
p. 103, lines 21-3: Robertson 1989, 364.
p. 103, line 34: Glover 1977, 185.

Sources of quotations

p. 105, lines 17-18: quoted in Ivy 1949, 132.
p. 109, lines 13-16: Veatch 1989, 97.
p. 109, lines 19-22; 23-5: Ramsey 1978, 156-7.
p. 110, lines 39-41: *Chatterton v Gerson*, Weekly Law Reports 1980/3, 1003.
p. 111, line 16: Croom-Johnson LJ, in *Wilson v Pringle*, Weekly Law Reports 1986/3, 10.
p. 111, lines 32-3: *Chatterton v Gerson*, Weekly Law Reports 1980/3, 1013.
p. 114, lines 7-9: Parsons 1951, 466.
p. 114, lines 10-11: ibid., 468.
p. 114, lines 16-19: BMA 1993, 14.
p. 114, lines 37-9: Brazier 1992, 87.
p. 116, lines 13-16: quoted in BMA 1993, 328.
p. 116, lines 18-21: ibid., 333.
p. 118, lines 26-7; 28-32: Brazier 1987, 311.
p. 121, lines 27-30: BMA 1993, 71.
p. 121, lines 36-9: *Sunday Times*, 17 May 1992.
p. 125, lines 7-10: BMA 1988, 21.
p. 125, lines 31-3: *Oldie*, 22 July 1994.
p. 126, lines 19-23: Bliss and Johnson 1975, 79.
p. 127, lines 22-7: *Lancet*, 19 January 1985, 177.
pp. 129-30: Bliss and Johnson 1978, 78.
p. 130, lines 5-7: Miller 1967, 1216.
p. 130, lines 10-12: Kennedy 1981, 158.
p. 130, lines 27-8: Lloyd 1978, 140.
p. 130, lines 29-31: ibid., 143.
p. 130, lines 41-3: Kennedy 1981, 156.
p. 131, line 1: ibid., 158.
p. 131, lines 3-5: ibid., 156.
p. 131, lines 27-9: quoted in House of Lords 1994, vol. 2, 63.
p. 132, lines 40-2: Foot 1978, 52.
p. 133, lines 38-41, Harris 1985, 249.
p. 134, line 6: Phillips and Dawson 1985, 43.
p. 134, lines 10-12: Glover 1977, 156.
p. 134, lines 12-13: ibid., 157.
p. 136, lines 9-10, 11-12: Institute of Medical Ethics 1990b, 97.
p. 137, lines 29-30: *Airedale NHS Trust v Bland*, Weekly Law Reports 1993/1, 325.
p. 137, lines 31-2: ibid., 331.
p. 137, lines 33-4: ibid., 332.
p. 137, lines 35-7: ibid., 363.
p. 138, lines 30-3: ibid., 394.
p. 138, line 36: ibid., 400.
p. 143, lines 24-8: Ayer 1964, 112.
p. 144, lines 30-1: Rachels 1986, 3.
p. 144, line 33: ibid., 8.
p. 144, lines 35-9: ibid., 70.
p. 145, lines 5-9: F.J. Taylor in Alan Richardson, *A Theological Work Book of the Bible*, SCM Press, 1957, 34.
p. 145, lines 22-3: Rachels 1986, 5.
p. 145, lines 24-5: ibid., 26.
p. 145, lines 36-7: McCormick 1974, 175.
p. 146, lines 14-18: Gillett 1989, 58.

Sources of quotations

p. 146, lines 20-2: Rachels 1986, 131.
p. 147, lines 16-18; 23-4: Foot 1978, 37.
p. 147, lines 19-21: quoted in ibid., loc. cit.
pp. 147-8: ibid., 54.
p. 149, lines 28-30: Rachels 1986, 6.
p. 150, lines 26-8: quoted in Lockwood 1985, 126.
p. 151, lines 35-8: Gillett 1989, 16.
p. 151, lines 39-42: ibid., 17.
p. 152, lines 8-11: ibid., 57.
p. 152, lines 23-5: ibid., 30.
p. 152, lines 41-2: Rachels 1986, 157.
p. 162, lines 22-5: Lee 1986, 68.
p. 162, lines 38-9: ibid., 70.

Index

abortion 72, 109, 151
administration, of health service 41
advance directive 30, 104, 136
advertising 4, 19
Age Concern 119
AIDS 57-8, 72, 118
'allowed to die' 115, 120, 128-9, 131, 134
alternative therapies 66, 75
authoritarianism 5, 30, 33, 42, 90, 108, 141
Ayer, A.J. 143, 152

battery 107, 110-12
Bland, Tony 37, 88, 102, 134-7
Bliss, Brian and Johnson, Alan 26, 47, 52, 104, 126, 129
blood transfusion 15, 117
Brazier, Margaret 36, 61, 114, 118
British Medical Association 7-8, 26, 30, 37, 44-7, 51, 55, 57, 65, 88, 104, 107-8, 114, 121-5, 131, 137-8
British Paediatric Association 61
Brown, Sir Stephen 120, 137

Caesarean births 77-8, 107, 117, 120
Catholic Church 128
child abuse 29, 35, 42
childbirth 76-7, 85
Christianity 87, 92, 128, 144-5, 154
Church of England 92
Cleveland 29, 37, 38, 42
coercion 11, 34, 36, 104, 107, 109, 146, 165
collectivism 21, 42, 52, 146, 154, 156, 164
competence
  of medical staff 4, 36, 39

of client to decide 11, 30, 47, 61, 66, 115, 118, 121, 123-4, 160
competition 3-4, 17-20, 22, 31, 40, 48, 58-9, 67, 79, 81, 126, 140, 155
confidentiality 57-9, 72, 116, 157
consumer satisfaction 9-10, 55
contraceptive pill 72
corpses 32, 168
counselling 65, 72, 93
courts 18, 33, 37, 58, 70, 88, 91, 95, 97-8, 107, 110-14, 117-18, 121, 131-2, 137, 152, 160
Cox, Nigel 26, 79, 88, 91, 95, 99, 132
CPR (cardio-pulmonary resuscitation) 126, 128-9

deregulation 10
discretion of doctors 5, 9, 11, 22, 27-8, 34-5, 44, 88, 105, 112, 124, 156
'do not resuscitate' (DNR) 126, 128
Donaldson, Lord 110, 117, 121
drug users 13, 68

efficiency
  of market 140
  of medicine 4, 19-20, 27, 41, 53, 86, 95, 156
  of monopoly 3, 49-50
  of pain relief 78-9, 86, 95
  of treatments 110, 157
elderly clients 34, 40, 88, 90-2, 98, 102-4, 119-20, 125-7, 164
emergency treatment 110, 116, 118, 120, 139, 157
ethics committees 60-1, 116, 123
euthanasia
  generally 9-10, 12, 28, 31, 41, 47, 52, 56, 58, 79, 87-9, ch.8, 109, 113, 144-53, 158-60

DAS (doctor-assisted suicide) 97-105
involuntary euthanasia ch.10
experiments 8, 27, 60-3, 116, 168
exploitation, of medical power 19, 22, 27, 35, 40, 43, 79, 81, 153, 163

Food and Drug Administration 67, 74
Foot, Philippa 132-3, 147-8

Gillett, Grant 146, 151-2
Glover, Jonathan 27, 93, 98, 103, 134, 144
'go slow' 124
Greece, Ancient 91, 130

handicapped clients 61, 88, 125, 134, 157
harassment 43-4
Hippocratic Corpus 51, 58, 87, 130, 164
HRT (hormone replacement therapy) 73-4
Humphry, Derek 101-2

Illich, Ivan 42, 82
infanticide 134, 151
influenza vaccination 6, 10, 48, 69, 127
informed consent 112, 114, 116, 120
interferon 74-5
intervention
    medical 76, 85-6, 90, 107, 120, 127-30, 160
    paternalistic/coercive: generally 14-15, 68, 147, 156; by doctors 11, 94, 121; by state 20, 53, 59

Japan 33, 92
Jehovah's Witnesses 116
judges 28, 33, 37, 58, 80, 82, 102, 110-13, 117, 136, 138, 149

Kennedy, Ian 31-2, 39, 52, 74, 82, 130, 168
kidney dialysis 56, 86, 127

laetrile 74-5
legal advice 15-18, 39, 80
legislation 28, 52-4, 97-8, 101, 105, 115, 119, 161

libertarianism 125, 147, 149
liberty 28, 39, 46-7, 58, 65, 104, 146-9, 158-9
life support 27, 133, 135
life-saving treatment 5, 41, 87, 90, 107, 116, 120, 123, 126-8, 139, 162-3
lottery, allocation by 9, 56, 87
lying, of doctors to clients 32, 70, 129

malpractice 77
markets 3-4, 10, 16-9, 22, 49, 68, 74-5, 79-82, 113, 139-40
Mason, J.K. and McCall Smith, R.A. 33, 96, 136
medical examination 29, 37, 42, 69, 107
medical insurance 8, 19, 50, 53, 56, 89
mental illness 35, 48, 56, 104, 115, 125, 127
Milgram, Stanley 62-3
minors 6, 13, 29, 32, 41, 46, 50-2, 57, 61, 100-3, 107, 110, 119, 121, 138, 145, 153-4, 157, 160, 162
monopoly 3-4, 10, 19-21, 49, 58, 67-9, 75, 81, 87, 103, 130, 139
motivation, of health care workers 7, 26, 31, 35, 48, 58, 81, 130, 140
murder 26, 28, 36-7, 88, 91, 100, 102, 138, 146, 153

National Assistance Act 119
NHS 5, 20, 53, 56
National Health Service Act 20
National Insurance subscriptions 41
nationalisation 42
Nazi Germany 27, 70, 101, 151
negligence, medical 27, 36, 70, 78, 110-13, 155
Netherlands 97
nicotine patches 75
nurses 25, 28, 35-6, 43-4, 71-2, 78, 91, 96, 115, 125, 152, 159

pain relief 77-9
palliative care 86, 95, 127
Parsons, Talcott 43, 114, 168
paternalism 8, ch.2, 31, 33, 42-3, 45, 49, 51, 53, 65-9, 72, 74, 82, 108-13, 150, 154, 158, 163

Index

Phillips, Melanie and Dawson, John 29, 54, 168

philosophy 15, 18, 27, 51, 56-7, 60, 78, 100, 109, 114, 132-3, ch.11, 156
Plato 91
police 34-5, 37, 42, 57, 102
politicisation, of medicine 82
pregnancy 76, 107, 117-18, 157
prescribing 29, 65-6, 71-2, 75, 82, 130
prisons 34-5, 147, 151
privacy 58-9, 72
private medicine 8, 48, 82, 89, 152, 161-2
public good 18, 51, 57-8, 70, 158
public health 52, 90, 152
public relations 45, 48
PVS (persistent vegetative state) 135-8

Rachels, James 94-6, 100, 144-6, 149, 152
Ramsey, Paul 47, 109, 131
rationing 10, 55
refusal of treatment
 by clients 5, 15, 33, 41, 107-9, 115-18, 120-1, 135, 155, 157, 164-5
 by doctors 5, 9, 12, 23, 40, 43, 48, 56, 69-73, 123-4, 127-8, 130, 139-40, 148, 152, 163
regulation, of medicine 10, 36, 58-9, 139
relatives 34, 52, 92, 99, 101, 103, 126, 130, 136-8, 159-60
religion 41, 52, 97, 100, 117
research 60-1, 86, 116, 131
resource allocation 8, 9, 27, 53-7, 86, 126, 140, 152, 157, 161-3

sanctity of life 109, 144-6
Savage, Wendy 77
scarcity, of medical resources 9, 27, 41, 51, 102, 123, 140
screening 72, 118
second opinion 20, 40, 42
Shaw, George Bernard 26-7
side effects 7, 35, 44, 74, 95, 113, 131
Singer, Peter 144, 153
slavery 22-3, 30
slippery slopes 150-1
smoking 5, 14, 29, 40, 43, 75, 89, 123-4, 139, 151, 157, 163
socialism 156
Stengel, Erwin 92
sterilisation 111, 118, 157
suicide 14, 49, 68-9, 87, 89, 91-9, 102-3, 128, 159

taxation 8, 41, 54, 89, 100, 139
technology, medical 6-8, 10-11, 27, 53, 55, 66-9, 72, 76-7, 85-9, 93, 161, 164
television drama 25
terminal illness 79, 88, 93, 99, 128, 133, 158
torture 27, 70, 152

unconscious clients 25, 31, 43, 110, 116, 119, 132-3, 137, 145

volition 34, 94, 101, 104, 146, 149, 164

Welfare State 33, 41, 53, 55, 155-7
Williams, Glanville 28, 150

X-ray 10, 58, 66, 123, 149

Upstate Author

```
W 62 T211p 1995
Tassano, Fabian.
Power of life or death
```